TESTIMONY IN THE SPIRIT

This book explores the ordinary beliefs and practices of Pentecostal and Charismatic Christians in relation to the Holy Spirit. It does this by means of a congregational study of a classical Pentecostal church in the UK, using participant observation, focus groups and documentary and media analysis. This approach develops a framework in which the narratives of informants can be interpreted. Focusing on specific areas of interest, such as worship, conversion, healing and witness, each contribution from respondents is situated within the context of the congregation and interpreted by means of the broader Christian tradition.

This book makes a unique contribution to scholarship by offering a rich and varied picture of contemporary Christians in the Pentecostal and Charismatic traditions, enabling a greater understanding to be appreciated for both academic and ecclesial audiences.

Mark Cartledge has taken David Martin's concept of rescripting which he applies to (in Jeff Astley's language) the 'ordinary theology' of a local Pentecostal denomination and has pulled off a remarkable study of interdisciplinary sophistication which is both faithful to Pentecostal self understanding of their lives, yet deeply reflexive sociologically, and reflective theologically. If that were not enough he offers this rescription to Pentecostal practitioners in a spirit of critical engagement. This study is so rich and rounded that I am tempted to throw caution to the wind and say with confidence that this lifts practical theology to a higher level. Testimony in the Spirit is a tour de force.
Andrew Walker, Professor of Theology, Culture and Education,
King's College London, UK

Finally, a practical theological methodology that ably and adequately closes the loop between the vibrant and widely heralded 'Pentecostal spirituality' and the second-level discourse of Pentecostal theology. Cartledge not only writes here in service of the church, but further solidifies his reputation at the vanguard of the increasingly important field of practical theology through his expert translation of Pentecostal experience, that remains quite enigmatic to those outside the movement,.
Amos Yong, J. Rodman Williams Professor of Theology, Regent University School of
Divinity, Virginia Beach, USA

This is theological reflection that questions and listens discerningly to a local Pentecostal congregation in the light of a larger theological conversation. The result is a fruitful exchange that provides much needed clarity of thought, not only for Pentecostals, but for everyone interested in understanding how theology can serve the life and mission of the church.
Frank D. Macchia, Professor of Christian Theology, Vanguard University, USA

In a lucid and compelling style, Cartledge takes the reader inside the 'ordinary theology' of contemporary British Pentecostalism. He raises issues of great importance to leaders of diverse religious communities, while sharing ground-breaking scholarship in Pentecostal/ Charismatic studies and Practical Theology.
Richard Osmer, Thomas W. Synnott Professor of Christian Education,
Princeton Theological Seminary, USA

Explorations in Practical, Pastoral and Empirical Theology

Series Editors: Leslie J. Francis, University of Warwick, UK
and Jeff Astley, Director of the North of England
Institute for Christian Education, UK
Martyn Percy, Ripon College Cuddesdon and
The Oxford Ministry Course, Oxford, UK

Theological reflection on the church's practice is now recognised as a significant element in theological studies in the academy and seminary. Ashgate's new series in practical, pastoral and empirical theology seeks to foster this resurgence of interest and encourage new developments in practical and applied aspects of theology worldwide. This timely series draws together a wide range of disciplinary approaches and empirical studies to embrace contemporary developments including: the expansion of research in empirical theology, psychological theology, ministry studies, public theology, Christian education and faith development; key issues of contemporary society such as health, ethics and the environment; and more traditional areas of concern such as pastoral care and counselling.

Other titles in the series include:

Hospital Chaplaincy in the Twenty-first Century
The Crisis of Spiritual Care on the NHS
Christopher Swift
978-0-7546-6416-1

Entering the New Theological Space
Blurred Encounters of Faith, Politics and Community
Edited by John Reader and Christopher R. Baker
978-0-7546-6339-3

Evangelicalism and the Emerging Church
A Congregational Study of a Vineyard Church
Cory E. Labanow
978-0-7546-6450-5

Theological Foundations for Collaborative Ministry
Stephen Pickard
978-0-7546-6829-9

Testimony in the Spirit
Rescripting Ordinary Pentecostal Theology

MARK J. CARTLEDGE
University of Birmingham, UK

ASHGATE

Published by
Ashgate Publishing Limited
Wey Court East
Union Road
Farnham
Surrey, GU9 7PT
England

Ashgate Publishing Company
110 Cherry Street
Suite 3-1
Burlington
VT 05401-3818
USA

www.ashgate.com

British Library Cataloguing in Publication Data
Cartledge, Mark J., 1962–
    Testimony in the Spirit: Rescripting Ordinary Pentecostal theology. –
    (Explorations in Practical, Pastoral and Empirical Theology)
    1. Pentecostalism – Great Britain – Case studies.
    I. Title II. Series
    230.9'94–dc22

Library of Congress Cataloging-in-Publication Data
Cartledge, Mark J., 1962–
    Testimony in the Spirit: Rescripting Ordinary Pentecostal Theology /
    Mark John Cartledge.
        p.   cm. -- (Explorations in Practical, Pastoral and Empirical Theology)
    Includes bibliographical references and index.
    1. Pentecostalism. 2. Pentecostal churches. 3. Hockley Pentecostal Church
    (Birmingham, England) I. Title.
    BR1644.C38 2010
    230'.9940941–dc22   2010008290

ISBN   9780754663522 (hbk)
ISBN   9781409409472 (ebk)

Contents

List of Figure and Tables

Figure

Tables

Acknowledgements

To conduct a research project of this nature is a major undertaking and it could not have been completed successfully without the assistance of a number of people.

The pastors and leaders of Hockley Pentecostal Church have been most gracious in allowing me to use their church as a case study, even as they welcomed me into their midst. It has been a pleasure to visit them and, most of all, to worship with them. The congregation is one of the friendliest I have known. Pastor John was especially helpful in assisting me to arrange the focus groups and he offered transport to those who would not have otherwise been able to attend the groups. He also provided information about the congregation and helped me to understand it better. I am most grateful to him. The members of the church who participated in the focus groups did so with enthusiasm and good humour and my heartfelt thanks goes out to all of them. The church elders read at least two versions of the full manuscript and I am grateful to them for the care and attention which they gave to this task. I am also indebted to Pastor Angela for allowing me to use lyrics from three of her songs. I was not alone in this project and I need to register my sincere appreciation to Doreen Morrison, a postgraduate student at the University of Birmingham, for being willing to assist me in managing the focus groups, thus allowing me to concentrate on the task of leading the group discussion.

A good number of people read the full manuscript or specific chapters at various points and I continue to be in their debt. These include: Allan Anderson, Jeff Astley, Andrew Davies, Jaco Dreyer, Helen Ingram, William Kay, Frank Macchia, David Petts, Sigvard Von Sicard and Amos Yong. It goes without saying that any remaining weaknesses or errors in the text are solely my responsibility.

I am also grateful to colleagues and students who have given feedback to me regarding material presented as conference or seminar papers, including students from the Centre for Pentecostal & Charismatic Studies at the University of Birmingham. This Centre is truly an important resource for scholarship in the field and I am very pleased to be associated with it. Study leave, which allowed relief from teaching and administrative duties in the School of Philosophy, Theology and Religion, made it possible for the final stages of the project to be completed more or less on time. I am grateful to the University of Birmingham for such a concentrated spell of research. I am also very thankful to my colleagues at Birmingham, Allan Anderson and Richard Burgess, for cover during my study leave.

I was able to use the Donald Gee Centre, which is the Assemblies of God Archive based at Mattersey Hall, and this proved an invaluable resource for getting to know some of the historical material. I am grateful to all the staff who welcomed me to the college and especially to Dave Garrard for his hospitality.

I am extremely appreciative to the staff at Ashgate for their professional support in the publication of this book. My thanks go to Joe Gregory, Sarah Lloyd, Nicole Norman, Joanna Pyke (freelance copy editor), Nora Weber and Kirsten Weissenberg.

Once again my family have shared in the highs and lows of empirical research as they occasionally visited the church with me, engaged in Sunday lunch-time discussions after the morning services and entered into conversations with me following the focus group meetings. To Joan and Becky, as ever, thanks so much for your love and support.

Finally, I would like to dedicate this book to my friends in Pentecostalism. I have the privilege of knowing Pentecostals from all over the world: students, church leaders and members, as well as academic colleagues. Thank you for your distinctive witness, or perhaps I should say your 'testimony'! I expect that you may not necessarily agree with everything I have written; nevertheless I hope you find it interesting, thought-provoking and a stimulus to your own theologising.

Scripture citations are from the New International Version (NIV) © 1973, 1978, 1984, by the International Bible Society.

Chapter 1

Introduction

In the Acts of the Apostles, Luke records the departure of Jesus Christ from the earth with the following words still ringing in his disciples' ears: 'But you will receive power when the Holy Spirit comes on you; and you will be my witnesses in Jerusalem, and in all Judea and Samaria, and to the ends of the earth' (Acts 1.8, NIV). Following this promise, he records the extraordinary scene on the day of Pentecost, as 120 followers experience the powerful presence of the Holy Spirit resting upon each one of them and inspiring them to 'declare the praises of God' in languages other than their own (Acts 2.1–11). It is this very presence of God with his people that Luke records in the remainder of his second volume, as the Spirit inspires and energises the church in its expansion and mission. This promise and its fulfilment on the day of Pentecost and beyond has inspired a strand of Christianity throughout the history of the church and can be found in other New Testament documents. For example, Paul addresses it in his Corinthian correspondence, especially its use of certain giftings (*charismata*) that the presence of the Holy Spirit brings to Christians in their worship and service of God (1 Cor 12–14). It is these biblical texts that have informed and inspired Christians in their lives around the world as they participate in what can be called the 'charismatic tradition' (Cartledge, 2006a).

Over the course of the history of the church, there have been individuals and movements that have stressed aspects of the charismatic tradition, although there has often been marginalisation through the rise of institutional and formal features of Christianity. The continued presence of this spiritual tradition can be seen by reference to prophecy, healing and exorcism in the writings of the Apostolic Fathers, the Montanist movement in the third century and Athanasius' Anthony of the Desert (251?–356). Accounts of the work of the Holy Spirit and the use of *charismata* can also be found throughout the history of the church, for example, in the writings of Gregory the Great (540–604), Symeon the New Theologian (949–1022), the Cathars (condemned at Orlean in 1022), Hildegard of Bingen (1098–1179) and Ignatius of Loyola (1491–1556). The tradition can be traced throughout the seventeenth century (the Quaker movement) and the eighteenth century (Moravian Brethren and John Wesley), before providing the immediate backdrop to the rise of Pentecostalism in the nineteenth century (Edward Irving, the Holiness movement emerging from the Wesleyan tradition and the wider Evangelical movement). This means that over the course of the centuries the charismatic tradition has accompanied other forms of Christianity and can be described as a kind of 'plug 'n' play' tradition: always working alongside other traditions and absent without them (Cartledge, 2006a: 132–133).

At the beginning of the twentieth century there were a number of different Evangelical revivals around the world, each with different characteristics yet emphasising the work of the Holy Spirit and expressing aspects of the Spirit's work through giftings, signs and wonders and conversions. There is a debate among scholars regarding the historiography of Pentecostal origins, but it has become clear that the view suggesting Pentecostalism was 'made in America' is probably untrue despite its towering impact on Pentecostal identity. For example, the revival at Pyongang in Korea in 1903 predated both the Welsh revival (1904) and Azusa Street revival in Los Angeles (1906). The Indian revival associated with Pandita Ramabai's Mukti Mission in Poona (1905–1907) also began before the Azusa Street revival (Anderson, 2004: 172–173). However, the Azusa Street revival is probably the most famous centre associated with Pentecostal origins. It built upon the Wesleyan holiness tradition and stressed the experience of being baptised in the Spirit as empowering for witness, as evidenced by speaking in foreign tongues. It was an experience subsequent to conversion and sanctification, for power followed on from purity. With the gift of tongues, many missionaries were sent off to distant lands with the expectation that they could now communicate with the inhabitants in their own language. Unfortunately, they proved to be disappointed. These centres of Pentecostal revival were gradually mirrored in other countries around the world (e.g. Sunderland in England, 1907). From these revivals developed a global movement and classical Pentecostal denominations began to emerge that enshrined key beliefs and practices: powerful personal experiences of the Spirit especially in the context of worship, holiness of life, missionary endeavour, signs and wonders, *charismata*, and an expectation in the soon-coming return of Jesus Christ. It was this final expectation that motivated mission, and the outpouring of the Spirit in the revivals was regarded as the 'latter rain' in preparation for the harvest of souls that would usher in the return of Christ.

The contemporary Pentecostal movement maintains most of these beliefs, although eschatological expectation has been modified over the course of the past hundred years. It is a tradition that has found a home in the mainline denominations, such as Roman Catholicism, Anglicanism and other Protestant and independent denominations. In this form it has been labelled either the Charismatic movement or the Charismatic Renewal movement, and it has had a significant impact on these denominations in different countries around the world. Thus, it exemplifies once again its capacity to plug into and play alongside different Christian traditions. Therefore, Pentecostalism can be defined in both a narrow and broad sense. In the narrow sense it refers to those classical denominations that emerged over the course of the twentieth century having their roots in the early revivals. In the broad sense it also includes the historic 'charismatic tradition' and especially its contemporary expression through mainline and independent church life.

Today Pentecostalism, defined in its broad sense, is regarded as the second largest form of Christianity, with an estimated 520 million adherents worldwide in 2000. It is suggested that approximately 27% of the total population of Christianity can be classified as Pentecostal. There are 740 Pentecostal denominations, with a presence (often referred to as the Charismatic movement) in 6,530 non-Pentecostal mainline denominations and 18,810 independent denominations and networks. This means that Pentecostal and Charismatic Christianity is incredibly diverse and covers 95% of the world's population, represented by 9,000 ethnic groups and expressed in 8,000 different languages (Kay, 2009: 12). If these figures are correct (there is always an element of doubt about such large figures), then it could be suggested that there is only 5% of the globe remaining until a Pentecostal presence is found at 'the ends of the earth'(Acts 1.8).

It is this form of Christianity that lies at the heart of this book, even if the picture that I wish to paint is rather modest compared to the global reality behind these rather grand figures. This book is concerned with an analysis of the 'ordinary theology' of members from one classical Pentecostal congregation in Birmingham, England. It has connections with global Pentecostalism, and some of these connections will become apparent in the narratives that follow. But it also has its roots in the early Pentecostal movement in the UK, and from which the established classical Pentecostal denominations emerged.

In order to set the scene for this study, I shall briefly describe both the history of the Assemblies of God denomination in the UK and the nature of the particular congregation under study. The narratives of the adherents need to be placed within these two contexts in order for us to better appreciate their nature and significance for the overall study. Having described these two contexts, I shall define the central aim of the book and outline the main thematic chapters.

The Assemblies of God

British classical Pentecostalism has its roots in the Welsh revival (1904–1905) but especially the early Pentecostal revival meetings conducted by Alexander A. Boddy at All Saints' Church, Monkwearmouth, Sunderland, between 1908 and 1914 (Kay, 1989; Wakefield, 2007). I have argued elsewhere that this early movement stressed a (Wesleyan Pentecostal) five-fold gospel between 1911 and 1917, namely that Jesus is conceived as: saviour, sanctifier, baptiser in the Spirit, healer and coming king (Cartledge, 2008a). From these annual Whitsuntide Conventions and other conferences early Pentecostals, especially in the aftermath of the Great War, formed their identity and eventually established their own denominational structures. However, it was not until a decade or so later that denominations began to appear on the scene. One of the denominations to emerge was the Assemblies of God of Great Britain and Ireland. An initial meeting was held in Sheffield in May of 1922 at which a preliminary statement of fundamental truths was proposed and included articles concerning 'the present latter outpouring of the Holy Ghost, accompanied by speaking with other tongues', the restoration of 'all the gifts of the Holy Ghost to the church', church offices based on Ephesians 4.11, deliverance from sickness provided in the atonement and the 'personal and pre-millennial return of our Lord Jesus Christ' (Massey, 1987: 38–39).

On 1 February 1924 a meeting called by J. Nelson Parr was held in Aston, Birmingham, England, at which the decision to form a fellowship of Pentecostal churches was formally agreed. This was followed in May 1924 by the denomination's first conference held in London, at which the revised 'Statement of Fundamental Truths' was ratified and 74 assemblies indicated their willingness to join the fellowship (Allen, 1990: 115; Massey, 1987: 157). This statement of faith was not regarded as a creed but as a basis for unity for a full gospel ministry (see Appendix A). It has been argued that the reasons for the emergence of this denomination in the 1920s was to preserve 'a distinctive Pentecostal testimony' (especially the significance of the Day of Pentecost: baptism in the Spirit evidenced by glossolalia), co-ordination of fellowship and witness (especially in the face of societal hostility) and protection against error and indiscipline (especially the inappropriate use of the *charismata*) (Massey, 1987: 213–298; 1992: 57–77).

Thus, existing independent assemblies were 'united' together and established as a denomination under the leadership of J. Nelson Parr (1924–1933), succeeded in turn by Howard Carter (1934–1945) and Donald Gee (1948–1966). A quarterly magazine was published called *Redemption Tidings*, which was edited by Parr as a means of inculcating Pentecostal values and identity (1924–1985) alongside annual conferences and revival campaigns. At the time of writing, *Joy* magazine had replaced *Redemption Tidings* as the main publication for the denomination. Within one year of its establishment the number of assemblies in the fellowship had grown to 100 and by the 1930s it had increased to 300 assemblies (Allen, 1990: 160). Although its membership has subsequently waxed and waned, especially in the 1960s, the denomination continues to grow and to benefit from its association with what is now a global Pentecostal force in world Christianity. Today there are more than 600 congregations aligned with the Assemblies of God in the UK. It is affiliated to the Assemblies of God World Fellowship, the Worldwide Pentecostal Fellowship, and the Evangelical Alliance (UK).[1]

The denomination provided theological education for missionaries and pastors by means of the Hampstead Bible School founded in 1921, with Howard Carter as its principal until 1948. It had no fixed curriculum other than Bible study and the key doctrines of baptism in the Spirit (an experience distinct from and subsequent to conversion) and gifts of the Spirit, regarded as completely supernatural (Kay, 1989: 120). Later Bible colleges, at Kenley in Surrey and then at Mattersey Hall near Doncaster, provided a more established curriculum. Today the Assemblies of God denomination continues to train its pastors at Mattersey Hall and it now offers the full range of educational programmes up to doctoral level.

Over the course of the years the five-fold emphasis of the early Pentecostals was superseded by the language of the 'full gospel' (e.g. Squire, 1935), with the

---

[1]   http://www.aog.org.uk/pages/14-our-history/content;   http://www.agcongress. org/01_abot/abt_agfellowship.html;   http://www.worldwidepf.com/go/default/index.cfm; http://www.eauk.org/; accessed on 25 September 2009.

Wesleyan doctrine of 'entire sanctification' simply replaced by the need for 'holy living' (Boffey, 1939). The front cover of *Redemption Tidings* for 8 September 1939 proclaimed a four-fold gospel – namely, Jesus as saviour (Isa 43.11), baptiser (Mt 3.11), healer (Ex 15.26) and coming king (Jn 14.33). Pentecostals built upon the tradition of Holiness and Evangelical groups by defining their theological identity through short statements of faith (Kay, 2009: 224–225). The British Assemblies of God statement of faith has indeed remained fairly stable over the course of the twentieth century. In 1967 the Executive Committee proposed a revision but this was not accepted at the General Conference (Allen, 1990: 235). Various discussions over recent years have been held and the most recent statement was ratified at the General Council in 2004 (see Appendix B). It is interesting to compare the changes that were made from the origins of the denomination to 2004, as this gives a sense of how the tradition developed theologically over the course of 80 years. The following can be observed when the 1924 and 2004 statements are reviewed.

Both statements are biblicist, in the sense that all doctrine is to be normed by Scripture, with the language of infallibility remaining constant. The doctrine of God changed in article 2 to include 'One being co-existing in three Persons', probably reflecting a greater awareness of the dispute with the oneness Pentecostal tradition, especially from the USA, and it affirms more explicitly orthodox trinitarian theology. A new article 3 has been inserted, with the person and work of Christ preceding the fall of humanity. The new article also contains material that was previously contained under original article 10, namely eschatology. Now the whole ministerial life of Jesus is affirmed, including the language of substitutionary atonement and his 'personal, visible, bodily return' but now detached from a premillennial scheme. Article 3 on the fall of humanity is now article 4. Article 4 on salvation is now article 5 and expanded to include explicit reference to new birth, while article 5 on baptism by immersion is now article 6 and is reworded slightly. Article 6 on baptism in the Spirit is now article 7 and reads slightly differently. It is now explicitly defined as an enduement of power for service, with the 'initial evidence of which is speaking with other tongues' being replaced by 'the essential, biblical evidence of which is speaking with other tongues as the Spirit gives utterance'. This suggests a reinforced position. Article 7 on holiness now becomes article 9, with the wording being changed slightly. Article 8 on divine healing is now article 10 and remains unchanged. Article 9 on the Breaking of Bread is worded differently, with emphasis on reception by those who have 'repented and believe in Christ as Lord and Saviour' as a regular activity, while 'until the Lord comes' is dropped, thus suggesting a further blow to imminent eschatological expectation. Article 10 on the premillennial return of Christ, as stated above, has been incorporated into the new article 3, with premillennial language now dropped. Article 11 concerning everlasting punishment for those whose names are not written in the Lamb's book of life is now article 12 and includes a statement on the bodily resurrection and everlasting conscious bliss or punishment, thus becoming more explicit. Article 12 on the gifts of the Spirit is now article 8 and has been expanded to include 'gifts of Christ in the Church today', referring to the ministry gifts of Ephesian 4.11, previously implied but now made explicit.

These changes no doubt reflect aspects of Evangelicalism and broader Christianity in the UK and the denomination's concern to position itself within this setting. These statements will be used to inform the discussions on the themes in later chapters.

We now turn to the particular congregation that is the focus of this study, bearing in mind that the changes just mentioned in relation to official theology are to some extent reflected in the congregation. It was founded during a period when the original 1924 statement of faith was in operation and this current study is placed within a context in which the 2004 statement is now normative.

Hockley Pentecostal Church

Hockley Pentecostal Church (hereafter HPC) was founded by two women, Miss Harriet Fisher and Miss Olive Reeve, who had intended to be missionaries in India and were subsequently accepted into fellowship with the Assemblies of God of Britain and Ireland. Due to the outbreak of World War II they were prohibited from travelling overseas. Harriet Fisher was brought up in Smethwick and her parents were influenced by the Sunderland revival as it was mediated to them via members of the 'Apostolic brethren from Rolfe Street Mission, Smethwick' (Fisher and Reeve, n.d.: 25–26). Olive Reeve was converted during the ministry of George Jeffreys in Birmingham 'a few years later' in the 'aftermath of World War I' (27, 30). She was one of 300 converts baptised during the evangelistic campaign before a gathering of 10,000 people (Littlewood, 2010: 32). However, they were both deeply influenced by the ministry of George Jeffreys in Birmingham around 1932 and as a result of a prophetic message from a hostel matron, Miss Rae Arnott, decided to work together (Fisher and Reeve, n.d.: 31). During the war they hired a room and began a Sunday School ministry. Out of this ministry emerged a mission and then a church as they needed to hire larger premises because of numerical growth. In 1945 they began to acquire a bombed-out Baptist church, guided by a prophetic message and the enthusiasm of Olive Reeve, who commented: 'Oh it's not too bad, it only needs dusting!' (45). The church building was finally purchased in March 1955 and fully restored for services in October of the same year. Later, in 1979, a new church building was erected on the same site in order to accommodate the 800–900 people who attended the Saturday evening meetings. Kay observes that in many respects the work of these two women differed from other Pentecostal churches:

> First, Miss Fisher and Miss Reeve continued to live 'by faith' all their lives. They had no fixed income agreed with the church. Second, and most noticeable, the Hockley congregation emphasised praise, worship and dancing at a time when this was squashed and criticised by the majority of pentecostals. At some stage,

when the Sunday night Gospel meeting became the prime means of attempting to win the unconverted, pentecostal churches forbade or strongly discouraged the exercise of charismatic gifts on Sunday evenings. Not so with Hockley! So far as they were concerned, the most vital ingredient of the Christian life was to worship the Lord and nothing would stop them raising their hands in the air, jumping, clapping and singing. They really did not care whether people thought them mad or not, or whether the Executive Council of the Assemblies of God felt they gave pentecostals a bad name. (Kay, 1989: 196)

Joy and liberty in worship were celebrated features during the time of Fisher and Reeve, especially through dancing, singing and clapping in the Spirit, as well as 'the operations of the gifts of the Spirit, and the honouring of the Word of God' (Fisher and Reeve, n.d.: 69–70; cf. Allen, 1990: 233; Littlewood, 2010: 32). This attitude continues to be present among the church members, with many of the older members having direct and personal memories of joining the church during the time of these two 'lady pastors'. Although Miss Fisher died in 1984 and Miss Reeve in 1987, their memories and influence are still significant for the identity of the church. Indeed, two theologians from the University of Birmingham attended HPC during this period, Daniel W. Hardy and David F. Ford. They note HPC in the acknowledgements to their 1984 book and reflect on the Pentecostal tradition.

At its best it is distinctive by being able both to combine pattern and dispense with pattern. It revels in improvisation, innovation, an ability to play with themes in the Bible or in music. It has 'the jazz factor' (and jazz has the same black American origins). (Hardy and Ford, 1984: 20)

One suspects that both Fisher and Reeve epitomised the 'jazz factor' and that the 'pulpit culture' of dance and movement they represented was reciprocated by the congregation (Amoah, 2004: 70–71). Hardy and Ford's experience of HPC, as well as their engagement with colleague Walter J. Hollenweger, informed their understanding of Pentecostalism's distinct contribution to a theology of praise.

Today HPC continues to be located on the same site as the church purchased by these two women at the end of World War II. It lies within inner city and multi-cultural Birmingham, located approximately 1 mile from the city centre. The area of Hockley scores extremely highly on measures of social deprivation.[2] The working population is categorised as: managers and senior officials (6.7%), professional occupations (9.0%), associate professional (12.4%), administrative or secretarial (13.1%), skilled trades (11.4%), personal service (10.2%), sales and customer services (6.0%), plant and machinery operatives (10.6%) or elementary occupation (20.6%). In terms of stated religious affiliation, the area is 64.0% Christian (compared to 59.0% for Birmingham), 1.0% Buddhist (compared to

---

[2]   Office for National Statistics: www.neighbourhood.statistics.gov.uk, accessed on 7 September 2009.

0.3% for Birmingham), 1.2% Hindu (compared to 2.0% for Birmingham), 0% Jewish (compared to 0.2% for Birmingham), 5.5% Muslim (compared to 14.3% for Birmingham), 0.9% Sikh (compared to 3.0% for Birmingham), 14.0% for no religion (compared to 12.4% for Birmingham), 0.4% for other religion (compared to 0.4% for Birmingham) and 13% for religion not stated (compared to 8.4% for Birmingham). In ethnic terms, Birmingham is 67.2% White (compared to 88.7% for England), 3.2% Mixed (compared to 1.6% for England), 20.7% Asian or Asian British (compared to 5.5% for England), 6.6% for Black or Black British (compared to 2.8% for England) and 2.3% Chinese or Other (compared to 1.4% for England). HPC is attended by mostly Caribbean and African born Christians (approximately 60–70%) integrated within a Pentecostal denomination shaped by the Holiness, Evangelical and classical Pentecostal traditions of the British context of the twentieth century. It is within this denominational context that HPC flourishes as a church, with approximately 245 regular worshippers and 109 'signed up' members. The majority of these worshippers are women (65%). It is estimated that the majority of the worshippers would be classified as 'working class' (70%) with a minority being classified as 'professional class' (30%). It is estimated that the majority (approximately 80%) live within a 2 mile radius of the church building.

Miles and Judy Witherford were the successors to the founding pastors from 1984 to 2002. Miles had been a member of the Sunday school established by Fisher and Reeve and eventually succeeded them as they declined in health, ultimately working with his wife Judy. They became trustees of the church and significant figures in the life of the church during this period. Miles sought to emulate the work of Fisher and Reeve in Sunday school ministry but this proved difficult to sustain in the long term. Towards the end of their time the church experienced decline as the demands of inner city ministry proved difficult. At the present time, the congregation has another married couple as its pastors, John and Angela Butcher, who have begun to reverse the previous decline in church numbers. As a result the constituency of the church has changed, with greater numbers of Caribbean and African members. The church has a council or eldership group, which advises the pastors in their work and represents the wider congregation. The church programme contains Sunday services, morning and evening, mid-week meetings for prayer and fellowship, a monthly half-night prayer meeting, as well as membership meetings through which enquirers can learn more about the church and the Assemblies of God denomination. There are social events for families, men and women, and occasional celebratory events such as the Easter walk of witness with other similar denominations in the area.

Each week Pastor John conducts membership classes and the notes from these classes provide key information regarding the church's self-identity. A number of statements are important for acquiring a sense of the church's self-understanding. For example, the current church purpose statement reads as follows:

The Great Commandment – Loving:

Love God: 'Jesus said, "Love the Lord your God with all your heart…soul…and mind. This is the first and greatest commandment"' (Matthew 22.37).

Our purpose is to be worshippers (Matthew 4.10; John 4.23).

The primary calling of every true believer is to glorify and magnify God. It must come in priority and sequence before service. And we do so not out of duty or restraint but out of gratitude and celebration.

Love the Church: 'By this shall they know that you are my disciples, if you have love for one another' (John 13.35). Jesus also said: 'Love your neighbour as yourself'. Being worshippers drives us to service. We want to minister to others out of what we have received from God. We are called to 'care' for one another and that is why we have small group meetings in homes called 'Care Groups'. We are called to be 'ministers'. If we are church attendees and not ministers, then we are not being faithful to our call. Some believers just want to **sit, soak and sour.**

Love the World: 'Go and make disciples' (Matthew 28.19).

HPC exists to communicate the Gospel in word and deed to its community. To be both salt and light. Each of us will give an account on the day of the Lord as to how we administered the message of reconciliation – the coming, dying, rising, ascending, returning Christ. In all four Gospels and in **Acts 1.8** Christ makes it clear the Church is now the light of the Gentiles. It's more important than the fight against terrorism, or the plight of starving nations.

The Great Commission – Living:

In the Great Commission three verbs describe the act of discipling, and all are in the present continuous tense – an ongoing practise. They are **going, baptizing, and teaching**. We are all called to live out our Christian experience 24/7 (24 hours a day, 7 days a week). **Romans 12.1** exhorts us to present our bodies as 'living sacrifices'. We are to live out our walk with God, totally committed to God.

The Great Commitment – Learning:

'Teaching them to obey' (Ephesians 4.12) – … Teaching is insufficient. There must be a response to what is taught. Jesus calls us to teach people **to obey**. This is discipleship (Colossians 1.28). After reaching must come teaching – to process maturity. (Butcher, n.d.: 15)

These statements suggest that love is at the centre of the church's mission and that this is expressed primarily through worship and subsequently in acts of service through pastoral care of one another in the congregation and discipleship-making in the world. This purpose statement is articulated more succinctly when it states that: HPC celebrates God's presence in worship, demonstrates God's love through ministry, communicates God's Word by means of evangelism, incorporates individuals into God's family or fellowship and educates them through discipleship (16). These purpose statements are supplemented by two further statements. First, the HPC vision statement reads:

> The purpose of Hockley Pentecostal Church is to give every man, woman and child the opportunity of understanding the gospel and to provide ways in which they can grow and develop in ministry for the glory of God. (31)

Second, core values are defined as statements that join people together in common belief and govern choices, programmes and activities, and clarify strategic goals. HPC core values are stated as follows:

1. the value of biblical and theological integrity
2. the value of sensitivity to the Holy Spirit
3. the value of moral integrity
4. the value of unity-in-diversity
5. the value of transparent worship and consistent prayer
6. the value of quality relationships
7. the value of every member ministry
8. the value of mission orientation
9. the value of team ministry (32)

It is these statements that enable an observer to get a sense of the purpose, vision and values of the church. Clearly these values resonate with Pentecostalism generally, especially the emphasis upon the Bible and the Holy Spirit, worship and prayer, holiness, relationships, gifts of ministry and mission.

Aim and Overview

This study is an investigation into the contribution that ordinary discourse makes in the construction of a practical-theological account of Pentecostal identity. It utilizes the notion of ordinary theology, as proposed by Jeff Astley (2002) and develops it by means of the concept of 'rescripting' (Martin, 2006; Cartledge, 2008c). *Therefore, the central aim of this study is to listen to, record and reflect upon the 'ordinary theology' of congregational members in relation to a number of key themes.* It offers a reflection that intends to rescript the ordinary theology of Pentecostal church members through an engagement with denominational and wider Pentecostal tradition, social science perspectives and Pentecostal and Charismatic scholarship.

After this introduction follows a methodology chapter. This is written in order to explain where this book is placed in the sub-disciplines of theology – namely, practical theology as an empirical discipline in the field of Pentecostal and Charismatic studies. It also gives details concerning the research process and, in particular, discusses the ideas of ordinary theology, rescripting and levels of discourse. It is written for academic colleagues and students interested in these matters. For readers who are less concerned with methodological issues, you may wish to skip this chapter and begin with chapter 3, the first of the thematic chapters.

There are six thematic chapters in this book that aim to elaborate the contours of ordinary Pentecostal theology, while also paying attention to pneumatology. They relate to the themes explored through the focus groups, although a selection was made on the basis of word-limitation and the quality of the material that emerged from the focus group discussions. 'Worship' was chosen as the first theme because of its importance in Pentecostal spirituality. It lies at the heart of what it means to be a Pentecostal Christian in terms of identity. It was the initial 'way in' to the congregation, allowing me to become orientated towards the church community. It was also the entrée into the congregation for the purpose of research, and it allowed me to appreciate their ordinary theology as expressed through corporate worship. The chapter aims to analyse the nature of worship as observed and as reflected upon by the members. Following this, two chapters discuss entry and progression in the Christian life, namely 'conversion' and 'baptism in the Spirit'. They belong together because, as it will be seen, there is a connection between the way individuals come into Pentecostal churches and the way in which they are drawn into the centre of congregational life. Both of these themes are important to this process. 'Healing' is a central belief for Pentecostalism and this congregation exemplifies traditional attitudes towards the significance of it for theological identity. The worship services also provided a context in which to understand just how expectations about healing are given theological freight. Finally, the themes of 'life and witness' and 'mission and the second coming' belong together and provide analyses of how the beliefs and practices of ordinary Christians assist them to relate to the society in which they are located. They also enable congregation members to relate to the wider church through their understandings of world mission and global Pentecostal forces, together with eschatological expectation and its impact on their everyday lives. These beliefs resonate with central Pentecostal themes of salvation, empowerment for witness, health, relationship with the world and the return of Christ.

The concluding chapter makes recommendations for renewed congregational praxis based upon the testimonies in the context of the wider congregational study. Insights from the rescripting process are then applied to recent discussions in Pentecostal ecclesiology and a proposal is made based upon this concrete study. The contribution of the study is summarised before suggestions for future research are made.

Chapter 2
Methodology

In this chapter I shall first of all situate the nature of the study within the discipline of practical theology. I do this in relation to my own work in the field, as this study builds upon and extends my previous methodology. It is extended by means of the concepts of 'ordinary theology' and 'rescripting', which are both defined and explained here. After setting out this overarching methodology, I shall then describe the qualitative research tasks in this kind of congregational study: gaining access, participant observation, focus groups, documentary sources, data analysis and verification of the findings. Finally, the theological scholarship with which I am in conversation is described, namely Pentecostal-Charismatic theology, in order to understand the contribution that is being made through this enquiry.

Practical Theology as an Empirical Discipline

My *Practical Theology* book (2003) provided an opportunity to think through the methodological issues that I had engaged with in previous research and to move beyond them (Cartledge, 1996, 1998c, 1999a, 1999d, 2002b). I wanted to provide a text that was located within the discipline of practical theology, that took seriously the empirical approach to the subject coming from the Nijmegen school, associated with the *Journal of Empirical Theology* (Brill), and at the same time offered an explicitly Pentecostal-Charismatic perspective. In this sense it was a hermeneutically aware and constructive text. Pentecostal-Charismatic theology drives chapters 2 and 3 and in a sense is the key to that book. In those chapters I considered just how practical theology can be reconfigured by the notion of dialectic that is conceived in pneumatological ways, and also how truth and epistemology can be considered as forms of testimony, which are then subsequently applied to biblical and empirical material. The empirical studies that followed were intended as illustrations of the kinds of research that are possible and included both qualitative and quantitative data. The use of quantitative data may be regarded as problematic because of its positivist associations. However, I intended to locate such data explicitly within a hermeneutically aware approach that treated data not as bare facts but as influenced by values from the start. To acknowledge such commitments but nevertheless to use the approach of quantitative method is now widely accepted within the European context and the international academy represented by the International Society for Empirical Research in Theology. It is at this point that I perhaps need to explain some of the differences between 'empirical theology' in Europe compared to the same designation in the USA.

The phrase 'empirical theology' appears to mean different things in Europe and the USA. In the USA it is a type of modern liberal theology, a kind of natural theology that relinquishes 'any world of transcendental causes or principles' (Inbody, 1992: 11). It appeals to autonomous human reason as the arbiter of truth. But it also appeals to experience and is open to investigating the range of human experience using instrumental and experimental means of doing this. It believes that all theological claims are open to public inspection and correction; and it appeals to 'common human experience in one form or another as the source and justification' for theological assertions (Inbody, 1992: 12). This approach has its roots in both the British empirical tradition and the American pragmatism of John Dewey and William James. It was associated with 'The Chicago School' in three different phases: (1) the early socio-historical phase (1908–1926, associated with Shirley Jackson Case), (2) the philosophical-theological phase (1926–1946, associated with Henry Nelson Wieman) and (3) the constructive theology phase (1946–1966, associated with the arrival of Bernard Meland). It was during the second phase that Alfred North Whitehead's metaphysics was applied to develop process philosophy and theology. The key thinkers in this developing intellectual tradition were Charles Hartshorne and Bernard Loomer. Thus, there is an established link with process theology, even though there are differences of emphasis between the empirical and the speculative traditions.

The European tradition has been developed by practical theologians who are also, in some sense, committed to the Christian tradition (e.g. Heitink, 1993). Van der Ven from the Roman Catholic University at Nijmegen started publishing the *Journal of Empirical Theology* without any obvious and explicit commitment to the kind of process theology associated with the American tradition (van der Ven, 1993). Leslie J. Francis also uses the denotation 'empirical theology' in the British context, where is it perhaps most associated with his social-psychology of beliefs and values and descriptive theological accounts. I have positioned myself somewhere between these two figures, and indeed started to engage with van der Ven's work on methodology at an early stage (1999d). I added a specifically Pentecostal-Charismatic perspective to the discipline. That is, I used the empirical-theological cycle from van der Ven's empirical approach to practical theology, but studied aspects of Pentecostal and Charismatic Christianity, with a view to building academic discourse in the field (see especially 2002a; cf. Thomas, 2009).

However, in the *Practical Theology* text I moved from my reliance on the empirical-theological cycle of van der Ven to the idea of dialectic, which I understand as operating beneath the surface of most cyclical models (Cartledge, 2003: 20–30; cf. Cartledge, 2004). I suggested that the research process be framed as an oscillation between the 'lifeworld' (concrete reality) and 'system' (theory or theological metanarrative). The individual theologian or research team of theologians move between these two poles and in Pentecostal-Charismatic theology are in dialogue with the charismatic spirituality that also informs the process. It is this dialectical model that continues to inform my approach to empirical studies (see Cartledge, 2003: 22). It appeared to me that this oscillation is basic to the kind of enquiry that practical theology is interested in because it attempts to connect two quite distinct areas. The empirical-theological model is a rigorous research tool but it is too unwieldy for most studies of a more limited nature (two distinct stages of empirical investigation is extremely time-consuming). On the whole, practical theology uses a methodology as a guide that allows researchers and students to understand the process through which the study has progressed in order to better evaluate the conclusions and recommendations for renewed action, or in this case *rescription and renewed praxis* (see below). It is a *heuristic* tool that is as good as the quality of engagement with each different type of source, be it empirical or theoretical.

Practical theology conceived as an empirical discipline uses the tools and methods of the social sciences to map out the beliefs and values, attitudes and practices of individuals and communities. Prior to the contributions noted above, theology had not done this before in a rigorous way but instead relied on *ad hoc* approaches or insights and intuitions. These are important and, no doubt, much has been learned from this kind of reflection, but if lived faith is to be understood in all its complexity then a more rigorous methodological approach must be taken. The danger, of course, is that this kind of work could become just another branch of social science and the danger is very real. However, I am alert to the danger and believe that a theologically normative discipline rooted in the Christian tradition, as well as engaged with contemporary faith practices, will be less likely to fall into this trap if theological discourse is given priority from the start. This raises the important question of how practical theology relates to the social sciences and I have opted, following van der Ven (1993), for an intra-disciplinary approach (Cartledge, 1999d, 2002a). That is, ultimately the study constructs *theological* discourse, but in critical dialogue with the contributions of the social sciences. It can be illuminated further in relation to the different kinds of discourses with which academic practical theology in its empirical mode now interacts (see below).

Rescripting Ordinary Theological Testimony

Ordinary Theology

This study aims to map out the contours of what Jeff Astley calls the 'ordinary' theology of Pentecostals (Astley, 2002; Astley and Christie, 2007; Christie and Astley, 2009), or what some theologians have called 'local' (Schreiter, 1985), 'contextual' (Bevans, 2002), 'non-academic' or indeed 'irregular' theology (Macchia, 2002) at the 'ground level' (Cruchley-Jones, 2008). In practical theology it has been called *Laientheologie* (Dingemans, 1996: 86). Contemporary anthropologists and sociologists use similar categories, such as 'lived' (McGuire, 2008), 'everyday' (Ammerman, 2007) and 'elementary' religion (Stringer, 2008). Astley defines ordinary theology in the following way:

> Ordinary Christian theology is my phrase for the theology and theologizing of
> Christians who have received little or no theological education of a scholarly,
> academic or systematic kind. 'Ordinary', in this context, implies non-scholarly
> and non-academic; it fits the dictionary definition that refers to an 'ordinary
> person' as one who is 'without exceptional experience or expert knowledge'.
> (Astley, 2002: 56)

He continues by saying that this type of theology is grounded in attitudes, values
and commitments, experiences and practices of individuals and communities,
often categorised as 'folk' or 'common' religion.

Astley contends that religious beliefs should not be called 'theology' unless
they are articulated to some extent and reflected upon. However, he assumes that
most believers do engage in some measure of reflection, even working out answers
to their own theological questions (Astley, 2002: 139). This would certainly be
the case for a good number of Pentecostals. There are some 'lay' members of
these churches who, though they have never studied theology formally, have
nevertheless read various accessible (and perhaps less accessible!) theology texts.
Over time they may have built up a good understanding of theological concepts.
Alternatively, they have attended church-run discipleship courses and, in that
sense, may have studied theological ideas systematically if not academically.
Pentecostals take their beliefs seriously and therefore take time to engage in Bible
study, so while they may not have experienced academic study their theology
cannot be regarded as *necessarily* naive or simplistic. But even if Pentecostals
have not had exceptional experiences of academic theology (although what might
count as one of these experiences is perhaps an interesting question!), they have
had exceptional experiences of religion, which is why they have been studied with
such energy over the past 40–50 years. Moreover, they claim that their experiences
are directly from God, and that such experiences impart knowledge. They have
built up a kind of common-sense expertise in relation to how these experiences
should be handled. This should not be dismissed as irrelevant or indeed inferior
and Pentecostal scholarship has recognised the value of this 'ordinary expertise'.
Therefore, the definition of theology and theologising that Astley refers to as
'ordinary theology' appears appropriate to Pentecostal and Charismatic studies;
and it allows us to start with the people in the pew, so to speak, even if they no
longer use pews but portable, comfortable chairs!

Rescripting Testimony

David Martin (2006) suggests that ordinary Pentecostal discourse should not
be interpreted too quickly by standard sociological concepts, for example
'deprivation' and 'alienation', because this may distort the reality that is being
interpreted. Instead, he argues that people should be allowed to speak in their own
terms first because that way scholars are able 'to stay respectfully and attentively
close to whatever discourse is produced' (2006: 20). And the ways in which

scholars rescript can vary between weak or strong, with over-strong rescriptions potentially damaging the evidence and misrepresenting those under study (2006: 23). Martin proposes that attention should be given to the autobiographies, images and artefacts in order to appreciate fully the nature of their beliefs and values, especially their narrative of betterment (2006: 35). Thus, Martin provides an important metaphor, namely 'rescription', for how one might approach the study of ordinary theology. If ordinary theology can be said to exhibit a kind of 'script', then a scholarly engagement can be said to be a form of rescripting which maintains the proper scholarly values of both respect and attentiveness. The focus of attention is therefore the script of the verbatim testimonies located within the broader congregational narrative. But what exactly is testimony in this context?

It can be argued that the concept of testimony, the telling of one's personal story of God's activity, is central to the ordinary expression of faith. This is because Pentecostalism is rooted in oral culture, rather than literary culture, and oral culture is shaped by narrativity (Hollenweger, 1997: 18; cf. Camery-Hoggatt, 2005). Indeed the kind of rationality employed within Pentecostalism is more likely to be narrative in shape: a story about what happened and its consequences, rather than a set of abstract propositions. As I have argued elsewhere (Cartledge, 2002c; 2003: 52–57), testimony is a means of social knowledge construction and indeed integrates other forms of knowledge such as perception, memory, consciousness and reason (Audi, 2000). In Pentecostal spirituality it functions as a mechanism of reinforcement and commitment (McGuire, 1977), whereby the worldview is both legitimated and energised in the community through the art of telling testimonies about the grace of God as it has been made concrete in the lives of believers (Plüss, 1987: 10; 1988; De Matviuk, 2002). It is used largely in an informal manner, although in the formal setting of a worship service, it can take on some more routinised characteristics (Coady, 2000: 27–53). Essentially it provides not just a way of entering into the world of ordinary Pentecostal theology, but also enables members of this world to share their theology with one another in an holistic way and with reference to Scripture (Ellington, 2000; 2001; 2007). Its function, as a means of integrating social knowledge, makes it significant for this type of research.

Therefore, it has currency both as a mode of theology and as a research strategy whereby ordinary beliefs and values can be accessed in a natural manner (cf. Green, 1999). It is found principally in worship services, so methodologically this has also provided an entry point into the life of the congregation, which is why worship is the first thematic chapter. Indeed, Pentecostal testimony could be said to function by means of three interrelated modes: (1) personal story, expressed in dialogue with others, (2) congregational story expressed in corporate worship and public life and (3) denominational story expressed through its historical and contemporary tradition. I am interested in the relationship between all three modes but seek to rescript (1) in relation to (2) and (3).

The nature of rescripting in this context takes seriously the authenticity of the witness of ordinary theology. The narratives reflect a combination of personal values, corporate beliefs and particular circumstances. In them there is resonance with both the wider Assemblies of God and other Pentecostal traditions; as well as exhibiting unique expressions of the faith, which can be dissonant with the wider ecclesial narrative. The rescripting process produces neither a damaging revisionist account, which seeks to supplant Pentecostal presuppositions with alien ones, nor a re-envisioning of classical Pentecostal confessionalism. Rather, it seeks to maintain a tension between a revised script that is *both* in continuity with *and* in discontinuity with the existing script. It seeks to move ordinary theology forward through a deeper analysis of its testimony mode and a broader dialogue with the Christian theological tradition, illuminated by the insights of the social sciences. Rescription in this practical-theological orientation aims to be careful in its representation, sensitive towards the denominational tradition, sympathetic towards Pentecostal spirituality, yet also critical in its analysis and constructive in its proposals.

This notion of rescripting also builds on practical theology's concern with praxis. Praxis is usually defined as value-laden practices, or what might be called operationalised theology – that is, theology that is intimately bound up with action and behaviour (Cartledge, 2003: 249; Forrester, 2000: 7). But it is also concerned with espoused theology via sermons, leaflets and regular everyday conversation. The script to be examined is constructed through an analysis of these sources (see below), and within Pentecostal discourse is encapsulated in the notion of testimony. It connects with what has been called the theology of the heart, the personal contructed narrative and the canonical narrative approach to theological reflection (Graham et al., 2005, 2007). A theological rescripting exercise, as opposed to, say, a sociological rescripting exercise, will of neccessity wish to engage with the norms of Scripture (the Christian script; Vanhoozer, 2005) and Christian tradition (interpretations of the script historically), although, of course, how this is done will vary according to the nature of the subject under study and the approach of individual theologians. For the purposes of this book, I shall take contemporary Pentecostal and Charismatic theological scholarship as my main dialogue partner. So, how will this proceed and what kind of discourse will be constructed? In order to answer this question, I turn to matters of process and discourse (that is, language as it is used in particular ways).

Process and Levels of Discourse

In this study, each thematic chapter will reflect the practical-theological dialectic and contain different kinds of material relevant to the theme, but taking as its starting point the ordinary theology of adherents. It does this by bringing different voices into a conversation, and allowing these different perspectives to reinterpret the verbatim testimonies, or (in one case) a dialogue and a sermon summary. The testimonies are not only interpreted in the light of other testimonies, the dynamics of the focus group, but also in relation to the wider context of the congregational study (through participant observation and documentary analysis). They are regarded as 'windows', however imperfect, into the beliefs and practices of the congregation as a whole. But in order to appreciate the historical context of this Pentecostal tradition, in which these testimonies are located, a discussion of British classical Pentecostal material relevant to the theme is also presented. These voices are brought into dialogue with theoretical perspectives from the social sciences, and (in one case) philosophical theory, allowing theory to illuminate the narratives and the ordinary narratives to interact with the relevant theoretical perspectives. In each chapter a discussion of Pentecostal-Charismatic theology enables insights from scholarship to influence the theological construction by developing the ongoing conversation. What emerges from this dialectic between multiple voices is a distillation of the conversation in a rescripted ordinary theology. In the conclusion to the book, I make these rescriptions more concrete by suggesting recommendations for renewed congregational praxis (cf. Osmer, 2008). Finally, this is supplemented by a contribution towards Pentecostal-Charismatic theology, by suggesting a constructive proposal for the sake of academic theological discourse.

In anthropological language, this study will explore the emic categories (i.e. the ideas and concepts that are common to the people under study) and expressions that participants in a Pentecostal congregation use as they are embedded in corporate and individual praxis and sustained by a Pentecostal worldview and belief system. But I do not wish to leave it simply at that. I wish to employ etic (overaching theoretical) concepts in order to rescript these emic or ordinary ideas and expressions (Cartledge, 2008c; cf. Bowie, 2000: 92). In effect, I shall be working at three conceptual levels. The first is the 'ordinary' level of participants in the movement, who have the Pentecostal tradition mediated to them by means of corporate worship, small group meetings, their pastors and their own experiences and personal commitments. The second is the 'official' theology of the British Assemblies of God denomination, which seeks to offer parameters within which authentic Pentecostal expression may move. There is often a dialectic between these two levels mediated via official teaching expressed at the local level and through academic theology that is rooted in confessional theology. The third level is the academic discourse on Pentecostalism, which can either be theological discourse about Pentecostalism from within its own ranks or non-theological religious and social science discourse. This level attempts to use etic categories to abstract from the emic and theorise more generally about religious experience and processes. Obviously scholarly Pentecostal-Charismatic theology will stand nearer to official denominational discourse and may even be constrained by it. Scholars in social science and religious studies may appear to have greater freedom, although in reality there are theoretical positions policed by peers.

Figure 2.1 represents the different levels of conversation in the methodological process. Ordinary discourse is represented as level 1, which in anthropological terms is the emic domain or sometimes called first order theology. It is the theology of the people on the ground and is the focus of this study. Denominational or confessional theology is represented as level 2. It is a second order reflection on the first order theology from the pew and is articulated in denominational material, official statements of faith and policy documents; it is ecclesial discourse. It functions to give denominational identity and a focus for community and fellowship. It therefore intersects with ordinary discourse and the mediators of these levels of interaction are often the church leaders. Academic theology also intersects in two directions and functions as the mediating discourse and is represented as level 3. It is theology that is not tied to confessional Pentecostal theology but nevertheless shares similar sources and concerns. It has a broader agenda in relation to non-Pentecostal theology and non-theological academic discourse. It is here that practical theology functions as a mediating academic discourse between levels 1, 2 and 3. It advances theological discourse in dialogue with the Christian tradition and the social and human sciences by means of original empirical research. The rescripting sections of each chapter are written at level 3, while the recommendations for renewed congregational praxis are written at level 2 for translation into level 1 by the church leaders themselves, should they wish to do so (see the discussion of 'open-ended guidelines' or 'rules of the art' in Osmer, 2004). The application of the research findings in the proposal towards a Pentecostal ecclesiology is also written at level 3.

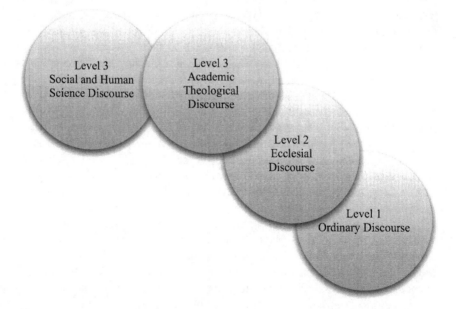

Figure 2.1   The Interrelationship between Different Kinds of Discourse

The Researcher

At this point, some readers will want to know where exactly I stand in relation to those whom I am researching. In other words, can I come clean about my own location? In terms of epistemology, given the current awareness of practical theologians towards 'reflexivity' (Swinton and Mowat, 2006: 59; Osmer, 2008: 57–58; Ward, 2008: 3–4, 18–20), I confess that I am an insider to the field of Pentecostal and Charismatic studies and an insider to the spirituality of the Charismatic movement. This has given me insight into the nature of how Pentecostal spirituality functions on the ground and how it has been theorised by theologians and social scientists (cf. Arweck and Stringer, 2002). However, I am an outsider to classical Pentecostalism and have never studied *classical* Pentecostals on the ground before, so this strand of tradition also brought with it some surprises. My previous fieldwork experience has been with mainline Charismatic Renewalists and the New Church movement. This meant that I could not take for granted either my academic understanding, from general knowledge of the literature, or indeed my previous fieldwork experience as providing the necessary lenses through which to interpret the congregation. I needed to investigate this congregation in a fresh way, which is what I have attempted to do. Therefore, I found myself in an unfamiliar place of being an insider in some respects and an outsider in other respects. The creative tension that this epistemological location gives me contributes to the exercise of rescripting: allowing me to be sensitively critical and yet constructive (cf. Dreyer, 2009). In the end, I am not constructing a theological account for myself, but for others (in that sense, an outsider) even if I have some sympathy with what it is that I am recommending (in that sense, an insider) and its contribution to the overall discourse of academic Pentecostal-Charismatic theology (cf. Schreiter, 1985: 19–20). Of course, there is the possibility that the congregation and leadership may reject my recommendations and that is their prerogative to do so. Nevertheless, and even if that is the case, this study offers an example of how empirically orientated theology, paying attention to both espoused and operational content can potentially rejuvenate both the ordinary and the academic through a focused study that brings the two together in a rigorously methodological manner.

Research Methods

The project focuses on one Assemblies of God congregation (HPC) in order to attend to the ordinary theology of the members in a particular context and takes an inductive qualitative approach that treats the congregation as a case study (Yin, 1989; 1993). It is best described as a case study because it is a 'bounded system': bounded by time (eight months' data collection) and place (single congregational site), using multiple sources of information (Creswell, 1998: 37). It can also be further described as an 'instrumental case study' because the study focused upon a specific concern, namely the ordinary theology rather than the intrinsic nature of the congregation (Stake, 1995: 3). In this sense the project can be understood as an explicitly theological enterprise and could also be classified in congregational study terms as 'extrinsic-theological' (Woodhead et al, 2004: 8–9). This classification refers to studies that consider a congregation in relation to an external concern, such as 'social capital' or a desire to hear congregational voices for their distinctive contribution (2). The present study falls within this category, as it aims to take the perspectives uncovered 'on the ground' to another place, namely an engagement with academic theological discourse in Pentecostal and Charismatic scholarship. But it also seeks to understand the nature of the congregation in its own terms, and in this way fulfils something of the 'intrinsic' agenda as well (cf. Cameron et al, 2005; Swinton and Mowat, 2006; e.g. Labanow, 2009).

The congregation of HPC in Birmingham, England, was chosen because I wished to study a church that was authentically Pentecostal and reflected the multi-cultural context of where I live: Birmingham. After considering the lists of churches available in the Assemblies of God and Elim church denominations, and after a discussion with colleagues and local students, it appeared to me that HPC fitted the type of church I was interested in. Importantly it takes only 15–20 minutes to travel there by car from my home; therefore its geographical location was also ideal. In the context of a busy schedule, this is an important consideration for a researcher! Therefore, I decided to make an approach and see what transpired.

Gatekeepers

Initially I approached Pastor John after a visit to an evening service during the summer of 2007. After the service I explained who I was and that I was interested in conducting a congregational study. He seemed genuinely interested and happy to assist me. This was followed by a meeting at which I explained the project and answered questions. He said that he would need to discuss the matter with the church council and that if they agreed, then they would probably wish to meet up with me and ask questions directly for themselves. I met with the council in September 2007 and explained the project. It is fair to say that the meeting was an occasion for a rigorous analysis of my proposal and as a result of the meeting I wrote a letter highlighting what I wished to do and enclosing my research ethics statement, which I had prepared when designing the project (Swinton and Mowat, 2006: 137–138). One of the key issues in this kind of research is representation and the church council members were quite naturally concerned about how I would represent them in a text, and, importantly, how congregation members would react to any negative representation and its repercussions for congregational life. I agreed that this was a serious ethical concern, that Pentecostals have sometimes felt victimised by social scientific research; and that in order to alleviate this concern that I would be prepared for them to read the draft manuscript to check for factual accuracy and raise questions of representation (Creswell, 1998: 203; cf. Kimmel, 2007: 319). I also stated that academic autonomy should be respected.

In addition, I agreed to share the findings from my research in a preliminary way with members of the congregation so that they could challenge or verify my initial findings (see below).

The research material contained three types: participant observation of worship services, focus group interviews and documentary analysis of material produced by the congregation. This enabled these different sources of data to be triangulated – that is, themes were viewed from at least two of these sources collected by different methods (Creswell, 1998: 202, 213; Stake, 1995). It allowed findings from one source to be verified with another, or perhaps developed.

Participant Observation

I attended Sunday morning worship services over the course of eight months (September 2007 to April 2008). During the worship services I took the stance of a participant observer. This meant that I took notes throughout the service as well as participating in liturgical acts, such as singing the songs, praying, standing for prayer when the congregation was asked to stand, receiving the sacrament of Holy Communion and listening to the sermons. I did not respond to any of the altar calls or ministry times; instead I watched what happened and made notes of the practices and how these were interpreted. During my second morning service (September 2007), I was introduced to the congregation briefly by Pastor John, who explained that I worked at the university, that I was doing some research and visiting the congregation over a period of months. After my introduction I had a few conversations with members who expressed an interest in what I was doing. My notes from the observation were written up as soon as possible after the service and formed a description of the service structure, the hymnody, use of biblical texts as well as the liturgical rites that formed part of the worshipping life of the church. Much of this material has been used in relation to the chapter on worship. Other aspects have been used to inform other themes as they are expressed in the liturgy of the congregation.

Documentary Sources

During my time of participant observation I was able to gather the monthly newsletter, Bible reading notes and any special event information as I attended these services. In addition, Pastor John kindly gave me his membership class teaching material as well as general information about the demographic constitution of the church. The church has a website and I was able to use this through the course of my study, especially in relation to additional teaching material that was published there. I was also able to compare the church website with the denominational Assemblies of God site and this enabled me to contextualise the information I was gathering at HPC vis-à-vis the wider tradition. The church also posted a number of video clips on YouTube and these proved informative.[1] I acquired several copies of the denomination's magazine, *Joy*, during this period and was able to analyse material from this magazine in relation to HPC. Finally, the founders of the church, Miss Reeve and Miss Fisher, had produced a booklet that outlined aspects of the history of the church (n.d.), which provided a useful source of information. A member of the church kindly lent me a video of the church that had been broadcast by the BBC in the 1970s. This included an interview with Reeve and Fisher and helped me to understand the historical context of the church.

Focus Groups

In order to understand the ordinary theology of the members, I used the practice of testimony as a way of helping members participate in conversation. Realising that most would be familiar with the giving and receiving of testimony and that this was best done in a group setting, I decided to conduct 'focus groups'. I used this title because most members would have been familiar with this idea through its use in research by commerce and government. It was a way of getting people with a common spirituality to talk together in depth about a theme in a non-threatening environment (Krueger, 1988: 18, 27–30). It was also a means of listening to a conversation between members of the church and noting their interaction as a group (Bryman, 2004: 348). In order to select an appropriate number of participants, the adult membership list was used as a sampling frame and a diverse group of ten people were invited to participate. Therefore, each focus group contained Pentecostal Christians – that is, homogeneous in relation to spirituality, but also stratified so that there was a mixture of people in each group according to gender, age, ethnicity and lack of close knowledge of each other (Bryman, 2004: 349; Krueger, 1988: 92). In the end, the groups were sufficiently varied so as to suggest that a genuinely stratified sample had been selected from the 100 people who were invited. From those invited, 82% participated in the ten focus groups; therefore 18% exercised their freedom not to participate. Ten individuals were invited to participate in each focus group on the assumption that at least two would drop out, thereby leaving an ideal size of six to eight people (Krueger, 1988: 18). In the event, the average group size was nine.

The great advantage of using this strategy was the interaction between the members of the group. Whereas a set of interviews with individuals might gather a fair amount of information, with a focus group one is able to watch and analyse the interaction between the members of the group. This means that different viewpoints are brought into dialogue before the researcher's very eyes and the way in which ordinary theology is negotiated at a group level can be observed. It was the best way to appreciate testimony in this context, because participants are completely

---

[1]   See: http://www.hockleypentecostal.com/about/;   http://www.youtube.com/watch?v=YCStZJhzZ4g; http://www.flickr.com/photos/faster1974/2859880733/; accessed on 25 September 2009.

at ease about sharing their personal stories with one another. Indeed, the problem was not to do with a lack of engagement, so often considered a problem with focus group research, rather it was ensuring that only one person spoke at any given time during the exchange. Thankfully, the group was also willing to comply with the process as a whole, including the need to watch the clock.

The focus groups contained 31 men (38%) and 51 women (62%). The age range for men was 16% in 18–29 years; 19% in 30–39 years; 26% in 40–49 years; 3% in 50–59 years; 16% in 60–69 years; 13% over 70 years; and 7% did not give their ages. The age range for women was 10% in 18–29 years; 16% in 30–39 years; 18% in 40–49 years; 23% in 50–59 years; 14% in 60–69 years; 15% in over 70 years; and 4% did not give their ages. The church is very international and multi-cultural, with worshippers from many different countries, although some have now become British citizens. The men originated from: Africa (Nigeria 10%; Togo 3%; Uganda 10%; Zambia 3%); Asia (India 7%); Europe (Ireland 3%; Macedonia 3%; the UK [Black 7%; Mixed Heritage 3%; White 32%]); and the Caribbean (Barbados 3%; Jamaica 10%; Montserrat 3%; St Kitts 3%). The women originated from: Africa (Ghana 2%; Nigeria 10%; Uganda 4%; Zimbabwe 2%); Europe (Ireland 6%; Germany 2%; the UK [Black 2%; Mixed Heritage 2%; White 33%]; and the Caribbean (Barbados 6%; Dominica 2%; Jamaica 21%; Montserrat 6%) and the Turks and Caicos Islands (2%). Not everyone specified their occupation, especially if retired. The men gave the following occupations: hospital porter, cleaner, caretaker, crane worker, heavy goods driver, accountant, legal practitioner, college tutor, local government manager, business adviser, teacher, engineer, IT consultant and student. The women gave the following occupations: home-maker, care assistant, cook, hospital domestic, housekeeper, cleaner, factory worker, support worker, administrative assistant, teaching assistant, administrator, traffic enumerator, sales representative, nurse, PA executive, student, evangelist and unemployed.

The focus groups were conducted between January and March on a weekday evening in 2008. They were usually held in a medium-sized lounge room in the church complex with tea- and coffee-making facilities nearby. I was assisted in the management of the focus groups by a postgraduate student, Doreen Morrison, who kindly took notes and helped me with running the evening. As the participants arrived, they were shown to comfortable chairs and invited to take refreshments. During these refreshments, I also handed them a short questionnaire, which enabled them to give me some basic background information so that I could contextualise their contributions later. They were also invited to write their names on a folded piece of card. Once refreshments were taken, I invited them to sit around a table and put the name cards in front of each of them (Krueger, 1988: 86). I welcomed them to the focus group and invited them to introduce themselves. Doreen and I introduced ourselves at this time. I explained the process by distributing a statement about the nature and purpose of the project and what they could expect over the course of the next hour or so. This explanation informed them as to how the event would be managed and that it would be recorded by notes (Doreen) and by two tape recorders (one backup). I also explained that before we could proceed I needed to obtain signed consent forms. I informed the participants that their involvement was entirely voluntary, that their privacy would be respected and that they could withdraw from the event before the discussion began, after the discussion had ended and at any time subsequently by writing to me directly. I also explained that there would be no negative consequences for them should they choose to withdraw (Bryman, 2004: 356).

A series of open questions was used to guide the focus group discussion and each group generally used similar questions but addressed to different themes (Bryman, 2004, 355; Krueger, 1988: 59). Thus, ten groups were conducted and addressed different themes: (1) conversion, (2) baptism in the Spirit, (3) healing, (4) prayer and inspired speech, (5) worship, (6) pastoral care, (7) gender and culture, (8) evangelism, the secular and other religions, (9) world mission and the second coming and (10) community and social action. In keeping with Pentecostal spirituality, each discussion began with an invitation for two or three participants to give a testimony of their experience in connection with the subject in question. This usually gave the desired result of helping the participants to relax and engage in a conversation as I gently probed and began to ask subsequent questions. Each focus group recording was subsequently transcribed and examined using content analysis, and forms the starting point in the chapters that follow (Krueger, 1988: 79–80, 106, 118; Robson, 2002: 459–460). This meant that key categories could be traced across the different focus groups and compared with other sources of data from participant observation and documentary analysis (Dey, 1993; Creswell, 1998: 140–146). All the excerpts from the focus group discussions are from the verbatim transcripts. In order to protect the identity of the participants, all names reported are pseudonyms. The only exception to this is the names of the pastors, John and Angela, who did not participate in the focus groups in any case.

After the data had been analysed and reflected upon (Creswell, 1998: 153–154), I conducted a feedback session at which all those who had attended a focus group could be informed of the preliminary findings (Creswell, 1998: 202; Stake, 1995: 115–116). This occurred in December 2008 on a weekday evening, at which approximately 30 people attended. I used a PowerPoint presentation to highlight key points and gave participants a form with a set of headings and space to write comments for me to consider. In the process of the feedback, there was a consensus that I had captured the beliefs, values and practices of the participants accurately and I received only one form back with additional comments for me to consider. In the chapters that follow, I have selected key themes that are important for Pentecostalism and are based on the quality of the data that emerged from the focus groups themselves.

Pentecostal-Charismatic Theology

Academic Pentecostal-Charismatic theology is a relatively young branch of theology. It began to emerge in the 1970s, with the founding of the Society of Pentecostal Studies and the publication of its journal *Pneuma*, but asserted itself further in the 1990s with the publication of the *Journal of Pentecostal Theology* (initially published by Sheffield Academic Press in 1992, now published by Brill) and its supplementary monograph series (initially published by Sheffield Academic Press, now published by Deo Publishing). The editors of that journal (Rick D. Moore, John Christopher Thomas and Steven J. Land) argued for a 'critical-constructive' approach to Pentecostal scholarship in its broadest sense (Land et al., 1992). This approach recognised that Pentecostal scholars had previously engaged in historical and social scientific research on Pentecostalism, but had not intended to re-envision the tradition. Now, with the advent of 'critical-constructive' scholarship, Pentecostals are able to integrate their own commitments with the Pentecostal tenets of faith, thus contributing to the whole range of theological scholarship. This development not only reflected the emergence of postmodern theologies within the academy, but also built upon the work of the Society of Pentecostal Studies. This premier society provides a network of scholars engaged in the study of various forms of Pentecostalism and its work continues to be reflected in its journal, *Pneuma* (now also published by Brill). These scholars associate themselves with the Pentecostal or Charismatic movements, but are not necessarily Pentecostal (although most members would classify themselves as such), so, for example, many Roman Catholic charismatics are included in this society, as well as other non-Pentecostal charismatics. In recent years there has been a convergence in the material published in these two journals, although *Pneuma* claims to be interdisciplinary in a way that the *Journal of Pentecostal Theology* does not. Other significant journals publishing scholarship in the field include: *PentecoStudies: An Interdisciplinary Journal for Research on the Pentecostal and Charismatic Movements* (Equinox), the *Journal of the European Pentecostal Theological Association,* the *Asian Journal of Pentecostal Studies* and the *Cyberjournal for Pentecostal-Charismatic Research.*

The key dialogue partners that I use to engage with the social science analysis of the ordinary theology emerging from this congregation will be largely drawn from this domain of the Pentecostal and Charismatic theological academy. Other dialogue partners will be used as appropriate to the particular rescripting exercise and they will be used in a 'critical-constructive' manner within the discourse of academic practical theology. However, there is one important distinction to stress, given how I have situated the nature of my contribution above. I am not 'rescripting', to use my terminology, from within the classical Pentecostal tradition. Rather, I write from within the broader domain of Pentecostal and Charismatic scholarship that is more critical of classical Pentecostal theology than classical Pentecostals themselves. In this sense, while I advance a *theological* position, I do *not* advance a denominationally confessional theological position. The intention, as stated above, is to critically rescript ordinary Pentecostal theology in ways that are both continuous and discontinuous in order to advance theological thought and action on the ground, but also in relation to the broader academy.

Chapter 3
Worship

This chapter begins the analysis of key themes associated with Pentecostalism, which are reflected in the congregational life of HPC. Pentecostals are enthusiastic worshippers and it has been argued that it is the worshipping life of congregations that form communal identity and assist members in negotiating the issues of everyday life. This is because faith is informed by worship and worship is informed by faith: *lex orandi, lex credendi* (Wainwright, 1980).[1] In other words, belief can be understood from what and how people pray because people normally pray what they believe. It is certainly the case that worship is at the heart of the community of HPC, especially the Sunday morning worship. In order to appreciate the style and content of this worship, the physical setting of the church interior will be described and related to the service structure, because the church space connects to the activities that occur. From the focus group convened to discuss worship, beliefs and understandings are captured and analysed. This material is subsequently contextualised within the discussion of Pentecostal and Charismatic worship, especially with regard to the Assemblies of God denomination. In order to interrogate the overall worship of HPC, the work of Daniel Albrecht is used. This is because he has analysed the practice of worship by means of ritual theory and HPC data will be reflected upon in the light of his ritual studies. Subsequently, the material is recontextualised by placing it within a broader discussion of the Pentecostal-Charismatic theology of worship, before rescripting the ordinary theology.

The Worship Service

In 2006/7 the whole worship space was changed from a traditional long east-facing arrangement with static pews to a south-facing, stage-orientated fixture with portable chairs. The space has been 'opened up', carpet has been laid, coloured lighting has been fitted, a sound system and projector system are fully installed and operational. This means that the words of songs can be projected onto two screens, the weekly notices can be delivered by means of a DVD recording and sermons

---

[1]   *Lex orandi, lex credendi* is normally translated as 'the law of prayer is the law of faith'.

can be followed by the congregation with the use of PowerPoint presentations (cf. Gold, 2006). Therefore, this church is 'hi-tech' in its use of media resources.[2]

The Service Structure

The pattern of worship observed suggests that there are seven main units and these units are present at virtually every morning worship service (Appendix C). But in order to knit these units together, so that the worship service flows, there are links. Key individuals link the units together but they do so in relation to specific locations. There are three locations in which activities occur: the platform, the main body of the congregation and the space between the platform and the congregational seating, which has been labelled the 'between zone' for convenience. Key individuals mediate these three zones, notably: (1) the music leader, which is most often Pastor Angela, but occasionally another church council member, Jack, (2) Angela's husband, Pastor John, gives the notices and manages key links, (3) both of the pastors share most of the preaching and response times, (4) other preachers such as Brian, another church council member, or invited guests who are given permission to function in a given service, and (5) other elder members of the church who lead Holy Communion or occasionally preach. The minor links, as I have labelled them, function as transitions between the major sections and members of the congregation can participate in these activities depending on the nature of the transition (e.g. praise shouts and clap offerings).

The service starts with a greeting and welcome, a prayer and usually an exhortation to leave one's burdens behind in order to worship with freedom (unit 1). Regularly, the congregation will be asked to stand for this act of preparation. On occasion a member of the congregation will be invited to the platform in order to give a testimony of healing or answered prayer. Then the music leader and the band lead the congregation in a time of singing worship songs (unit 2). This normally follows the pattern of two phases. In the first phase there is the singing of around three songs that have an upbeat tempo, and between these songs there will be praise shouts from the congregation as a whole, or from individuals in the congregation and led by the worship leader on the platform. The congregation moves in time with the rhythm of the music as Hillsong (Australian) and African/ West Indian culture appear to combine (Amoah, 2004: 69). In the second phase the songs become quieter and more reflective; in between the songs there might be exhortations from the platform or from the main body of the congregation.

After this quieter and more reflective period of sung worship there is often some form of response (unit 3). This can be in terms of prophecies, when between one and three people stand and offer a short message in sequence. There can be a message in tongues followed by an interpretation. This is followed by a call by one of the pastors for a reponse in prayer for healing or as a response to the content of

---

[2]   See http://uk.youtube.com/watch?v=7EYXWttofHA; accessed on 11 August 2009.

the message. On a number of occasions it is the pastors, mostly John, who have encouraged prayer for healing irrespective of whether a prophecy or a message in tongues has been delivered. For prayer ministry, members are called out to the front to stand in between the platform and the front row of chairs. Other members of the church are then called forward and asked to pray for them. After this ministry time has finished, and again this ending is usually managed by Pastor John, people might be asked to put up their hands if they have experienced an answer to prayer or a healing. This may be shared via a testimony and a clap offering made to the Lord by the whole congregation in thanksgiving. The ministry time may occur here or after the sermon, especially when there is a visiting preacher so that members can respond to the message preached.

After sung worship and a response, the congregation always receives the sacrament of Holy Communion (unit 4). A senior member of the church, and not necessarily a pastor, first reads one or more Bible passage in order to prepare the congregation to receive the bread and fruit juice and explains something of the significance of Holy Communion. Then he (and very occasionally she) prays a thanksgiving over the elements (referred to as emblems) and they are passed around the congregation by the stewards. The fruit juice is delivered in small cups. Anyone who is a born-again Christian may receive the elements whatever Christian tradition they belong to. During the administration of the elements a song is sung quietly, usually focused on the sacrifice of Christ on the cross. Occasionally there is silence. In between the reception of the elements a member of the congregation might stand up and deliver an extemporary prayer thanking God for the blood of Christ or read out a Bible verse or passage. Afterwards the pastors may take up the theme of the prayers and build on it, encouraging particular attitudes or action. This unit of worship may be closed by inviting some congregational building exercise, such as greeting one another or by turning to the person next to them and passing on a word of encouragement – for example, 'you are special to God'.

At this point in the service Pastor John normally offers further welcome, especially to visitors, introduces the weekly notices, which are projected onto screens in the form of a DVD recording, and supplements them as necessary (unit 5). He then invites the congregation to give their tithes and offerings to the Lord. These are collected using traditional offertory bags and prayed over by Pastor John. The children go to their groups at this time, normally during a song. This is followed by the sermon, which is preached either by one of the pastors, or by a senior member of the congregation or a visiting preacher (unit 6) . Occasionally, during the sermon, a member of the congregation may shout out: 'Praise the Lord' or 'Thank you, Jesus'. Most often the preacher punctuates the sermon with 'Amen', which usually means 'Are you still with me?', and the congregation reply 'Amen' with varying degrees of enthusiasm. A prayer ministry time may follow, linked by a song, if this has not occured earlier; and the service is closed with a prayer and an invitation to tea or coffee in the church hall with a reminder that the evening service starts at 6.30 pm (unit 7). Very often, because of time, the ending can be quite rushed because it is expected that the service will finish at 1.00 pm, having started at 11.00 am. During these final three units (5–7) there is normally very little congregational participation, unless there is a prayer ministry time after the sermon (a relocation of unit 3). In general, therefore, the most participation from the congregation is in units 1–4, with 5–7 providing less opportunity for spontaneous contributions.

Thus, it can be seen that despite the lack of written liturgy there is a clear sequence of expected events. The seven units are sown together by minor units of congregational participation, normally led by one of the pastors. These minor links include: praise shouts, exhortations, tongues and interpretation, testimony, song, instruction and prayer. There is also a relationship between the different zones of the church, with a clear intensity of encounter with God expected in the 'between zone' linking the main seats and the platform. This is symbolised by the seating of Pastor John who normally sits on the front row, either on his own or with guest preachers, but who has easy access to the platform for leading and preaching. He symbolises the connection between the platform, with the music led by Pastor Angela (and the band), and the congregation. He mediates between the two zones and is the chief master of ceremonies that ensures there is a smooth transition between the different units. Pastor Angela accompanies him through the music as she links the various units through song. On occasions she will invite him on to the plaform in order to exercise his authority, while she provides a musical atmosphere to match the action in the 'between zone'. They work in partnership and while she enables the congregation to enter into sung worship, he manages the response times. On other occasions Pastor Angela manages the response time herself.

Testimonies

The Focus Group

The focus group contained five women and four men. The women were from Nigeria (Megan), Ireland (Charlotte) and the UK (Amelia, Hannah and Lily). They were largely middle-aged (Amelia, Hannah, Lily) although Megan was younger. Their occupations were home-maker (Megan), nurse (Amelia), hospital domestic (Hannah), traffic enumerator (Lily) and unemployed (Charlotte). The men were all middle-aged and originated from Montserrat (Joshua) and the UK (Brian, George and Lewis) They worked as a caretaker (Joshua), maintenance assistant (Lewis), teacher (Brian) and college tutor (George).

I invited the participants to give testimonies of their experiences of worshipping God, and especially any memories of the Holy Spirit in worship. Five participants offered testimonies.

Charlotte: I can't explain properly other than I just feel weepy, I mean I'm not sad, but it just brings tears to me eyes. That's the only way I can describe it for me. I just feel the presence of the Lord when I'm worshipping and the music is on, you know, and everyone is singing and it's just that lovely peaceful atmosphere, it's joyous ... It doesn't happen to me all the time but occasionally, especially certain choruses, and I just feel I think it's the Lord touching me, you know [sounds of agreement in the group].

George: I remember an occasion in a previous fellowship where the pastors, who were husband and wife, were due to travel to Australia on a particular mission and the [...] gave me a, during worship, the Holy Spirit gave me a very acute awareness of the presence of angels. The whole place was full of angels. I didn't see one, everywhere I turned the Spirit showed me that the place was absolutely crammed full of angels. The Spirit was really moving me. Every time I turned towards an angel, wow, the presence of God, that's something I shall not forget in a hurry.

Brian: I got saved in effect when the Spirit came upon me in worship as ... [an] atheist, who denied the existence of God. And then in the middle of the first Charismatic Pentecostal service I'd ever been to in the middle of a particular song, which now obviously holds great meaning for me ... The Spirit came upon me and I tried to fight it and ended up at the front down on the floor with tears falling down my eyes. And I got saved that day.

Megan: Yea, so many times, even when we worship here, the atmosphere changed. People begin to worship God in tongues. There's the crying of the goodness of God and the Spirit of God just takes over [sounds of agreement] when the songs are being sung. Like this song [starts to sing]: 'How great is our [God]'. You know you begin to imagine the greatness of God in your life, in your personal life [agreement], in your surrounding. Everything happening around you is the Spirit of God just taking over.

Mark : How would you describe the effect on you in terms of worshipping? What would be the effect, either at the time or maybe afterwards? How would you say ...?

Megan : You begin to, you just have that personal encounter. You know when you are a Christian, a real Christian, you should be able to know when you encounter God. And you just have that inner peace within you,... that something has happened to you, inner peace.

Lily: I find that I have a lot of trouble with my joints and a lot of times I'm very tense. It's a way of protecting your joints. And I come to the church and we start off with something quite lively ... and suddenly with regard to something that you've just said [agreement] and I normally can't lift my arms too high, but when I'm praising something changes [agreement] and you know something is happening to you. It reduces [me] to tears and you can sob and sob and sob, and my arms just come up [agreement]. It's a lovely feeling, a lovely feeling.

I explored the idea of encountering the Spirit in worship further by asking about the focal points as the service progresses. The following extract gives a flavour of the discussion.

Mark: So, how would you connect other aspects of worship and encountering the Spirit? Would you say there's one area that [is] more intense for you ...? Is there one place in the service which is really quite an important time for you, or it just varies from week to week?

Lily: Sometimes, as soon as the Pastor starts to speak, something changes [agreement]. I don't think I always feel that straight away but something sometimes changes. Another one, sometimes I get stuck, I can't even sing the song. I have to start praying in tongues.

Amelia: 'Cos sometimes the atmosphere changes. You can just [agreement], it's like almost tangible [agreement], the atmosphere in the church changes. So I find that no matter what mood I've come in with. Sometimes I come in feeling irritable [agreement], you know and at odds, you know, things that have happened during the week. It sort of washes it off me somehow [agreement].

Brian: For me, I would say that in terms of connection with the Spirit generally it's during the slower songs because when we sing the faster songs I love it, I absolutely love it. But it's more about me, you know, to the praising, isn't it? It's me declaring how I feel about God [agreement]. And I wouldn't, although I feel in connection with God, I don't necessarily feel very spiritual in terms of the general meaning of the word. But when we come to the slower songs [agreement], then it's heavenly, literally in the sense that [agreement] I do not feel I'm still on earth [agreement]. I do not feel that I'm still just connected to the physical. I actually feel [connected] to heaven ... and actually, you know, you feel a sensation inside you, which you don't feel at other times. It's different to what you feel normally and it's different to when, you know, if you're just happy about something or anything else like that, or something. You've got that connection with God and [agreement] and you absolutely feel not of the earth [agreement]. For me, it tends to be during those slow songs.

George: I think that there are some songs that we all individually connect with perhaps more than others [agreement] for one reason or another. And I think that when we have such songs, I think the Holy Spirit can move more freely within us [agreement] and work more deeply within us. For example, the one with the chorus 'here I am to worship, here I am to bow down' [agreement], is something that I connect with very deeply and I can just give myself to the worship. Now I have to say that with some lyrics I just have to set the question mark. Because they seem to have to do more with the Old Testament than they have to do with the New Testament [laughs]. I can't connect with them as liberally, as freely as I can with lyrics that connect directly with the teaching of Jesus [agreement].

Regarding Pentecostal practices, one comment by Brian captured so much of the Pentecostal attitude and he made insightful remarks on the role of the worship leader.

Okay when you've got a good worship leader, like Pastor Angela, then they encourage you with certain practices. So very often at the start of the service it will be, you know, 'Look, are you ready to worship? Have you got the correct mindset?' We teach on praise and worship. And I was thinking when you were saying earlier about, you know, dancing and why do you dance, and why do you do certain things. I was thinking, it didn't come out at the time, because I've been taught, because when I've heard a sermon on praise and worship they've shown me scriptures which talk about dancing, which talk about lifting your hands [agreement], which talk about clapping, which talk about a joyful noise and raising a shout and they said this is what God wants and because we're taught these things, you feel, well, that's a good thing to do [agreement]. And in various practices, you know, there'll come times when they say, look, let's give a clap offering to the Lord. So we'll all clap and go for it and we're clapping for God. Do you know what I mean? It's not just because the worship leader said 'Let's clap', 'oh alright'. It's like no, well, this is right and it connects in your spirit that this is something that we should do [agreement]. And at a time of quiet when we'll sometimes say, 'Well, seek God, seek God for what he is speaking to you about now'. And sometimes when there's tongues or interpretation and prophecy and things like that then we'll stop and respond and say, 'Look, God is speaking to us now in worship [agreement], as we're worshipping God is speaking. We must respond.' We must be in tune with what's happening and you don't need [to] ignore what's happened, you let the service focus change maybe. How many times have we gone on longer in worship because we've had a word about that or [agreement] we've called people to the front because God has said, 'Here's a time to get your healing, here's a time to receive your needs' [agreement]. So okay, well, it doesn't matter that we're due to put the sermon on at 12 o'clock. He can go [on] at quarter past or twenty past today [agreement]. And I think these are the kinds of practices which actually show that it is an important thing that God through the Spirit is speaking to us in worship [agreement].

Summary of the Testimonies

There are a number of important aspects to note from these testimonies and the following discussion. First, worship is affective: it connects at a deeply emotional level. This is illustrated in the references to tears and feelings of peace and joy. Second, there is an atmosphere in worship that is interpreted as the 'presence of the Lord'. This can be associated with music, especially the slower songs, or with speaking in tongues, or other rites within the worship serivice, such as the sermon. There is a clear view that in the worship services the atmosphere changes at times quite suddenly and this is associated with God's intense presence and power. Third, in relation to the second point, there is a cosmology that also informs Pentecostal worship, namely that humanity is joined in worship by the heavenly host. It is not something that humans do alone, but when the presence of the Lord is really felt then there are angels involved in worship as well. This was indicated by the idea that worship is heavenly, that worshippers are drawn into the heavenly realm because that realm has come down to earth. Fourth, worship and an experience of the Spirit in sung worship can be deeply transformational. In fact, it can be a means of evangelism, as even atheists are converted. Fifth, there are a range of practices such as dancing, clapping, prophesying and speaking in tongues that are in fact taught from the Bible. Worshippers are formed by both their experience and by an explanation of practices of the church. Sixth, there is an openness to God whereby the agenda set by the leaders can be changed because the Spirit has spoken and led the congregation as a whole in a different direction; therefore there is a degree of spontaneity in how the service will run. Seventh, the role of the worship leader is very much respected and Pastor Angela is understood as having gifts in leading the church in worship. In this regard the element of trust is significant.

Worship in British Pentecostalism

The worship of the Assemblies of God in the UK has its roots in the early Pentecostal worship of the Sunderland Conventions. At the very first Convention, the chairman, Alexander A. Boddy (1854–1930), set out the rules that should govern this worship in the Spirit (1908). In this description of what should take place, it is expected that 'praise and prayer' should take up a third of each meeting. Quiet prayer should precede each meeting and there should be no talking in the room prior to each meeting. The choruses should be controlled by the leader, with participants praying that he should be 'led aright' in the choice of songs. Confusion should be avoided, although it is acknowledged that sometimes the Holy Spirit works so powerfully that 'there is a divine flood'. But in order to minimise any confusion the chairman's decisions should be 'promptly and willingly obeyed in cases of difficulty' and earnest prayer be offered in silence. Thus speaks a Victorian gentleman in an Edwardian era! Nevertheless, it is these early experiences of worship that formed the theology and practices of the emerging classical Pentecostal denominations in the UK.

Three extracts from different generations of Pentecostals capture something of the nature of worship in the tradition. Donald Gee, a key leader of the denomination (1948–1966), commented on the nature of Pentecostal worship in the Assemblies of God, stating:

> One of the distinctive features of a British Pentecostal meeting will be the singing of many choruses, most of them bright and catchy, expressing the joy of salvation, and others very sweet and beautiful, full of worship and all about the Lord Jesus. They love the old Methodist hymns too, and the congregational singing in British assemblies is always thrilling to visitors from overseas. Perhaps the fact that they seldom have choirs has helped to develop this feature – they are 'all in the choir'. Before very long there will probably be an utterance in 'tongues' that will be duly interpreted, usually by the leader of the meeting: for the two gifts of the Holy Spirit listed in 1 Cor. 12.19 as 'divers kinds of tongues' and 'the interpretation of tongues' are exercised very generally through all the British Assemblies of God. Quite often you will hear the gift of prophecy also and find other spiritual gifts manifested. (Gee, 1935: 10; cf. Gee, 1936, 1937)

This element of spontaneity and full participation in worship is also captured in the words of an Elim Pentecostal leader, Tom W. Walker, when he writes:

> The spontaneous adoration, exaltation, praise and worship of God by the congregation occupies a large part of the time, however. Reverent cries of 'Amen!', 'Hallelujah!' and 'Praise the Lord!' are heard from time to time. There is a precious sense of the presence of the Lord as those gathered are rapt in their devotions to the praise of God. The climax is when the emblems of the Breaking Bread are distributed by the elders, deacons and other leading brethren. The weekly act of Communion has not in any way devalued it; on the contrary, the partaking of the bread and wine has become ever more deeply appreciated. (Walker, 1976b: 43)

Again, a more recent description from Assemblies of God historian David Allen reinforces the above accounts:

> Sunday services, often known as 'meetings', are characterised by great informality and spontaneity. Though hymns common to virtually all Protestant churches – except Unitarian – are sung, shorter songs, the majority of which are paraphrases of Scripture, are more popular. It is not uncommon for these to be sung through several times, the whole congregation not infrequently standing with arms raised in an attitude of worship. Messages 'in tongues' i.e. brief glossolalic utterances, are a regular feature – these are interpreted by a member of the congregation or by the leader of the 'meeting'. 'Prophecies' – short

exhortations in the vernacular – are not unusual. Preaching is invariably lively and intensely personal and practical. Preachers expect and call for an outward response to their messages. The recording of messages is not uncommon, thus enabling the housebound to hear the Sunday sermon and those interested in doing so to study it further or pass it on to a neighbour as an evangelistic tool. Though the traditional two- or three-day convention, once very popular amongst Pentecostals, has declined, a few churches still hold these at Whit, Easter or to coincide with a church anniversary. (Allen, 1990: 126–127)

Of course, like other Christian denominations during the majority of the twentieth century, it has been the hymnbook that has provided the texts of the hymns and the songs. It is only recently, with the advent of the overhead projector and latterly with the use of computer and projector technology, that words have been made available on a large screen placed at the front of the church sanctuary. The character of Pentecostal worship is revealed in the preface to the classic hymnbook of British Pentecostalism, the *Redemption Hymnal*, which reads as follows:

This collection of hymns has been compiled to meet the need of companies of believers all over the British Isles who are rejoicing in a scriptural experience of the grace and power of the Holy Spirit similar, they humbly affirm, to that received by the early Christians on the day of Pentecost, and enjoyed through the primitive apostolic churches … The inconvenience of not possessing an adequate compilation of hymns in one book suited to their distinctive testimony eventually led to a decision to prepare and publish such a collection …

[T]hese hymns emphasize the Deity of the Lord Jesus Christ, and glory of His cross as central in the redemption, by His blood, of sinful men (sic). They provide for the worship of the Father in spirit and truth, and express the aspirations of those who long to be holy as He is holy. Their basis of doctrine is belief that the Bible is the word of God that liveth and abideth forever, by which men are born again and through which they grow in grace and in the knowledge of our Lord and Saviour.

All these truths have new and deeper power and beauty through the baptism in the Holy Spirit received as a definite experience with scriptural evidence …

Arising from this testimony has been a fervent evangelism proclaiming the gospel of full salvation which includes divine healing for the body and the hope of the coming of the Lord. Resultant assemblies of believers delight to continue 'steadfastly in the apostle's doctrine and fellowship, and in breaking of bread, and in prayers'. A hymnal is now proferred that combines rich devotional hymns in abundance with stirring revival hymns that present the Gospel in all its depth, winsomeness and simplicity. It is equally suitable for the regular life and work of the local churches, for great conventions and for evangelistic campaigns …

The hymns of the Methodist Revival, many of the best of which will be found in this collection, served to impress its great doctrinal and experimental truths upon the multitude who sang them up and down the country. In publishing this grand collection in the middle of the Twentieth Century the Committee believe that these hymns also will indelibly impress the burning truths of the Pentecostal Revival upon the many thousands who will sing them with the spirit and with the understanding also. (*Redemption Hymnal*, 1951)

It is interesting that themes emerging from wider British Pentecostalism from the twentieth century resonate with this congregational study in a number of ways. First, singing is an important component of Pentecostal worship, drawing material from its Methodist and early Pentecostal revivalist roots (Sykes, 1931; cf. Steven, 1997). Second, it is expected that songs and hymns will carry theological freight and mediate the central beliefs of the movement. Third, strong leadership of the worship is required, especially in the selection of songs and in the management of the gifts and manifestations of the Spirit. Fourth, this worship is regarded as biblical and primitive, thus signifying an experiential continuity with the early Christian communities, especially for Christology and soteriology, trinitarian grammar and sense of holiness. Fifth and finally, it is the Christian life, and, in particular, regeneration and baptism in the Holy Spirit, that allows the believer to appreciate both the power and beauty of true worship. It is worship that holds together both doctrine and experience based upon the Bible: *lex orandi, lex credendi*. These themes will be returned to below. In the meantime, Pentecostal worship is considered through the lens of ritual studies.

Ritual Theory and Pentecostal Worship

Daniel E. Albrecht has researched Pentecostal and Charismatic worship using the lens of ritual studies (1997, 1999). He defines ritual as 'those acts, actions, dramas and performances that a community creates, continues, recognises and sanctions as ways of behaving that express appropriate attitudes, sensibilities, values and beliefs within a given situation', which he applies to the corporate worship service (Albrecht, 1999: 22). He also uses the term 'rite' to refer to a portion of the worship service or a distinct practice, enactment or set of actions recognised as part of the overall ritual. In his analysis he describes the ritual field as comprising the locus of ritual practices and the totality of the ritual's structures and processes (122). Within this field there are three ritual elements: time, space and identity. First, ritual time refers to the weekly and annual cycle of worship: Sunday and mid-week services in the main. But other lifetime rituals are marked, such as conversion (Baptism), Spirit Baptism and healings. In the Sunday worship, Albrecht suggests that ritual time can be divided into three main sections (which he also calls 'foundation rites'; see below): praise and worship, the sermon, and the altar call or response. There are also short moments of encounter or 'ecstasy' within the overall progress through these sections. Second, ritual space provides the physical boundary and Pentecostals create 'a ritual place, a micro-world' in which to encounter God (127). Most Pentecostal churches function with three main spaces: the congregational space, the leadership space (platform) and the altar space ('the front'), which is the space in between the platform and the first row of the chairs or pews. 'The altar space is the meeting place' (131). This is where the communion table is placed and the communion rail is used for prayer. It is thus symbolically defined as the key meeting place (cf. Williams, 1974: 146). It is at this place that leaders from the platform and congregation members from the main body come to stand, kneel or bow before God. It is also the case that Pentecostals are encouraged to 'transcend' this space by taking their encounter with God outside of it, back into the world (Albrecht, 1999: 135). Third, ritual roles and identity include the role of the congregation. This is defined as active participants playing the functional roles of worshipper, prophet, listener/learner and doer/disciple. Liturgical leadership is democratised by the *charismata* and any member can lead a moment in the service through prophecy, speaking in tongues, prayer or testimony. However, the overall ritual leader is regarded as the facilitator or co-ordinator of worship and they have the authority within the meeting to evaluate the 'spontaneous charismatic demonstrations' (140). They are the experts or specialists who have been trained and anointed to lead the congregation, and usually they are one of the pastors.

Albrecht also suggests that there are three sensory domains within the ritual field, termed icons of encounter. Icons refer not only to visual portraits but also to intersections between the human and divine, or windows into prayer (142). He suggests that for Pentecostals three ritual icons stand out: sounds that surround the worshipper, sights that stimulate the worshipper and kinaesthetic dimensions of the ritual field. First, in terms of ritual sound, music functions as an auditory icon. The song seeks to usher the worshipper into the presence of God and the sound of other worshippers praising God provides 'surround sound' to the individual. Second, with respect to ritual sights, the band, the large screen upon which the words of songs are projected, the lectern from where the pastor preaches, the altar rail from where people are prayed for and, most of all, other worshippers gathered around provide an overall visual context. Third, the kinaesthetic dimension refers to the use of the body in ritual. If God is expected to move, then so are the worshippers by swaying or dancing, clapping and applauding (clap offering), raising hands in celebration and joining hands in prayer or extended to others in prayer. On occasion worshippers may fall under the power of the Holy Spirit, or bow, kneel, stand, sit or lie prostrate before God (148).

In this context of ritual studies, Albrecht understands worship as human expressions directed to God that denote appreciation, devotion, love and the like in response to divine revelation and it is contextualised by communities over time. It is a responsive interaction by the worshippers to God (Albrecht, 2004: 71). For Pentecostals, worship is understood as a way of life, or the entire liturgy of the Sunday service, or as a specific feature or aspect of the service. Albrecht considers Pentecostal worship as experiential and containing an encounter with God, a hierophany (Albrecht, 1997: 5), especially through praise and worship, and attentiveness to God through specific liturgical acts, which produces a sensitivity to the needs of humanity (Albrecht, 2004: 72–73). '[I]n worship, the believers minister to God and then God in turn ministers in and through the believers to others' (73; cf. Cartledge, 2006a). He explicates this theology of worship by reference to (1) values, (2) expressions or 'rites' and (3) liturgical sensibilities or embodied attitudes.

Regarding values, Albrecht notes the importance of personal experience of God through the Holy Spirit, which is at the centre of Pentecostal spirituality. The order or sequence of liturgical events is secondary to this overall value. Biblical authority is affirmed both in the sense that God has spoken through the biblical writers and in the sense that God continues to speak through the Bible, and through other 'words' of revelation today. This is expressed through preaching, testimonies and inspired speech. The Pentecostal tradition is appreciated for its orality, enabling active participation by its members because the basic contours of the liturgy are easily memorised; it is dynamic and emerging, and the congregation exerts liturgical leadership, not just the pastors. From this oral and narrative character emerges spontaneity as the Holy Spirit leads the group, for it is the Holy Spirit who is understood as the supreme worship leader. This spontaneity is a form of improvisation even though there is an underlying liturgical 'script' and it infuses new life each Sunday. Spiritual gifts are also linked to this spontaneity and symbolise this feature. Ministry and mission are valued in the worship context, where ministry is offered to everyone present through prayer, especially for healing and any problems or burdens. The worship service is the natural context in which ministry begins and is a launch pad for mission in and to the world (Albrecht, 2004: 77).

Albrecht observes a number of expressions or rites that undergird a Pentecostal worship service. He identifies an adaptable pattern, which he describes as 'foundation rites' (78). These have already been noted under 'ritual time'. The pattern includes: (1) the worship and praise rite that initiates the service, beginning with up-tempo songs and moving into slower and more contemplative songs (Boone, 1996: 139), (2) the sermon rite and (3) the altar or response rite which identifies the climax of the liturgy. These foundation rites are also accompanied by other 'microrites' which assist in gathering and dispersing or in transitions between these foundation rites or in accompanying the foundation rites (Albrecht, 1999: 152–170). Thus, the foundation rite of worship and praise is characterised by the microrites of clapping, dancing, swaying and the raising of hands. The sermon may be accompanied by 'sacred expletives' such as: 'Hallelujah', 'Thank you, Jesus', or simply 'Glory'. The response rite may display the microrite of concert prayer as people lay hands on each other, or hold hands and pray. The role of *charismata*, testimonies or visions and dreams also fulfil this role as mircorites, or what he also terms 'charismatic rites' – that is, particular expressions of microrites (171–174). Transitional rites act as an adhesive to connect the whole service together and include prayer led by the pastor, a musical or choir item, notices and congregational business including the collection (160–162).

Finally, Albrecht describes the sensibilities that Pentecostal rites enact (177–195). By 'sensibility', he means 'an embodied attitude which is the result of abilities to feel or perceive, as in receptiveness to impression or an affective response to something' (Albrecht, 2004: 79). These attitudes assist the worshippers to orient themselves towards and enliven the liturgical practices. He identifies at least seven types of sensibility that are found within Pentecostal worship services: celebration (which characterises expressiveness and spontaneity) marking the 'transition from the mundane to the sacred' (Boone, 1996: 139), contemplation (marked by a deep receptivity and openness to God), transcendental efficacy (which participates in 'pragmatic ritual work' in relation to the transcendental reality, expecting to 'accomplish a hoped-for empirical result' [Albrecht, 1999: 182]), penitence (marked by sorrow and remorse), ecstasy (the sense that one is directly influenced by God), improvisation (creative innovation within the rite or gesture) and ceremony (the commitment to the larger liturgical task) (Albrecht, 2004: 80). These sensibilities intersect with the rites in the context of the values described by Albrecht. Thus, the values 'support and inform both the rites and sensibilities' (82).

Reflection

In many respects the ritual interpretation offered by Albrecht can be mapped onto the worship of HPC. It is 'encounter-centred' and reflects the values, rites and embodied attitudes that Albrecht identifies.

The values noted by Albrecht are observable. There is a focus on personal experience of the Holy Spirit, which permeates all of the worship, although the name of the Holy Spirit is not necessarily invoked as often as might be anticipated. Biblical authority is affirmed as demonstrated through a sermon by Pastor John (January 2008 on the subject of 'revelation'). The use of prophecy is very frequent, either in terms of a message in English or through an interpretation of a message in tongues (Cartledge, 1994, 1995, 1998a, 1998b, 1999b, 1999c, 2000, 2002a). The 'orality' dimension is also demonstrated, with no books being used except Bibles brought by worshippers. All other 'texts' are mediated by two large projector screens and the sequence of the liturgical units is memorised and internalised. All of the members have the opportunity to contribute spontaneously at the appropriate time, as led by the Holy Spirit through the use of spiritual gifts.

The foundational rites described by Albrecht are also present in this church but the rite of Holy Communion must be added to the main three of praise and worship, sermon and response. Therefore, this rite modifies the foundation rite theory of Albrecht. Hudson observes that for older classical Pentecostal churches, the 'breaking of bread' was the central event of the service but that in recent times this has been replaced by the 'worship time', by which is meant the sung worship unit (1998: 191). HPC stands in this older tradition, with the Holy Communion rite situated at the centre of the worship service, marking the transition from the more lively part of the service to the more reflective part. It also symbolises the fact that the centre of this spirituality has come into view: the sacrifice of Christ upon the cross and the benefits won by his victory over sin and death.

The 'microrites' are also in evidence and reflect the practices identifies by Albrecht. I would suggest that these microrites do indeed enliven the foundation rites as Albrecht suggests, but I would also want to emphasise their transitional role. They function as minor links in between the major units and these transitions are essentially managed by the pastors as the ritual leaders. For example, prophecy may be explained and given further interpretation if deemed necessary. Prayer is also used to link one unit to the next, almost as a way of closing one section and opening up another. Applauding by means of the 'clap offering' is important and offers what Csordas calls the 'percussive element' to praise and contributes to Albrecht's notion of the auditory icon (2001: 109). There is a discussion to be had as to whether the Notices/Family business/Offertory slot is indeed a transitional rite or a foundational rite. In my structure it is certainly a major unit because of the importance it plays within the ritual time in the service. It is the time when the community of the church is affirmed and developed in a significant manner. Therefore, I consider it to be of greater significance than other transitional rites for HPC worship. This denotes another modification of Albrecht's theory.

The use of space is also important and I have been able to identify the importance of the platform, the main congregational space and the space between the platform and the main congregational space, which I simply called the 'between zone'. The spaces correspond to the ones identified by Albrecht. There is a dynamic between the platform and the main space, as certain activities are associated with them. People move from one to the other, but especially Pastor John. He moves freely and without permission (as the main authorised person) in all these spaces whereas other members are either on the platform or in the main body and are guided to other sections of the building (cf. Hudson, 1998: 189). The key space is, of course, the 'between zone' where the response rite is located and where the introduction to the Holy Communion is given. This is a place of prayer, as people are prayed for or as the leader prays over the 'emblems' for Holy Communion. In a sense, prayer permeates all aspects of the service, but in this place its importance becomes heightened. Jerome Boone identifies prayer as 'a rite performed with the expectation of results' (1996: 140). He would also suggest that altar calls provide an opportunity for contemplation, to receive from God in the context of 'liminal space', drawing on the work of Victor Turner (142). Cheryl J. Sanders (1997) also notes that music undergirds everything in the worship service along with prayer and that these features cannot be simply limited to certain elements of the worship sequence (cf. Amoah, 2004: 67). But it is often the case, during the response rite and the introduction to the Holy Communion, that music and prayer are combined in these units: prayers are spoken over a musical background, enhancing the reflective mood and reinforcing the sensibility of contemplation.

Pentecostal Theology of Worship

There have been a number of studies of Pentecostal and Charismatic worship that identify the various components or specific issues, such as those by Boone (1996), Parker (1996), Hollenweger (1997), Sanders (1997), Percy (1997), Hudson (1998), Stringer (1999, 2005), Steven (2002), Cartledge (2003) and Ward (2005a, 2005b, 2008). For the purpose of engaging in a theological reflection on Pentecostal worship, Hollenweger, Boone and Hudson will be chosen as the key voices with which to dialogue, although other contributions will be referred to in various sections.

Walter J. Hollenweger (1997) famously raised awareness of the oral liturgy of Pentecostal worship and suggested that the elements of historic liturgies (Invocation, Kyrie, Confession of Faith, Gloria, Eucharistic Canon and Benediction) are present under different guises (271). Oral liturgy is memorised by the congregation so that it does not need to be written down. It means that there is order and sequence as well as the possibility for creative divergence. Oral liturgies flourish among people whose most natural means of expression is oral/verbal rather than literary/written.

> Oral people are not necessarily people who do not read and write – although illiterates surely belong to them; they are people whose main medium of expression is the oral form – story, proverb, parable, joke, dance, song … – in short, all the forms in which (as form-criticism has shown us) were framed the elementary, original source material of the Bible. Today the fact that not only illiterates, but also people from middle-class backgrounds and highly trained intellectuals find the 'oral order' more satisfying than the written one is demonstrated by the great attracting power of the charismatic movement within mainline churches. (Hollenweger, 1997: 270)

In this medium, every member of the congregation participates in the dancing, singing and praying, as well as appreciating and judging the sermon! He reflects that Pentecostalism can move in one of two directions. Either it can become like other denominations, being formalised with written liturgy and structure, thus down-playing its oral cultural roots, or it can discover a 'post-literary liturgy', in which the main means of communication is not written texts but proverbs, parables, stories and choruses (273). By maintaining its oral roots, rather than attempting to become like traditional forms of Christianity (and perhaps resisting the 'textualisation' of Evangelicalism; cf. Smith, 1997), Pentecostalism will continue to connect with the majority of people who function, or prefer to function, within oral rather than literary media. In Hollenweger's view, it is this orality that will continue to facilitate the global spread of Pentecostalism.

Boone (1996) argues that Pentecostal identity has been transmitted primarily through the community and its worship. It is the community that communicates a worldview and socialises its members into it, which it does primarily through its liturgy and corporate devotional practices. The community manages the spiritual growth of its members by providing an environment of contradiction and confirmation. Contradiction is illuminated through the work of the Spirit, who exposes prejudice, ignorance and sin, which is reinforced by the dissonance between the members' stories and visions and God's story and vision. Contradiction is resolved in the community by means of an environment of confirmation, through dialogue, shared values, similar views, common concerns and goals, and mutually affirming liturgical practices. It is the liturgical rites that dramatise the theological commitments of the community and give expression to its worldview (Boone, 1996: 136). This is focused around a theology of encounter (Cartledge, 2006a, 2007; Warrington, 2008), as Pentecostals 'meet God' in their worship. The *charismata* signal the presence of Spirit and therefore have a theophanic quality. But songs can also contribute to this 'narrative of encounter' (Ward, 2005a: 202–204) as there is a palpable shift in mood from celebratory to receptivity type songs, accompanied by a shift in the atmosphere associated with the Spirit's presence (Boone, 1996: 139). Prayer allows burdens to be released through speech, while testimonies give expression to personal confession directed to the congregation and God, allowing members to tell something of their stories. The sermon offers a counterpart to the testimony by declaring the story and vision of God. Thus, together they give expression to the contradiction/confirmation dynamic (140). Both the testimony and the sermon can contradict and confirm the community's worldview, perhaps in unpredictable ways. The high point of Pentecostal worship is the altar call or ministry time as a response to the preached word: giving opportunity for the interim resolution of life's contradictions amid an ethos of confirmation. This enables members to journey forward in their *via salutis* as they experience episodes of transformation and growth (Ward, 2005b: 34).

Hudson raises a number of concerns and issues around the contemporary Pentecostal theology of worship. He is concerned that the content of the songs that are sung leave little room for doubt 'or a recognition that for many people change is a gradual process' (Hudson, 1998: 196). The fact that Christians experience the 'dark night of the soul' is missing from the discourse. He is concerned that this can lead to a dualism, namely that people live one thing at home and sing another in congregational worship. In order to resolve this tension, he suggests that there needs to be a place for honesty within worship, just as the Psalms contain lament as well as joy and celebration. He also notes that there has been a shift in the content of songs from a focus on relationships between believers to a focus on society; and this has often been accompanied by spiritual warfare and militaristic rhetoric. Thus, as the church retreats into its own ghetto it sings songs of spiritual warfare engagement with greater enthusiasm. Questions regarding the political and structural issues in society are never addressed in worship; therefore worship does not spill out into the community with a view to changing the power structures (199). Confession and intercession are often neglected in worship, being relegated to the mid-week meeting. Without corporate acts of confession and intercession there is a danger of individualism, whereby even public acts of worship are accessed by individuals working at the level of personal piety alone. Hudson suggests that Pentecostals are pragmatic because of the experiential basis to their spirituality and this leads them to chase the latest fad. Instead, they should be prepared to quarry their own treasures and those of other Christian traditions, with a view to renewing their own worshipping practices. A greater focus on the sacrament of Holy Communion would be one way in which they could do this. This emphasis could mean that a theology of the cross, linked to sacramental theology, as well as divine sovereignty and a theology of the resurrection might influence the content of sermons. One outcome of this influence, especially in relation to the sovereignty of God, might be a modified Pentecostal attitude towards revival, seeing it as graciously given rather than as earnestly sought (203).

Rescripting Ordinary Theology

There are a number of theological themes that can be identified from analysis of this material and rescripted in dialogue with Pentecostal theology.

Theology: Speaking of God

The first is the 'theology' proper of the ordinary discourse expressed through worship. With no written liturgy to give a language to worshippers, which has been debated by theologians and liturgists as to the precise content and shape it should take, what theological language is displayed? To answer this question I turn initially to the local hymnody. One of the unique features of HPC is that Pastor Angela is not only a musician and music leader, but she is also a songwriter herself. Thus, she represents local and oral culture, if necessarily influenced by wider Pentecostal and Charismatic hymnody. In addition to singing well-known Pentecostal and Charismatic songs there is a strong local flavour to the hymnody. During my time at the church, Pastor Angela launched a CD with songs that she had written specifically for worship, entitled *No Other Name*.[3] This album contains eight songs, five of which are based on Bible passages, especially the Psalms (Pss 91, 100, 34, 66, 97). Psalm 91 speaks of God being our refuge and fortress in whom we trust. Psalm 100 is a psalm of praise. Psalm 34 encourages singers to taste and see that the Lord is good. The writer of Psalm 66 praises God for his intervention in turning the sea into dry land. Psalm 97 extols the creation, including God's people, to praise him. The psalm-based songs are generally theistic, addressed to God or the Lord, but the others are distinctly Christological in focus. Even the hymnody that is based on the Psalms is interpreted Christologically, since the 'Lord' is interpreted as referring to Jesus. I would like to quote the texts of the other three songs, as they give a flavour of the genre.

---

[3]   © Angela Butcher @ HPC 2007, cited with permission.

1. Isaiah 53
Verse 1
He was despised and rejected by men
A man of sorrows and acquainted with grief
He took our suffering and He carried our pain
The punishment was upon Him, by His wounds we are healed
Refrain
I love you Lord
For you died on Calvary
I love you Lord
You gave your life for me
Verse 2
All we like sheep have gone astray
Each has turned into His own way
He was led like a lamb to be slaughtered for us
For the Lord laid on Him the sins of us all

2. To the Son of David
To the Son of David I will lift my hands (× 4)
For He is Jesus Son of God
The blind He healed the dead He raised
For He is Jesus Son of God
And I will praise His Holy Name
Yes I will praise His Holy Name

3. No Other Name
No other Name no one the same
Jesus is the sweetest Name I know
Gave His life a willing sacrifice
Jesus is the sweetest Name I know
Bridge
No other Name but Jesus
No one the same but Jesus
His Name is the sweetest Name I know

The songs cited above show a clear Christological centre to the worship language because of the sacrifice of Calvary and its link with salvation and healing today. They could be said to stand in continuity with emphasis of the Assemblies of God hymnody, as stated in the Preface to the *Redemption Hymnal* of 1951 (Kay and Dyer, 2004: 152). This Christological centre is given a general theistic context and is not placed within an explicitly trinitarian framework. In this emphasis the church continues within the traditional Pentecostal focus on Jesus as saviour and healer. Jesus as sanctifier, baptiser in the Spirit and as coming king do not appear to be represented in the hymnody.

When people pray in the worship services, they tend to focus on Jesus, although the Father is mentioned to a limited extent. Once, when introducing Holy Communion, Rodney specifically mentioned the Godhead as three in one and that the Holy Spirit came because of Jesus. However, two days earlier I had conducted my focus group conversation, which Rodney attended, during which I asked the group about the doctrine of the Trinity. It is the only mention of this doctrine during my time observing worship and I suspect it reflects the focus group conversation.

The prophecies that I observed also reflect a mixed pattern of theism with Christology. For example, messages that indicate that (1) the Lord is in the midst and that members could reach out and touch the king; (2) that God is their Father and has their best interests at heart, and that God loves them; (3) or simply: 'Open your hearts to me', with no designation of who is speaking; (4) the Lord comes and bowls a boulder (at the church members); (5) 'I have been down and you have lifted me high'; (6) consider God who is above our circumstances; (7) there is someone here with financial needs to whom God wants to minister; (8) there is someone here with a pain in the shoulder to whom God wants to minister; (9) 'You need to be broken in order that the fragrance may flow out of you'; (10) burdens fell off Christ at the cross and can fall off us; (11) 'Reach out this morning, he is never too busy ... You did not choose me but I chose you and ordained you to go and bring forth fruit (Jn 15.16)'; (12) focus on Calvary and the great price (interpretation of a message in tongues during Holy Communion); and (13) 'You are searching and longing, but you are still going to the broken cisterns, to the empty vessels.' 'Come to him who is all you need. He alone gives you water that satisfies'.

Therefore, the theological discourse is either generally theistic, with occasional 'Father' language, or strongly Christocentric. In this regard, it resonates with the existing characterisation of Pentecostal theology as being 'theocentric and Christocentric' (Warrington, 2008: 34). There is an easy transference from the LORD of Old Testament discourse to the Lord Jesus Christ. The Holy Spirit does not appear to be explicitly addressed as a person in worship, neither does there appear to be a full trinitarian structure at work in the discourse. In this respect the ordinary discourse echoes the comments of David Allen when he observes of Pentecostal worship that:

> It is not at all unusual, in open worship, to hear *Jesus* invoked in prayer. Whilst this is not necessarily wrong – though Jesus himself did clearly lay down prayer to the Father as the norm – it is nevertheless a measure of the Christ-centredness of Pentecostalism and also (possibly) the lack of clear teaching on the Trinity. This is perhaps confirmed by the occasional extemporary prayer which runs, 'We thank you, Father, for dying on the Cross for our sins ... (Allen, 1990: 124).

There is a very limited expression of what James Steven calls 'instinctive trinitarianism' (2002: 171), which only very occasionally hits the surface. He is able to quote examples of extemporary prayer that includes trinitarian language, even if it is imprecise (173). He observes how the liturgical tradition of the Church of

England provides resources for such 'instinctive trinitarianism', which is missing from the classical Pentecostal tradition. He also notes the trinitarianism located in the congregational songs, which I have observed to be lacking. Therefore, there appears to be a significant difference between his empirical studies and this congregational study with regard to the ordinary theology of worshippers. Robin Parry, addressing the issue of Charismatic hymnody, refers to what he calls trinitarian syntax: '*The Trinity functions in Christian God-talk in such a basic and foundational way that it starts to function something like a syntax – a set of rules about how Christian language works*'(2005: 131–132, italics in the original). He argues that, overall, the songs should be consistent with this syntax even if they are not explicitly trinitarian (140). HPC songs are at least theoretically consistent with such a syntax, even though explicit trinitarian grammar appears to be weak.

Atonement

The second area is soteriology and, in particular, the theology of atonement. Although this will be considered in greater detail in chapter 5, it is so deeply embedded in the discourse of worship that some comment is required at this juncture. The song cited above is based on Isaiah 53.4–6 and reflects the dominance of this text in the ordinary discourse of worship, as well as its wider connection with the Pentecostal tradition. This is illustrated in the Assemblies of God 'Statement of Faith', articles 3 ('Substitutionary Atoning Death'), 5 ('salvation through faith in Christ who … died for our sins, that through His Blood we have redemption') and 10 ('We believe that deliverance from sickness, by Divine Healing is provided for in the Atonement (Isa 53:4–5; Mt 8:16–17; James 5:13–16)'). Therefore, it is worth being reminded of these biblical texts, as well as another key text, 1 Peter 2.24.

1. Isaiah 53.4–6

4. Surely he took up our infirmities and carried our sorrows, yet we considered him stricken by God, smitten by him, and afflicted.

5. But he was pierced for our transgressions, he was crushed for our iniquities; the punishment that brought us peace was upon him, and by his wounds we are healed.

6. We all, like sheep, have gone astray, each of us has turned to his own way; and the Lord has laid on him the iniquity of us all (NIV).

2. Matthew 8.16–17

16. When evening came, many who were demon-possessed were brought to him, and he drove out the spirits with a word and healed all the sick.

17. This was to fulfil what was spoken through the prophet Isaiah: 'He took up our infirmities and carried our diseases' (NIV).

3. James 5.13–16

13. Is any one of you in trouble? He should pray. Is anyone happy? Let him sing songs of praise.

14. Is any one of you sick? He should call the elders of the church to pray over him and anoint him with oil in the name of the Lord.

15. And the prayer offered in faith will make the sick person well; the Lord will raise him up. If he has sinned, he will be forgiven.

16. Therefore confess your sins to each other so that you may be healed. The prayer of a righteous person is powerful and effective (NIV adapted).

4. 1 Peter 2.24

24. He himself bore our sins in his body on the tree, so that we might die to sins and live for righteousness; by his wounds you have been healed (NIV).

These texts connect the work of Christ on the cross both to the forgiveness of sins and to divine healing, and this is reflected in the way in which Holy Communion is introduced in worship. Out of fifteen services observed containing Holy Communion, the dominant text in use was Isaiah 53.4–6 (five times). This was often linked to other New Testament texts in the gospels. Jack, who led Holy Communion on a number of occasions, illustrates the importance of this text and how it is interpreted.

In December 2007 Jack read from Isaiah 53 and Philippians 2. He stated: 'By his stripes we are healed. He has laid on him the iniquity of us all. Taking the form of a bond-servant he was obedient to the point of death, even death on a cross. Thank God for the emblems. He has liberated us and set us free.' The congregation was invited to shout out prayers of thanksgiving to God. In March 2008, he read from Isaiah 6 and Isaiah 53.6, 'By his stripes we are healed. He was pierced for our transgression'. This was followed by a clap offering. He then read Revelation 5.6–9 and thanked God. He exhorted the congregation to examine themselves before they received the emblems: 'If you are not a believer this morning then pass on the emblems to the next person. If you need to sort something out, then talk to God'. Finally, in April 2008, Jack stated that God loves us and has demonstrated his love for us in the cross of Jesus. He read Isaiah 53.1–7 and said: 'If you are sorrowful, then lay it down at Jesus' feet. By his stripes we are healed' (congregational 'Amens'). He told the congregation: 'Jesus did this for you'. They should open their hearts and accept it because the table is for them. If anyone present is not saved, then they should pass the emblems on. If they have accepted Jesus then they are allowed to participate. The communion unites the body together but if they have anything against others, then they should put it right if they can now. This is because Jesus said: 'Lay not their sin to their charge'. Therefore, they should open their hearts, hearts of gratitude to the Lord, the saviour, the risen Christ.

In this context of worship, the music and the prayers come together to emphasise the healing nature of the sacrifice of Christ. Healing is the dominant soteriological metaphor. It requires worshippers to once again open their hearts to the importance of this gift and be grateful. The emphasis is on the objective and holistic nature of the effects of this sacrifice. Christ has already won these benefits so worshippers need to appropriate them through faith. The benefits are not just in relation to the forgiveness of sins but also in terms of lifting our burdens, solving our problems and healing our bodies. Almost every service starts with Pastor Angela inviting the congregation to offer their burdens to the Lord as a way of preparing for worship. Throughout the service there is a strong rhetoric of empowerment. This is typified in sermons preached by Pastor John. Two are especially pertinent. The first is a sermon preached on 1 Samuel 17 and David's battle with Goliath, in which John offers 10 steps to becoming giant killers for God. Thus, he encourages the congregation to face up to their weaknesses and trust in God's strength. The second is based on Moses' call at the Burning Bush (Ex 3), entitled: 'You can do it!'. He again encourages members to move forward in their walk with God and be open to what God has for their lives. The rite of Holy Communion may function as a memorial of atonement for sin, but it fundamentally reinforces the idea that Jesus can and does deal with our burdens just as he has dealt with the cosmological burden of sin. Isaiah 53 and the rite of Holy Communion mutually inform each other and without the liturgical control of other biblical metaphors they could contract towards personal therapy under the rhetoric of empowerment (see chapter 5). Its importance as a foundation rite at HPC is informed by the work of David Allen, who has bemoaned the fact of its general demise among recent Pentecostal worship practice (Allen, 2007). This demise could not be said of HPC, which upholds the classical British tradition of a weekly Sunday celebration.

While there is some trinitarian language within ordinary discourse, it is clearly underdeveloped and remains implicit rather than explicit. As noted above, the dominant discourse is a kind of general theism and Christology. While not wishing to displace the Christological focus, there is a need for theological language to be framed in a trinitarian manner. This would provide a theological grammar that is consistent with the broader Christian tradition (Cartledge, 2008b). Traditional hymnody can be a source of rich trinitarian grammar, which can be set to contemporary melodies, and which have a clear triadic structure and content (Parry, 2005: 123–128). The disadvantage of an oral liturgy is that the contribution of ancient liturgical texts is missing. This is especially the case with regard to traditional eucharistic liturgy, which is usually framed in a trinitarian grammar. Of course, it is perfectly possible to translate these texts into an extemporary form in order to resonate with the orality of Pentecostal liturgy. A trinitarian *inclusio* to the worship service using a greeting or opening hymn and final blessing would also enhance the trinitarian grammar and provide a liturgical framework to the congregation's worship.

The key activity of worship is praise; it is constitutive of the church and reflects the orality of the ordinary theological culture. In the Pentecostal tradition, praise is regarded as one of the key practices through which one encounters the Holy Spirit. It is also something that is corporate, led by the band and by the Holy Spirit, yet individual: there are moments in which one can shout out 'sacred expletives' to the Lord as inspired to do so. Time is given over to praise at the beginning of the worship because the temple is a place of praise (1 Cor 3.16). Therefore, praise constitutes the people of God, just as on the day of Pentecost (Acts 2.11). When God visits his people by his Holy Spirit then they declare his wonders. It is what they do, and it is what they become: a people of praise. Following the insights of Hollenweger (1997), it could be suggested that one way of focusing on this feature would be to explore more local and intercultural songs (given HPC's constituency) that connect affectively with the congregation as an important area for development. Clearly Pastor Angela has begun to connect with this orality in worship through her own song writing. Others from different cultural backgrounds could be invited to explore song writing for the benefit of the church community. In addition, as Hudson (1998) suggests, there are areas that appear to be lacking in Pentecostal hymnody, such as doubt or questioning, lament and wider society. Perhaps these themes could also be incorporated into new songs.

There is a tension maintained between clergy and laity, although these precise labels are never used. The key pastor, John, functions as overall master of ceremonies, and his wife, Angela, leads the praise; together they manage the liturgical space and invite people into specific roles. In this human temple of the Holy Spirit, there are indeed leaders, but all are 'priests' or, better, 'prophets' because all can be inspired by the Holy Spirit to praise, to pray, to prophesy and to read Scripture or give a testimony. There is both order and spontaneity, which is managed by the pastors, but they recognise that the Holy Spirit may move freely upon an individual for the benefit of all, thus exercising leadership as well. Therefore, there is a prophethood of all believers that is based on their reception of the spirit of prophecy, the Holy Spirit (Stronstad, 1999). In this context, the Spirit is an egalitarian Spirit who is poured out on all flesh (Acts 2.17; Joel 2.28), but especially upon the pastors, who are anointed to lead the church. In this context, there is room for the tension between contradiction and confirmation that Boone describes (1996). In an overall atmosphere of encouragement and confirmation (a hermeneutic of trust), elements of contradiction can be sown by the pastors to make members think afresh in order to grow in their understanding. In the Pentecostal tradition both clergy and laity are under the authority of Scripture and the text can challenge and affirm both in their Christian discipleship. The sermon is an appropriate locus of such confirmation/contradiction and understanding it in this light might be a fruitful development for preachers. Alternatively, testimony is an occasion when a member might publicly align his or her experience with a biblical text in order to explain how it has been either confirmed or contradicted, thus exercising the prophethood of believers. Such testimony would enable others to use Scripture in a similar manner.

This temple of the Holy Spirit is in the making and is eschatologically framed. It is a church that is both in the process of being and becoming. It is being moved from one degree of glory to the next. This is reflected in its ministry times, when the prophets turn from praise to pray for the needs of the ecclesial community. The sacrifice of praise turns to the sacrifice of intercession on behalf of the 'living stones', in order that they might be healed, helped and supported. Again this is led by the pastors, but members of the congregation are called forward to exercise a ministry of pastoral care, of love and support, for those in need through prayer. It is in this time of prayer ministry that the church celebrates the presence of the eschatological Spirit of God who is invited to become intensified in the lives of the people who constitute the temple. Following Hudson (1998) again, it could be suggested that personal transformation experienced through the times of prayer ministry could be taken out into the world through prayer and action. As people have had their needs met, so they might become more sensitive to the needs of others with whom they live and work. Intercession might concern not just those who are present within the worship service but the world outside, and not just individuals but political and structural issues in wider society. In other words, it could be suggested that the energy, care and devotion exhibited in prayer ministry might be extended during public worship to the wider world, with a view to preparing members not just to have their own burdens lifted but also to be instruments for the liberation and empowerment of others in the wider world through intercession and action.

Summary

Pentecostal worship is an important and fascinating way into exploring ordinary theology. This chapter has investigated the nature of congregational worship at HPC and discovered that it has a sequence of events or regular units, with minor links between them. The main activities are linked to the three key zones within the church layout, namely the platform, the congregational seating area and the space in between the two of them. The three foundation rites (as noted by Albrecht

[1997; 1999], namely the sung worship, the sermon and the response time), are always represented in worship even if the placement of the response time varies. However, the rite of Holy Communion is also present on a Sunday morning and this modifies the foundation rites of Albrecht. Worship is understood by the members to be affective, transformative, informed by biblical teaching, spontaneous and well lead. Prayer is expected to permeate all of the worship service. Not only does it correspond in broad terms with the analysis of Albrecht but it also demonstrates the oral culture of Pentecostalism more generally, as argued by Hollenweger (1997), which is transmitted and socialised through the community of the church (Boone, 1996). The theology espoused through the local worship songs is based on biblical texts, especially the Psalms, but it has a Christological focus that is placed within a general theistic context rather than an explicitly trinitarian one. This is also reflected in the prophecies and the prayers. The language of atonement is especially prominent, with specific biblical texts (Isa 53.4–6; Mt 8.17; 1 Pet 2.24) in regular usage, especially during the rite of Holy Communion. The dominant soteriological metaphor is 'healing', which is expanded and other metaphors are subsumed within it. But all of these elements are contained within an overall orientation of praise, which is constitutive of the church as a people, or temple, of praise, even as the Holy Spirit inspires both members and pastors to exercise gifts of ministry. It is an eschatological experience, as the Holy Spirit nudges the community along its path and encourages it to take its next step on the corporate journey of faith.

Chapter 4
Conversion

Classical Pentecostalism, as a subset of Protestant Christianity, has adopted some central Protestant themes, although it has to be noted that the wider Charismatic tradition embraces other forms of Christianity (Cartledge, 2006a). It is intimately connected to Evangelical revivalist Christianity of the nineteenth and the twentieth centuries. As part of this association it is inevitable that there is an emphasis on the concept of conversion and the imperative to engage in the work of evangelism. Early British Pentecostalism understood the work of conversion to be bound to the action of Jesus as Saviour (Cartledge, 2008a). The proclamation of the gospel and the expectation that individuals would experience regeneration, respond by committing their lives to Christ, be baptised and walk the way of discipleship is strongly held. In the revivalist tradition the expectation that individuals would have dramatic encounters with God and thus be 'turned around' dominates popular discourse. Therefore, conversion is regarded as *metanoia*, or *convertere* (Romain, 2000: 17; Flinn, 1999: 51–52), a turning away from the old life of sin to a new life of righteousness in fellowship with God and other Christians. Some traditions would understand conversion as a process rather than as sudden and dramatic (Kreider, 1999: 21–32). Indeed, there is a continuing debate in the literature about whether conversion should be regarded as sudden or gradual (Gillespie, 1991: 12–20), also based on the different Platonic-Augustinian (crisis) and Aristotelian-Thomist (process) traditions (Flinn, 1999: 54–55).

A classic definition of conversion, oft cited, is given by William James. He states that:

> To be converted, to be regenerated, to receive grace, to experience religion, to gain an assurance, are so many phrases which denote the process, gradual or sudden, by which a self hitherto divided, and consciously wrong, inferior and unhappy, becomes unified and consciously right, superior and happy, in the consequence of its firmer hold upon religious realities. (James, 1925: 189)

It is this kind of experience that is considered as reported and discussed by Pentecostal Christians attending HPC, although it is influenced by social and cultural factors (Flinn, 1999: 53). In this chapter, verbatim testimonies are given theological context by being placed alongside historical material, before being brought into conversation with the multi-disciplinary theory of Lewis Rambo. Pentecostal theology from the bilateral dialogue with Roman Catholicism provides resources for reflection and theological rescripting.

Testimonies

The Focus Group

The focus group that discussed the issue of conversion was comprised of nine individuals from different social and ethnic backgrounds. There were three men and six women. The two white British men were older middle-aged and elderly (Alan and Rodney), while the other was a younger middle-aged African from Uganda (Abraham). Five of the women originated from the Caribbean, although they had been living in the UK for some time (Jane, Rebekah, Emily, Ruth and Amy); the other woman was of white British origin (Ruby). Four of the women were middle-aged and one was elderly (Ruth). The men's occupations were hospital porter (Alan), retired college lecturer (Rodney) and accountant (Abraham). The women were employed as administrative assistant (Jane), personal assistant / administrative executive (Rebekah), care worker (Ruby), retired (Amy and Ruth) or semi-retired (Emily).

Four different testimonies were given during the beginning of the group discussion. They were all interesting and illuminating, so they are worth considering in turn.

> *Alan* : It's not a specific conversion. I can't really tell you the date, like most people can. I remember going forward at an Eric Hudson crusade somewhere in the '60s at Aston Villa football ground but it meant nothing to me, until many years later I was in a small kitchen having read the book *In His Steps* by Hugh Sheldon, which really witnessed to me. I decided there and then in this small little mission kitchen in an FIEC church to say yes to Jesus lock, stock and barrel.[1] Shortly after that somebody came and ministered the Holy Spirit to me in over two weeks … The first week all I did was I felt a love for everybody. I could have loved the whole world no matter who he was. In the second week he prayed again and [I] just spoke in tongues, supernaturally. I have not looked back since.

In order to clarify the nature of these experiences, I asked if the first experience was his conversion and the second his baptism in the Spirit. He replied by saying:

> Yea, it was. It was sometime later, having made the decision to go on with God, to make Christ the centre of my life. It wasn't easy because I come from a mental health background, and I was in and out of hospital for many years for mental breakdowns, in the Birmingham area, so I had nothing to live for in a sense … And so when the Holy Spirit entered my life I found, as the book said, I have a power for living … and that's made the difference. In my life that's been well over forty, forty-five years ago.

---

[1]   FIEC refers to the Fellowship of Independent Evangelical Churches.

Ruby: Well, I'll tell you one. I actually, well before I became a Christian, I was actually quite an alcoholic and like very depressed and at the point of basically committing suicide. And the only thing that was keeping [me] going was finding a job. And every job I went for nothing came and I just said to God, 'God if you really exist I need a job'. And God gave us a job in a Christian old people's home. And I walked into the old people's home and literally you could have cut the love, the joy, the peace with a knife. It was so tangible. And within six weeks I'd actually given my life to the Lord but, before that, I think it was a couple of weeks later, we were at a service and my head was absolutely throbbing and I actually felt it was going to burst. And all of a sudden I saw this cloud. The only way to describe it was this cloud come over the top of my head and literally I could still feel that actual presence go straight from the top of my head all the way to every single nook and crevice of my life and the next minute the headache had completely gone. The next second the headache had gone. And I gave my life to the Lord literally within a few weeks of that. Within a few days of that I'd actually been baptised. And again, like Alan, within a few weeks of that [I] was actually filled with the Holy Spirit and my life was completely transformed. And there was no depression there at all. The depression had completely left at that point altogether ... The alcohol gradually went, but different things went but on that night it was literally I could see a cloud and I could feel it just come straight into the top of my head. I was just dancing and everything. This joy came over my life, completely instantly.

Rebekah: Okay quickly here. Basically before my conversion,... actually there was an event that happened before which made an impression and the whole thing. You see I was really really down and out. I got to the stage where I used to be a party animal really and after that the fire burnt out after so many years. I got to the stage that there was really no point going on. I was just existing and it got to the stage of really rock bottom. Everything was going negatively and I think that the only thing that kept me going was my awareness of my responsibility towards my daughter. Because by then we were already in ... and she had nobody, so if anything had happened to me she would have nobody to look after her. But what I really contemplated seems like, I mean it is not worth living, sort of thing. So it was in that state that I really started talking to God and said, 'Well,' – I wasn't a Christian then, but – 'like you said in your Word, you give us the desires of our hearts, what you can provide', everything is his, 'So what about me?', sort of thing. And it [is] really amazing the transition that took place, because the transformation that took place, because it's material [for] the description here, but the miraculous that took place one after the other even when I wasn't a Christian so to speak, I believed. You know I got a job in one of the most prestigious companies worldwide. You know, things I was waiting for, you know, really, things that were really significant, you know, like mine and my daughter's came through and I can remember one of the prayers I had when I was gone. And I was saying, 'God, if you get me out of this situation, I'm gonna do everything that you want, I'm gonna pay my tithes and all that'. And so God paved the way, opened doors, and put me in a position that I had asked him to so then it was my turn to do my part serving, which I did. But the thing that I kept holding back on was this: speaking in tongues, even though I was aware of the presence of the Holy Ghost in me in my life. I simply refused to speak in tongues because, you know, I seen so many cases where people let's say abused speaking in tongues. And I didn't want to fall in[to] that category, but it was fine. You know God has ironed things out and yes it's go since then.

In order to clarify further, I asked whether speaking in tongues occurred with her baptism in the Spirit or later. She said:

It happened gradually. It happened gradually but I refused to actually do it, say use it properly so to speak, you know.

Rodney : I'll be as short as I can. My parents were full time in the Salvation Army. So I was brought up in a very solid Christian background, evangelical. I was saved between the age of 7 and 8 and I knew I was saved. Moving on rapidly, by the time I was about 26 I found the activity of the Salvation Army too much. I wanted a better career, so laid aside Christian values for the sake of pursing my career. That went on, I was reasonably successful. By the time I was in my 30s I came to this church for a funeral and then I came the following Sunday and I began to realise what I'd lost as far as my relationship with God was concerned. And it wasn't long after that I really made a complete dedication to the Lord. I had a problem because brothers were saying to me, 'You know, Rodney, you ought to be baptised in the Spirit'. And oh no, they were saying to me first 'You ought to be water baptised'. And I said 'I know I'm saved, so I don't need to be water baptised'. I'd got the wrong concept, you see. Anyway, eventually somebody spoke in tongues one Sunday morning; the interpretation came through: 'You've been searching books. You've been doing everything to try and find the solution to your problem. If you would be obedient to the Lord, the Lord will answer all your questions'. And what happened was at the end of that meeting, Miss Fisher, one of our lady pastors, stood up and said 'In a fortnight's time we're having a water baptismal service'. My name was on the top of the list! [Laughs …] And I got water baptised and only about three weeks or so after that I was in the meeting one Sunday morning and I just started speaking in tongues to myself really but, you know, speaking out loud, well, I was speaking loud but I wasn't giving a message. I didn't know what was happening other than the Holy Spirit came upon me. And that has just revolutionised my life, and I've been here ever since.

Summary of the Testimonies

All of the testimonies refer to a problem of one kind or another, which provides the person with a reason to attend to their spiritual lives. These include mental health problems, alcoholism and unemployment; although Rodney's preoccupation with his career at the expense of his spiritual life might also be seen as problematic in Pentecostal terms. Through various means they gain some spiritual insight into the nature of the problem and this provokes them to seek God, represented by either experiencing the Holy Spirit or praying or attending worship. In Rodney's case insight and worship probably belong together. In all the cases there is a transformation of some sort, usually an empowerment of one kind: love, power, healing or revitalisation, which is related to being integrated into the Christian community. For three of the four individuals there was a previous conversion experience, which was prior to, and set the context for, the problem-solving to follow. For two of the individuals, baptism was important and a gateway into a deeper spiritual life, although for one person there was a renewal of commitment, which functioned in a similar manner. For the two who were baptised this was followed within a short period of time by baptism in the Spirit, while the person who dedicated her life afresh experienced speaking in tongues gradually rather than dramatically. This summary is represented in Table 4.1

Table 4.1 Features and Sequence in Conversion

Alan	Ruby	Rebekah	Rodney
Conversion Experience		Conversion Experience	Conversion Experience
Problem	Problem	Problem	Problem
Insight	Insight	Insight	Insight
Experience of the Holy Spirit	Experience of the Holy Spirit	Prayer Answered	Experience of Worship
	Baptism	Renewal of Commitment	Baptism
	Baptism in the Holy Spirit	Speaking in Tongues	Baptism in the Holy Spirit
Outcome: Love Power	Outcome: Healing	Outcome: Revitalisation	Outcome: Revitalisation

Further Analysis

It is inevitable that these testimonies reflect an understanding of conversion that
is influenced by their current faith stance (Tidball, 2006: 87; McGuire, 1992: 73).
However, because these understandings are contextualised within the study of this
church, the degree to which they cohere with the corporate understanding can be
appreciated. These narratives display the characteristics of a punctuated process
and there are a number of important and common features within Pentecostal
conversion narratives. These include: (1) a previous experience of Christianity,
which is a common sociological observation (Savage, 2000: 3); (2) a problem that
is faced, resulting in (3) some form of spiritual insight; this is followed by (4) an
experience of the Holy Spirit or answered prayer at the centre of the process, and
(5) the sacrament of baptism or an equivalent form of rededication; (6) experience
of baptism in the Spirit or speaking in tongues, which leads to (7) important
consequences, which are some form of empowerment (love, power, healing and
revitalisation). This is a crucial feature: life is transformed onto a higher level as a
consequence of this set of experiences, which is why advocates are positive about
their experiences but also wish to share them with others. For three of the people,
an early Christian conversion experience proved to be inadequate and it was only
by experiencing the Holy Spirit that the situation was transformed.

The participants see the key to the involvement of the Holy Spirit in evangelism
as starting with the pastors and the church leaders, especially their willingness to
seek the Spirit for the life of the church. They see worship as central to the life
of the Spirit in the church and as a key event associated with evangelism. Emily
explained how it starts:

> I would say in the praise and worship, which is the first part of the morning's
> activity, reminding us that we should come with joy in our hearts to praise
> God and to explain what it does when you start to praise God. It releases the
> working of the Holy Spirit and it can change the tenor of the entire service. As
> you praise and you worship it releases people from stresses and strains and if
> you've come with a problem you are prepared to put your problem behind you
> and really worship God in humility. You can see [this] throughout the whole
> congregation.

It is interesting to observe how 'problems' and 'burdens' are dealt with explicitly
and regularly on Sundays before the congregation enters into worship. I asked
whether anyone had been converted in the context of a worship service at HPC and
the answer was in the affirmative. Emily again recalled what happened:

> There was a group of new people and the presence of the Holy Spirit [was such]
> that [there] was a powerful praise and worship; and during that [time] when the
> message was given and the announcement was made, one young lady she went
> forward. There were several who put their hands up but this young lady she

actually went up and you could see the excitement on her face; that something had transpired in her life. Whether she is still going on, because I don't think she was from this area, but I do know that she made a commitment.

Rebekah expressed the view that the pastors facilitate the empowering work of the Holy Spirit because they create space for the Spirit's work and everyone is given a chance to experience the Spirit. Testimonies are encouraged and there is 'speaking in tongues' and everyone, not just the pastors, can experience the Spirit.

In order to provide an historical context for this ordinary theology, it is worth outlining briefly the theology surrounding conversion in British Pentecostalism.

Conversion in British Pentecostalism

The Assemblies of God denomination is an inheritor of the Evangelical theology of the late nineteenth and early twentieth centuries concerning the need for lost humanity to be reconcilied with God through personal faith and trust in the work of Christ upon the cross (Bebbington, 1989: 5–10). It resonates strongly with Evangelical approaches to conversion and cannot be distinguished from them. To summarise, conversion in Evangelicalism of this period was largely considered an individual matter, whereby a person sought God for mercy and the forgiveness of sins. The prospective convert recognised that pardon could only be received through acceptance of the substitutionary work of Christ upon the cross: that Christ died in their place for them. Acceptance of this exchange resulted in a sense of divine pardon, emotional freedom and spiritual peace. As a result, the life of the convert had been surrendered to God for his purpose and plan (Bebbington, 1989: 5).

This understanding can be appreciated by glancing through the pages of the first British Pentecostal magazine, *Confidence* (1908–1926), where we read of a theology of new birth associated with conversion. For example, in April 1909 Alexander Boddy wrote an article entitled 'Born from Above', in which he articulated the standard Evangelical theology of conversion at the time based on John 3.2. The repentant sinner is to accept Christ Jesus by simple faith as his or her redeemer and ask the Holy Spirit to unite him/her to Christ, his/her Head, into his death and resurrection (Boddy, 1909). This was followed by an anonymous article years later (presumably written by Boddy), in which much of the earlier article is reiterated (*Confidence*, 1922). The standard creation-fall-redemption narrative is in evidence. The article closes with a statement to be used by those committing their lives to Christ and seeking the new birth:

A PERSONAL ACCEPTANCE OF NEW BIRTH

(i.) I fully believe that the Lord Jesus is willing to save my soul, and to save it to the uttermost.

(ii.) I do with my whole heart trust Him now and trust Him absolutely. I trust His precious shed Blood (His Redeeming Sacrifice for me).

(iii.) As one on a sinking ship gladly gets into a life-boat, so I confidently place myself in Thy merciful and mighty keeping, Lord Jesus. Thou wilt save me now and eternally. (Thy sheep shall never perish.)

(iv.) Though the great adversary of my soul may seem to gain the victory over me, I will continue to believe that I am saved by Christ ('Reconciled by his death and saved in His life', Rom. v., 10).

(v.) I read, 'Whosoever believeth in Him (the Lord Jesus) shall not perish, but have everlasting life' (John iii., 16). I believe, and therefore I shall not perish, for I accept the gift of God, eternal life.

(vi.) Holy Spirit of God, I trust Thee now to make all this real in my life. I accept in fullness this Birth from above as Thy Divine Gift. I am now a new creature in Christ Jesus. Dead indeed unto sin, but ALIVE unto God in Jesus Christ my Lord. (*Confidence*, 1922: 56; cf. 1926)

This understanding remained fairly constant in the Assemblies of God, as can be seen by advice to new converts (Parr, 1927a, 1927b, 1927c), as well as articles affirming the doctrine by John Carter (1932) and Cunningham Thomson (1934a, 1934b, 1934c). Carter (1932) argued that being 'born again' was not an option but a commandment of Christ (Jn 3.7). As natural birth is an entrance into life, so regeneration is an entrance into spiritual life, thus new birth is the portal through which we pass into the kingdom of God (Carter, 1932: 7). It means that the person has become a member of God's family, can call God 'heavenly Father' and receive the Spirit of his son, Jesus Christ (Gal 4.6). Carter makes a clear distinction between the reception of the 'Spirit of the Son' at conversion and the reception of the Holy Spirit as enduement for service, which refers to the doctrine of baptism in the Spirit (Carter, 1932: 7).

Some years later, Donald Gee was to summarise the Pentecostal view concerning conversion, when he wrote:

Now to be 'Pentecostal' is to stand for just that type of evangelicalism (touching and changing the most formative elements in human affairs) that aims above all at personal conversion, and emphasizes to each individual the gravity and importance of their own decision concerning repentance from sin, and faith in the Lord Jesus. (Gee, 1944: 42)

The current denominational 'Statement of Faith' states the relevant doctrinal themes in the following terms:

> 5. We believe in salvation through faith in Christ, who, according to the Scriptures, died for our sins, was buried and was raised from the dead on the third day, and that through His Blood we have Redemption (Titus 2:11, 3:5–7; Rom. 10:8–15; 1 Cor. 15:3–4). This experience is also known as the new birth, and is an instantaneous and complete operation of the Holy Spirit upon initial faith in the Lord Jesus Christ. (John 3:5–6; James 1:18; 1 Pet. 1:23; 1 John 5:1).

> 6. We believe that all who have truly repented and believed in Christ as Lord and Saviour are commanded to be baptised by immersion in water (Matt. 28:19; Acts 10:47–48; Acts 2:38–39).[2]

It is interesting to see how the language of faith in Christ is linked to atonement and new birth, which is regarded as instantaneous and complete upon initial faith in Christ. Those who have repented and believed are commanded to be baptised by full immersion in water as an expression of their faith and in obedience to the Scriptures, which was an early denominational position (cf. Parr, 1927c). With this background in mind we turn to the most extensive social scientific work that has been done on the subject.

A Multi-Disciplinary Theory of Religious Conversion

Lewis R. Rambo is probably the leading theorist on the topic of religious conversion and, therefore, it is important to engage with his theory in relation to this data. He uses a seven-stage framework in order to explain its nature (cf. Wakefield, 2006: 17; Percy, 2000: xi–xvi), regarding conversion as a process rather than an event, although he acknowledges that sudden conversions do occur. He also contends that all conversions are 'mediated through people, institutions, communities and groups' (Rambo, 1993: 1; cf. Rambo and Farhadian, 1999). Conversion can be a source of greater self-worth, participation in a community, and an envisioning, inspiring and guiding process. Rambo defines conversion in the following way. It is:

> [A] simple change from the absence of a faith system to a faith commitment, from religious affiliation with one faith system to another, or from one orientation

---

[2]   http://www.aog.org.uk/pages/17-statement-of-faith/content; accessed on 3 January 2008.

to another within a single faith system. It will mean a change of one's personal
orientation toward life, from the haphazards of superstition to the providence
of the deity; from a reliance on rote and ritual to a deeper conviction of God's
presence; from belief in a threatening, punitive, judgmental deity to one that is
loving, supportive, and desirous of the maximum good. It will mean a spiritual
transformation of life, from seeing evil or illusion in everything connected
with 'this' world to seeing all creation as a manifestation of God's power
and beneficence; from denial of the self in this life in order to gain a holy life
thereafter; from seeking personal gratification to a determination that the rule of
God is what fulfills human beings; from a life geared to one's personal welfare
above all else to a concern for shared and equal justice for all. It will mean a
radical shifting of gears that can take the spiritually lackadaisical to a new level
of intensive concern, commitment, and involvement. (Rambo, 1993: 2)

Rambo suggests that all of these meanings are associated with the central
concept of change or a 'turning' from that which is old to something 'new', even
if the precise meaning of the term in specific settings is contextually determined.
He advocates a process model of conversion that is multi-dimensional – that is,
containing various elements that are 'interactive and accumulative over time'
(17). This model has been constructed from observation, description, empathy,
understanding and interpretation, with a view to providing a theoretical explanation
of the phenomenon. The seven stages or dimensions of the model are as follows.

Context

The first stage is the overall context (20–43). This is less of a stage and more
of a total environment in which the religious change occurs and includes larger
cultural and local factors. This context not only includes external forces but also
internal psychological ones, such as motivations and aspirations. It includes
'social, cultural, religious and personal dimensions' (20). The macrocontext refers
to the larger environment of, for example, politics, organisations, ecological
landscapes and economics. The microcontext is the immediate world of family,
friends, ethnicity, religious community and neighbourhood, which influence a
person's sense of identity and belonging, feelings and actions. The macro- and
microcontexts obviously interact and there is inevitably some 'push and pull'
between them. How these two aspects relate will depend on other factors, such as
the dominant culture and society. In the Western context, Rambo identifies further
aspects, which influence the context. First, transportation and communication
influence conversion, making it easier for people to travel and network and for
ideas to be disseminated. This is made possible because of the macrocontext,
although it can also be hindered by such contexts which outlaw conversion (e.g.
in India, Israel and Sudan). Second, secularisation is noted as a factor influencing
the decline of religious conversion, especially in the modern West. In this context
there is religious plurality, rationalisation of public spheres and a relegation of the

religious to the private realm of personal belief. Rambo follows the work of Peter L. Berger and argues that secularisation's most important feature is pluralism: due to transportation and communication, many more people now know that there is a variety of religious options on the table from which to choose (Berger, 1969; 1977). In addition to these factors, Rambo also observes the influence of a person's myths, rituals, symbols and beliefs on conversion. The religious background is a significant factor and conversion needs to be understood within the context of religious traditions in transition, not just individuals. Individuals and groups form an understanding of conversion from out of a *religious matrix*, using the ideas, images and metaphors of a specific religious tradition (Rambo, 1993: 34).

These factors can either inhibit or facilitate change and thereby influence all of the other stages either directly or indirectly. Rambo notes how contexts may resist or reject conversion, create religious enclaves, shape conversion along established cultural or social lines, or according to some form of congruence between a religion and a context. He suggests that there are five types of conversion in relation to the context. (1) Tradition transition occurs when there is contact between two different cultures and an example would be a cross-cultural missionary setting, in which a foreign religion is exported. (2) Institutional transition marks the move from one form of a religion to another form of the same religion, for example from Roman Catholicism to Anglicanism. (3) Affiliation represents the move from little or no religious commitment to a group requiring a high level of commitment, for example the Unification Church (cf. Gillespie, 1991: 15). (4) Intensification occurs within a religious tradition and allows previously nominal members to become more active within the same tradition, for example through the Cursillo movement (cf. Lynch, 2006: 28). (5) Apostasy and defection tend to occur when there are few benefits from belonging to a particular group and the person leaves, even though there might also be risks involved (Ipgrave, 2006: 5; Cotterell, 2006). Some secular interpretations of religion have supported this understanding.

Crisis

A crisis usually precedes a conversion because it is regarded as a response to a problem of some kind (Rambo, 1993: 44–55). This means that converts are regarded as active agents in the process of conversion rather than passive recipients, although this feature has been debated (45). The nature and extent of the crisis that precipitates conversion is variable. Often social disintegration, political oppression or trauma are cited (e.g. Ullman, 1989: 18–20). However, other less dramatic events can cause a crisis, such as hearing a preacher or a speaker. Crises may prompt a fundamental shift in orientation or be the straw that breaks the camel's back: perhaps a change in worldview (Flinn, 1999: 58). Indeed, Rambo regards cummulative events as significant processes towards conversion. Often it is the discrepancy or dissonance between the ideal and the reality that prompts such a crisis (Lofland and Stark, 1965: 864), or dissatisfaction (Romain, 2000: 26). Rambo notes Max Heirich's study of Roman Catholic charismatics, which is pertinent here. Heirich's study found that charismatics were less likely to deny stress than non-charismatics but that this was insufficient to account for what was happening *in toto* (Heirich, 1977). The types of experiences that Rambo cites as prompting a crisis include: mystical experiences (e.g. Saul of Tarsus), near-death experiences, illness and healing, and general dissatisfaction with life and leaving a religious tradition (apostasy). Rather than simply framing this aspect as a crisis, Rambo suggests that it is also important to note the innate desire that humans have for transcendence of some kind and, in a constantly changing world, religious conversion can offer both an experience of transformation and refuge from the surrounding chaos (Rambo, 1993: 51). Different psychological perspectives offer conflicting accounts of the motivation for conversion, from fear, loneliness and desperation to the desire for fulfilment and meaning. Romain suggests that problems can be categorised as: spiritual, interpersonal, character, material or physical (Romain, 2000: 64–65).The moving on from the past into a new and uncertain future, however exciting, can be extremely painful for many people because the past cannot be eradicated in a moment but takes time and is a form of loss.

Quest

In this phase people aim to resolve the crisis in which they find themselves and establish greater meaning and purpose in life (Rambo, 1993: 56–65). This is a continual process but is intensified during the need to find resolution. Flinn prefers to see it as a state of 'suspension' or indecision (Flinn, 1999: 58). Rambo identifies three factors that explain the nature of this stage. First, there are two different kinds of response style: active and passive, and the assumption that Rambo works with is that converts are predominantly active rather than passive agents. This runs counter to the often held belief that they are passive recipients. Although Rambo acknowledges that people are situated at different points along the active–passive continuum, and at times are more passive than active, he nevertheless suggests that converts are located towards the more active pole. Second, there is the degree to which the person is free to move from one previous commitment to a new one (called 'structural availability'). Existing networks of family, employment and friends can inhibit or prevent change, despite the inner desire for fulfilment (Tidball, 2006: 89). Alternatively, the search for friendship can prompt an interest in faith (Romain, 2000: 37–38). Previous or profound emotional attachments can inhibit any active change, similarly 'old' intellectual or cognitive frameworks must have some compatibility or continuity with the 'new', and there is usually some compatibility between existing religious beliefs and practices and new ones. Third, motivation is significant for conversion and there are different theories that attempt to account for this aspect. Examples of motivations include the need to experience pleasure and avoid pain, the need for a conceptual system, the need to enhance self-esteem and the need to establish and maintain relationships (Epstein, 1985; cf. Ullman, 1989: 27–74). Rambo suggests that these factors, and two others, namely power (Beckford, 1983) and transcendence (Conn, 1986), are important for understanding motivation in its complexity and that they may change over time (Rambo, 1993: 63).

Encounter

There is a meeting between the person on a quest and an advocate of the new religious alternative (66–75). The advocate or evangelist has an important role to play in the process of change because they represent the alternative. The meeting between the advocate and the potential convert is regarded as a dynamic and complex process. Previous studies have focused on the convert without paying sufficient attention to the role of the advocate. But in reality there is a negotiation going on between the two and the effect is two-way: advocates are influenced by their potential converts as well as vice versa. Historically, Christianity as a missionary religion has been interested in the conversion of groups and societies regarded as 'pagan'. Advocates are motivated to engage in these encounters in order to do God's will, obey Christ's command and offer 'civilisation', as well as desiring to help others less fortunate than themselves. Building on the work of an anthropologist of mission studies, Thomas Beidelman (1974; 1981; 1982), Rambo describes five characteristics of the advocate. First, the social background of the advocate, such as his or her ethnicity, class and economic status will influence attitudes and outlook. Second, the religious system of beliefs is significant and will differ according to theological tradition. Third, the advocate's theory of conversion and its process will be influential in relation to the potential convert's rejection of previous ways – for example, respect for indigenous culture, use of strategies, segregation of new converts away from the community or a conversion of whole communities. Fourth, the advocate's missionary career can also be influential, depending on where they are in their own careers, and what experiences they have had, both positive and negative. Fifth, advocates are also able to offer inducements to converts, such as technology, medicine, education and resources, and this is often a factor in the outcome.

Interaction

This is a development of the previous stage as the encounter intensifies and seekers begin to 'negotiate' the meaning of the change and process their emotions and behaviour (Rambo, 1993: 102–123). In this phase converts learn more about their new religion and are socialised into a community of practice. The dynamic between the prospective convert and the advocate continues. Rambo argues that religious traditions encapsulate particular beliefs, values, attitudes and practices that create a new world for the convert to inhabit. The degree to which this is controlled and used by the religious group will vary depending on how it views wider society and if its boundaries are porous or tight. Rambo identifies four key components. First, relationships are the 'ties that bind'. Kinship and friendship are fundamental to most experiences of conversion. These relationships can compensate for previously poor relationships, inspire personal growth and provide confirmation of and validation for the religious orientation or worldview. It is also the case that religious leaders provide important examples of a particular religious life that can inspire converts. Second is the importance of ritual in religion. It has been suggested that people perform rituals before they rationalise or theologise them. Rambo asserts that ritual action being regular, sustained and intentional is fundamental to the experience of conversion and offers holistic and embodied knowledge. It enables converts to act differently, helps form new attitudes and consolidates faith communities while telling a story of its identity to outsiders. Third, the change in rhetoric is a significant feature of the conversion process. New conceptualisations and interpretations of what has happened develop by using new language. As there is prolonged interaction with a new religious group so the language of a potential convert changes as s/he absorbs a new vocabulary linked to the worldview and beliefs of the new religious group. The rhetoric of religious groups includes discursive language as well as the use of symbol and metaphor. It is also the case that how events are attributed changes and spiritual forces or God become agents in the human drama of salvation. Fourth and finally, there is the process of role change. A role is understood as the behaviour that is expected of an individual in a given social position. It contains shared expectations in relation to behaviour and specific enactments associated with the role. These expectations derive from institutions and beliefs and are reciprocal. One important role that the convert plays is that of a student in relation to a teacher, who may be a mature member of the religious group, and the interaction may be formal or informal.

Commitment

A specific step is made by the convert in which a decision to follow a new path or orientation is made (124–141). It is a stage of turning and the 'fulcrum of the change process' (124). Tidball's analysis of Evangelical conversion narratives suggests that this is the dominant rhetoric in that constituency (Tidball, 2006: 93). In many religions there is an important ritual that symbolises this decision or commitment and participating in the ritual can consolidate the decision. Rambo identifies five features. First, decision-making is crucial and can often be a difficult confrontation with the self. Turning to the new way, while still being part of the old way, can be a painful experience, and Rambo sees this as inherent in many forms of Christianity. However, once the decison has been made there is often joy, exhilaration and a new-found sense of freedom. Second, as mentioned above, rituals have a powerful role to play in the commitment of converts, and baptism in Christianity is an example of such a ritual. Through this ritual the convert says both 'no' to the past and 'yes' to the future. It functions to sustain loyalty to the group and is a symbolic act of 'bridge burning' (Hine, 1970), creating boundaries between converts and the outside world. Third, there is an inner process of surrender, which for many converts is *the* turning point produced by the grace of God not human endeavour.

It is regarded as essential to the new life and can be symbolised in the submission to an authority of some kind (leader, group, tradition). It is a complex feature that contains issues of desire, conflict, resolution, relief and continual affirmation. Fourth, conversions are told through testimonies, which include both transformed language and biographical reconstruction in the light of the change. Testimony is an important way of displaying commitment in a public context. Individual testimonies can remind the communities of its beliefs, values and overall theology, thus being overtly and covertly moulded by the group. Fifth and finally is the topic of motivation. It reaches its peak at the commitment stage because very often advocates question the motives of the potential convert. Language transformation and biographical reconstruction also influence motivation. Motivation is multiple, complex, changes over time and varies from person to person, but for conversion to continue some motives must be sustained.

Consequences

There are ongoing aspects of conversion and change, which follow as consequences of the experience and process (Rambo, 1993: 142–164). How one assesses conversion and its consequences will, of course, be influenced by personal values. Rambo makes an important observation concerning the positioning of scholars who attempt to evaluate conversion processes. The nature of the conversion is determined to some extent by its intensity and duration. Authentic conversion may, in fact, be an ongoing process of change and may take months or even years. He cites Donald Gelpi (1982) who argues for five dimensions of conversion: affective, intellectual, ethical, religious and social. Gelpi differentiates between initial conversion and ongoing conversion, including the integration of these dimensions into the whole of life. The consequences of conversion are not only personal, but can be social and cultural, bringing benefits in some cases, for example health and education, but also problems, such as affirming unjust social structures (e.g. the caste structure). Rambo avers that he would expect the results of conversion to be cumulative over time and that these would, in effect, be more significant compared to the short-term effects. Here he is considering the effects from the adoption of a religion by a particular society or culture en masse. Sometimes the consequences of conversion produce unintended socio-cultural consequences, such as challenges to the colonial powers, challenges to biblical interpretation because of vernacular translations, and restrictions on the role of the supernatural because of modernist assumptions. Religious traditions tend to evaluate the consequences of conversion by means of their own rituals and expected behaviour, as well as the sincerity and authenticity of the quest. Converts themselves may emphasise a number of features: that their relationship with God is now a living reality for them, including expressions of intimacy and love; that they have experienced relief from guilt and sense of sin; that they have gained a sense of mission and reason for living and that they have become members of a new community or family (Ullman, 1989:

169–181). They now understand the nature of reality in a new and more authentic way, with God positioned at the centre of their lives (Tidball, 2006: 91).

Reflection

The contextual analysis of the narratives provides important information. Three conversions are clearly 'institutional transitions' (Alan, Rebekah and Rodney), with initial conversions experienced elsewhere. The exception is Ruby, who falls into the 'affiliation' category. All of the conversions are mediated and in three cases real psychological difficulties are described (Alan, Ruby and Rebekah). Rodney seems to have exercised his choice not to affiliate religiously for a period of time, thus supporting aspects of Berger's secularisation thesis (Berger, 1969; 1977). His attendance at a funeral reawakened his faith commitment. All of the converts have exercised some degree of choice in affiliating to HPC (again supporting Berger's thesis).

All of the converts experienced some form of crisis prior to a Pentecostal commitment, or in Ruby's case her affiliation. All were active agents in the conversion process, seeking to resolve personal issues or find meaning. Clearly there is an acculumative effect of specific events and interaction with people leading to a new commitment, even if the role that existing networks play is less clear. The link between previous forms of Christianity and especially Evangelical Christianity supports the idea that conversion works best if the cognitive frameworks of the old and new are compatible. The self-esteem of all the converts appeared to be enhanced significantly by the experience and their continued participation in the life of HPC.

Three of the four converts speak of the role that an advoate had in assisting them to convert: Alan speaks of the Evangelistic rally, the book and a person coming to pray for him; Ruby identifies the witness of the care workers and experience in worship; Rebekah talks of answered prayer being the stimulus to her change; and Rodney mentions his parents initially, then the worship service and members of the church pressurising him to be baptised by immersion, about which he was finally persuaded through a prophecy.

It is clear from the narratives that all of the converts have had continued interaction with HPC, which has strengthened them in their faith commitment, and this is expressed through the rituals of baptism or an act of renewal and baptism in the Spirit. Participation in Sunday and mid-week worship sustains them in their Christian life and enables them to acquire the Pentecostal language of faith and behaviour in acceptable ways.

Ritual does play an important role in the conversion process of these people, especially in baptism and baptism in the Spirit, but also in weekly Holy Communion. Corporate worship is central to their lives and surrender to God is an important feature of the church rhetoric during these services. Testimonies also play a crucial role as individuals are encouraged simply to tell their story of what God has done or is doing in their lives. The testimonies offered through the focus group have been biographically reconstucted using the lenses of pneumatology and Pentecostalism.

As a consequence, this group of people is highly motivated and they are committed to their faith and church community. Their conversions and Pentecostal engagement have been long-lasting in some cases: Rodney has attended HPC for 38 years, Alan for 30 years, Ruby for 4 years and Rebekah has recently moved to the country and has attended only 18 months. All of the converts appear to be equally positive about their conversion experience and their ongoing life at HPC.

It can be said that the working model of Rambo is useful in analysing the conversion narratives of the participants. In general terms we may see these narratives as broadly fitting into the Rambo model, but the encounter and interaction phases are not as clearly distinguished in the Pentecostal model and they appear to blur into each other rather more. Also, it needs to be said that in most of these cases a prior conversion experience or Christian background provides the context for the conversion process proper. In these narratives the Holy Spirit and the ritual combine to give a distinctly Pentecostal interpretation of the process. This is also observed by Tidball in terms of the 'rhetoric of encounter' for charismatic Evangelicals (Tidball, 2006: 96). Participants, on the one hand, would regard their experiences as conversion plus a process of renewal and empowerment (context plus the rest of the stages). Conversion is the first step or a decision, after which there is ritual (baptism and baptism in the Spirit) followed by empowerment for the Christian life. This understanding stands in tension with the theory of Rambo, which sees conversion as belonging to the whole process. On the other hand, when asked what symbols or signs were associated with conversion, Alan and Rodney both referred to glossolalia and baptism in the Spirit, suggesting that the accent was not on the first conversion which was regarded as inadequate, but rather on their Pentecostal conversion, which was regarded as superior. Rebekah stated that she felt the 'consciousness of sin', which she connected to her renewal of commitment, and which stands in parallel to the accounts of Alan and Rodney. Clearly there is a particular Pentecostal reading of conversion that accommodates past and present experiences. It appears to be different to an Evangelical approach to conversion, defined as accepting a particular cognitive schema (Lynch, 2006: 30). Increasingly there is recognition that conversion is a form of socialisation, or resocialisation (Kreider, 1999: 21–32), even if acceptance of a cognitive schema is part of that process. Indeed, Tibball suggests from his analysis of Evangelical narratives that 'affection', due to relational attachments, is the key motif to be associated with conversion because it represents long-term, if low-level, engagement where participation precedes belief (Tidball, 2006: 101–102). This is an important factor in these narratives.

The above table (4.1) can now be modified to include the categories of Rambo (1993) for comparison (see Table 4.2).

Table 4.2 Features and Sequence in Conversion Compared to Rambo

Alan	Ruby	Rebekah	Rodney	Rambo
Conversion Experience		Conversion Experience	Conversion Experience	*Context*
Problem	Problem	Problem	Problem	*Crisis*
Insight	Insight	Insight	Insight	*Quest*
Experience of the Holy Spirit	Experience of the Holy Spirit	Prayer Answered	Experience of Worship	*Encounter/ Interaction*
	Baptism	Renewal of Commitment	Baptism	*Commitment*
	Baptism in the Holy Spirit	Speaking in Tongues	Baptism in the Holy Spirit	
Outcome: Love Power	Outcome: Healing	Outcome: Revitalisation	Outcome: Revitalisation	*Conse-quences*

A British study by William Kay of 907 Pentecostal ministers from the Assemblies of God, Elim, the Apostolic Church and the Church of God denominations showed that 19% had remained in the denomination in which they had been brought up; 54% with a church background had switched from another Christian denomination; 19% with non-churchgoing parents but who had switched from the denomination in which they had received a formal religious initiation as a child; and 9% had converted to Pentecostalism without any religious rite attending their birth (Kay, 2006: 116–118, percentages as cited in the original). This means that 73% of ministers had transferred into classical Pentecostalism from other Christian traditions, which generally began in childhood. For those switching Christian denominations, the commitment to Christianity had been a gradual one (64.2%). By contrast, it is those from non-churchgoing backgrounds who are likely to experience sudden conversions (58.9% for those with a totally irreligious background). It is ministers with a dramatic conversion experience who are likely to preach this kind of conversion to their congregations. It is also likely that the experiences of these ministers are also reflected in their churches, with the majority transferring from other Christian traditions. Interestingly, from the opposite angle, Romain observes that only 27% of Pentecostals move from one classical Pentecostal denomination to another, with 73% of Pentecostals leaving classical denominations for other churches (Romain, 2000: 95).

Given this analysis, is there a distinctly Pentecostal theology of conversion in contemporary scholarship? In order to secure a perspective with which to interact, we turn to recent Pentecostal and Roman Catholic ecumenical dialogue.

Pentecostal Theology of Conversion

Pentecostalism, as a missionary movement, has always emphasised the need to proclaim the gospel so that others outside of the church might both understand the message and accept the invitation to follow Jesus Christ (Anderson, 2007). The most useful statements concerning the theology of conversion and evangelism can be found in the reports of the fourth and fifth phases of the bilateral conversation between some classical Pentecostal churches and leaders and the Roman Catholic Church (1999, 2007). For the purposes of this discussion, the Pentecostal theology is distilled from these reports in order to provide a considered theological position with which to engage. Secondary literature will be used at various points to nuance the discussion. These reports will be taken in sequence.

First, the report entitled: 'Evangelization, Proselytism and Common Witness: The Report from the Fourth Phase of the International Dialogue (1990–1997) between the Roman Catholic Church and Some Classical Pentecostal Churches and Leaders' (1999) enables a Pentecostal theology of conversion to be gleaned in relation to issues surrounding evangelism.

Both Pentecostals and Roman Catholics believe that God has charged all Christians to announce the gospel to all people in obedience to the Great Commission (Mt 28.18–20).This proclamation centres on the reconciling work of God through Christ and it is central to the church's faith, life and witness (2 Cor 5.18–19). In particular, Pentecostals place emphasis on the proclamation of Jesus Christ as Saviour and Lord, with the expectation that where this is received it results in 'personal, conscious acceptance and conversion of an individual', a 'new birth' as in John 3.3. For many Pentecostals there is an urgency to evangelise the world before the return of Christ (Acts 2.14–17; Joel 2.28–32), thus making as many disciples ready for the return of the king: Jesus Christ. Therefore, it is expected that evangelism will contain the proclamation of the belief that salvation is offered through the life, death and resurrection of Christ as a gift of God's mercy and grace ('Evangelization, Proselytism and Common Witness', 1999: 13–14).They are motivated to evangelise by their love for Christ, their obedience to the Great Commission and their desire that unbelievers might receive the blessing of eternal life now and in the future. They also believe that the second crisis experience, known as the baptism in the Spirit, is essential for every believer to receive empowerment for witness to Christ (Acts 1.8) ('Evangelization, Proselytism and Common Witness', 1999: 15).

For Pentecostals, evangelism is understood to contain a missionary proclamation to the non-Christian as well as to those who have professed a Christian faith but now live a life indifferent to the faith. It is anticipated that the Holy Spirit prepares individuals and peoples for the reception of the gospel (Rom 1.20; Ps 19.1–4). The Spirit of Christ prepares those who are saved to receive Christ and they are saved without exception through the death of Christ. Many Pentecostals have tended to point to what they regard as demonic elements in other religions.

> While Pentecostals acknowledge the work of the Holy Spirit in the world, convincing people of sin, righteousness, and judgment (cf. Jn 16.8–11), they generally do not acknowledge the presence of salvific elements in non-Christian religions. Some Pentecostals would see a convergence towards the Catholic position ... in that the Holy Spirit is at work in non-Christian religions, preparing individual hearts for an eventual exposure to the Gospel of Jesus Christ. ('Evangelization, Proselytism and Common Witness', 1999: 16)

Pentecostals believe that there is one name whereby we can be saved (cf. Acts 4.12), and that people need to respond to the invitation to seek him and find him (Acts 17.27). They argue that the biblical mandate for mission is grounded in the redemptive purposes of God ('Evangelization, Proselytism and Common Witness', 1999: 17).

The content of the Christian message is Jesus Christ himself, the means of reconciliation with the Father, the good news (Gal 1.16), which was entrusted to his disciples (Mt 28.19). It is expected that the Holy Spirit gives dynamism to evangelism (Acts 2.17), enabling Christians to proclaim Christ in order to lead others to him (Acts 4.20). This proclamation of Christ is necessary because of the bondage of humanity to sin, because all are fallen and lost, resulting in an alienation from God and others. This means, as illustrated in the ministry of Jesus, that deliverance from 'the principalities and powers' is included in evangelism, which means exorcism in some cases ('Evangelization, Proselytism and Common Witness', 1999: 17). God always takes the initiative through his grace, which frees the human heart to respond. He acts through the Word, as well as signs and wonders. The role of humans is to respond positively and constantly in the power of the Holy Spirit to God's initiatives through Christ, the only mediator (1 Tim 2.5) and head of the church (Col 1.18) ('Evangelization, Proselytism and Common Witness', 1999: 18).

The ordinary context in which this gift of salvation is worked out is the church, the community of believers, which makes it possible for the church to become 'a servant, gift, and sign to the world' (18). This counteracts individualism and independence, on the one hand, and a tendency to sterile formalism, on the other. There is a recognition that the faith community evangelises through its common life, which means that proclamation and lifestyle are embodied in specific cultures. There is an acceptance of the idea that there is a considerable amount of good in all cultures, even though humanity is fallen from grace. 'Pentecostals emphasize the changing of individuals who when formed into a body of believers bring change into the culture from within. Catholics emphasize that culture itself in its human institutions and enterprises can also be transformed by the Gospel' (19).

Foreign missionaries need to be sensitive to a dominant non-Christian culture, to respect it and support positive elements while attempting to transform it from within. There is a genuine acceptance that no one operates in a cultural vacuum. Even so, Pentecostals claim that they have been most successful in cultures where they have been able to emphasise the 'freedom of the Holy Spirit, with their consequent openness to the diversity of forms of expression in the worship and praise of God (e.g. their recognition of dance as a genuine form of spiritual worship)' (19). Pentecostals also accept that there have been, and continue to be, 'great social changes in Western society', resulting 'in secularisation processes and consequently a decline in religious practice' (20). This is deplored when 'these attitudes become part of a political agenda which promotes a value-free society in the name of tolerance and liberalism' (20). Nevertheless, they accept that this developing context provides a challenge to find new ways of witnessing to Christian beliefs and values.

Sometimes Pentecostals have been accused of focusing on evangelism at the exclusion of responding to social and practical needs in the wider community of which they are a part. However, Pentecostals respond to this criticism by stating that:

> The sense of urgency which Pentecostals have concerning witness and salvation to the lost, like that of the early church, is not inconsistent with love and care for one another and for others. There are many examples of their sacrificial care throughout the world. The hope of the imminent coming of the Lord has sustained Pentecostals during persecution, harassment, imprisonment, and martyrdom during this century. They have consistently taught that the Church must be ready for the coming of the Lord by means of faithful witness and holy living. They have taught that all will have to give account to the righteous Judge for those things which have been done or left undone. ('Evangelization, Proselytism and Common Witness', 1999: 21)

Pentecostals have great concern for the eternal salvation of the soul, but they also have a concern for the present welfare of the body, demonstrated in their practices of healing. They have a real concern for the social, as well as spiritual, welfare of their members. Rebirth is understood as an anticipation of cosmic redemption (cf. 2 Cor 5.17; Rom 8.21), and this means that conversion and integration into a church community are connected to the transformation of society ('Evangelization, Proselytism and Common Witness', 1999: 21). It is fundamentally through personal conversions that Pentecostals understand that social change will be effected (22). Once converted, the person belongs to a local congregation and it is through this community that new purpose is given to the individual. The community functions as an alternative society that is able to protest against oppressive structures in wider society (cf. Yong, 2010). In this way, social change is made effective at the local and the regional level ('Evangelization, Proselytism and Common Witness', 1999: 22); and in this respect Pentecostals see themselves as exercising religious liberty, which they extend to others. This is a liberty which they believe the state should guarantee as a fundamental human right (36).

Second, the fifth phase report, entitled 'On Becoming a Christian: Insights from Scripture and the Patristic Writings with Some Contemporary Reflections' (2007; cf. Robeck, 2008), offers additional material that builds upon the previous report.

'Catholics and Pentecostals both agree that conversion is essential to salvation in Christ, and that its ultimate purpose is a life of committed discipleship', although it is admitted that there is a diversity of understanding ('On Becoming a Christian', 2007: 9). For example, it is recognised that conversion can be understood as an event or a series of events or a process; and that this variety is reflected in the biblical texts themselves. This diversity has been outlined by Wenk (2000) as embracing God's goodness and turning towards God as an ongoing process (Luke); the call to repentance (Mark, Matthew and Q); receiving life and light (John); and 'being saved' as a radical event (Paul). Pentecostals see conversion as a reorientation of attitudes, beliefs and practices that is linked to the 'proclamation of the Word, acceptance of the Gospel, profession of faith, repentance, a turning away from sin and turning to God, the bestowal of the Holy Spirit (Romans 8.9), as well as the incorporation of the individual into the Christian community' ('On Becoming a Christian', 2007:10).

The report, in a survey of biblical material, states that conversion embraces all aspects of humanity: rational, volitional and affective (Ps 51.10, 12; Jer 24.7; Ezek 18.30–31; Gal 2.20), such that the whole person is changed (2 Cor 5.17). In the New Testament conversion is uniquely connected to the person of Jesus Christ, in whom the kingdom of God is fulfilled (Jn 3.16). It is related to a number of key themes, such as sin, repentance, forgiveness, salvation, justification, baptism and faith, and it is often associated with the cleansing of heart and mind (Joel 2.12). It is often accompanied by zeal to testify to what God has done and to witness to the nations (Mt 28.19–20; Acts 4.20). 'The Bible presents various perspectives on conversion, and not just one definition' ('On Becoming a Christian', 2007: 13), but it is suggested that Roman Catholics and Pentecostals can agree on the following: (1) that conversion establishes a personal relationship with God so that the sinner can cry out with confidence (Ps 51.1); which (2) creates a 'mysterious interplay between the human and the divine', as the human responds to God's initiative; and which is (3) relational in both vertical and horizontal ways, being directed to communities as well as individuals ('On Becoming a Christian', 2007: 13).

The Patristic evidence supplied in the report suggests that the early Fathers regarded conversion as essential to the missionary life of the church. This material provides historical testimony to conversion and its influence. For example, the testimony of Justin Martyr (c.165), who tells of the impact that his observation of another's conversion had upon his own life in terms of 'a flame of love' being 'kindled' in his own heart (13; Wenk, 2000: 76). The moral transformation of Cyprian (c.250) after his conversion is highlighted, as is the famous conversion of Augustine of Hyppo (397–400). Concerning the latter, the report states:

> Conversion was the result of ongoing interaction between those converted and those already initiated, who shared the new religious life they had found with these newcomers. The change at the root of conversion is nothing less than transformation of the person through interaction of divine grace and human freedom. ('On Becoming a Christian', 2007: 15)

The Patristic writers were concerned with the way in which conversion affected behaviour and character, often in dramatic ways. They connected it to baptism as the beginning of the Christian life and often noted the role of human freedom in the decision to convert. Sometimes conversion was associated with new birth and sometimes with baptism (16; Wenk, 2000: 78).

Pentecostals and Roman Catholics both understand conversion as an entrance into a covenant that involves interplay between God and humanity ('On Becoming a Christian', 2007: 17). Baptism is a Christocentric act of personal commitment in the context of public worship, thus enriching ecclesial life and witness. Pentecostal views on baptism vary from understanding it as a public affirmation of faith to seeing it as a means of strengthening faith (17).

> … Catholics and Pentecostals tend to understand conversion and initiation, first of all, in terms of the kinds of testimonies reflected in the New Testament rather than in abstract concepts. For both groups conversion experiences are diverse, and all these experiences are something to be narrated and celebrated. ('On Becoming a Christian', 2007: 19)

They agree that generally conversion involves a need for formation and discipleship to be ongoing (cf. Robeck, 2008: 11). Conversions may vary in expression and be experienced at different levels or stages. Nevertheless, and despite its complex and varied nature, both Roman Catholics and Pentecostals agree that it is fundamentally a gift of God ('On Becoming a Christian', 2007: 20).

Rescripting Ordinary Theology

In order to rescript the ordinary theology of conversion, a number of features can be distilled from the discussion so far in dialogue with Pentecostal theology.

Even though people come from different religious backgrounds, it is likely that the majority of converts come from backgrounds in other Christian traditions; similar to Judaism providing the religious context in Acts (Dunn, 1996: 119). This is certainly the case with three of the four testimonies; and it is supported by wider research (Kay, 2006). Pentecostals, therefore, should appreciate the fact that converts will be mainly forms of 'institutional transition', with some affiliations from non-Christian backgrounds. This means that an attitude of openness and respect towards other Christian traditions would be not only courteous but advantageous. It would resonate with Pentecostal and Charismatic spirituality, which sees the whole of life as a search for an intimate and empowering relationship with God through the Holy Spirit (Cartledge, 2006a). It also resonates with the insight of Rambo (1993) that far from converts being passive, they are very much active participants in the process. Indeed a Pentecostal theology would expect there to be an ongoing interaction between the person and the Holy Spirit, such that the Spirit being active in previous experiences could be expected to lead a person from one stage to the next.

People have problems or crises and these are often crucial in the process of conversion. The accounts in Acts mention apostasy (9.1–30), ignorance (19.1–7), sin (2.1–41) and impurity (10.1–48) as forms of crises. Of these, only one is mentioned in the conversion narratives – that is, sin is stated by Rebekah. Earlier Evangelical and Pentecostal theologies of conversion majored on the problem of sin, which is solved by the act of Christ upon the cross and appropriated by faith in the event of conversion. It is interesting that in this generation the concept of sin is discussed less openly and frequently. There are, of course, good reasons for this, in that Pentecostalism has been accused of being legalistic and world-denying. Perhaps there is a shift in contemporary ordinary theology that seeks to play down the concept of sin for the purpose of greater acceptance in wider society. If so, a rescripted ordinary theology would recover a deeper understanding of sin (personal, holistic, corporate, societal and structural) that is nevertheless communicated with sensitivity and respect.

Insight is at the heart of Christian conversion, as the Holy Spirit allows the person to see what might be possible in relation to the problem. Rather than seeing the work of the Spirit in merely powerful ways, there should be greater recognition in the testimonies that the Holy Spirit is at work in providing insight and wisdom that open up new possibilities. The Holy Spirit is active in the ordinary routine of life and is intensified in the powerful and dramatic experiences associated with conversion. A theology of creation, which sees the work of the Holy Spirit as sustaining life, also needs to be articulated. This would not deny spontaneous 'signs and wonders' and 'works of power', but would see these as dramatic punctuations within an ongoing process.

Experience of the Holy Spirit and rites of commitment are part and parcel of the one complex. The clear stages of rebirth by the operation of the Holy Spirit followed by baptism by immersion are neither stated uniformly in the testimonies nor in the biblical texts (cf. Twelftree, 2009: 96–98). For example, Alan and Rebekah never mention baptism nor baptism in the Spirit explicitly, only an experience of the Holy Spirit; whereas Ruby and Rodney clearly emphasise baptism followed by baptism in the Spirit as distinct events. In Acts, Paul and Cornelius' household experience the Holy Spirit before baptism (9.17–18; 10.44–48), while the Ephesian disciples receive baptism at the hands of Paul and subsequently experience the Holy Spirit

(19.1–7). Here the witness of contemporary experience and Scripture cohere. There are experiences of the Holy Spirit that surround and intertwine sacramental initiation and locate important 'ritual milestones' (Poewe, 1999: 202–203). The picture, however, is variable. Nevertheless the components of insight, dramatic experience and sacramental ritual all combine at the heart of the process. It is here that Pentecostals recognise a certain fluidity in the patterns that are experienced, but stress the holistic nature of conversion and that it is rooted in relationships within the community of the Pentecostal church.

This discussion has identified the community of the church as vital to a theology of conversion. The church is a servant and a gift to those who wish to convert and a sign of God's grace to the wider world. A church that is open to the wider world is one that is a network facilitating movement of exploration and integration. Thus, it facilitates conversion through 'structural availability'. In this respect the worshipping life of the church provides a context in which to listen to narratives or testimonies of conversion, to learn the grammar of faith and to invite enquirers into their midst. It is important that lay leaders and not just the pastors recognise the importance and role that they have as advocates in the process of conversion. Rites of commitment are important for conversion, but these may differ according to the background of those seeking to convert. It may be that rites other than baptism, such as reception into fellowship, might assist in 'institutional transitions', which would appear to make up the majority of those joining Pentecostal churches.

The conversion process results in empowerment for the whole of life. It is not just the baptism in the Spirit that empowers for works of service, but the whole process of conversion. The testimonies do not distinguish between the baptism in the Spirit as the event of empowerment because it is set within a larger frame of reference. In this regard the theory of Rambo (1993) suggests that the overall process is one of empowerment and that conversion can refer to the overall process, not just the initial crisis and response. This means that the 'consequences' stage can also be significant for a theology of conversion. Pentecostal scholarship has suggested that this ongoing discipleship should include care for others, especially outside the church, for social concern to be understood as a form of holy living. Therefore, the new birth should be seen as an anticipation of the cosmic redemption that is to come and a means of exercising the glorious liberty of the children of God (Rom 8.21). Furthermore, glossolalia, as an important sign of the Spirit's presence, can be seen in the context of Christian discipleship as a whole, not just as marking the second stage of a distinct process. This is an important signification and reflects a new language for a new life.

Summary

Conversion is central to Pentecostalism as a missionary movement and the narratives displayed many of the characteristics one would expect to find. It is interesting to observe that most of the testimonies of conversion show that members had conversion experiences outside of Pentecostalism and that joining a Pentecostal church ('institutional transition') enabled them to build upon their experiences and extend them. The idea of conversion as a 'punctuated process' is evident within the narratives, especially if baptism and baptism in the Spirit are considered as part of the overall process, but the picture is variable to a certain extent. Rambo's (1993) theory of conversion was a useful means of analysing the testimonies and broadly fits their contours. However, some modification to Rambo's theory was suggested, especially with regard to the categories of the encounter/interaction and commitment. The theology of conversion from a Pentecostal perspective is very similar to standard Evangelical discourse, with emphasis being placed upon the proclamation of the gospel message of faith in Christ, and an experience of new birth (Jn 3.3) allowing reconciliation with God (Gal 1.16). Although a personal decision is still an important aspect of conversion for Pentecostals, the strong emphasis on community means that it is placed within a broader lifestyle context and culture. It must be seen as an aspect of salvation which affects the whole of the person (rational, volitional and affective) and their life in the world. It is suggested that Pentecostals would benefit from recognising that their numbers have been increased through many people transferring into Pentecostalism from outside. Therefore, an open approach to other Christian traditions would facilitate such transitions. Following Rambo, it should be recognised that many people who convert are active in the process and are agents of conversion themselves. It appears that many people turn to Christianity because of some kind of problem in their life and traditionally Christianity has associated these problems with the concept of sin. Although the testimonies did not make much of this feature, it was suggested that it could be explored and considered at a deeper level as a way of connecting to the broader Christian tradition. The role of the Holy Spirit is important in a theology of conversion and this can be understood not just by means of the dramatic and 'miraculous' but also in terms of the everyday and routine. Following Rambo again, it can be confirmed that, for those converting, the whole process is understood as empowering and fulfilling; and this should include the consequences of conversion for Christian discipleship.

Chapter 5
Baptism in the Spirit

One of the most important theological distinctives within Pentecostalism is an experience of the Holy Spirit, usually experienced as dramatic and significant, called the 'baptism in the Spirit'. In contemporary Pentecostalism it is often regarded as a post-conversion experience, that is symbolised by speaking in tongues, otherwise known as glossolalia (Cartledge, 2002a). The nature of baptism in the Spirit as subsequent to conversion and as signified consequently by glossolalia has received enormous scholarly attention. This attention has arisen from within classical Pentecostalism itself, as a theological distinctive, and from those in the Charismatic Renewal, especially Roman Catholics and others wishing to explore its sacramental significance (Laurentin, 1977). Therefore, it is an important theme for consideration. This chapter describes the testimonies of church members, before setting the narratives within their own interpretive framework. Once this has been done, the narratives are theorised by means of a philosophical typology proposed by Caroline Franks Davis (1989) and a sociological interpretation offered by Margaret M. Poloma (1989, 2003). Insights from these theories are placed in dialogue with theology, especially through the argument of Frank Macchia (2006) and others. Ordinary theology is rescripted in relation to these perspectives and an alternative proposal is advanced.

Testimonies

The Focus Group

The focus group was comprised of six women and two men. One man was a middle-aged Black British local government manager (Harry), the other was from Jamaica and retired (Joseph). The women were from Barbados (Helen), Uganda (Julie), Ireland (Alice) and the UK (Valerie, Ethel and Glenda). They were mostly middle-aged (Julie, Valerie, Alice and Ethel), although Glenda was a younger woman and Helen was elderly. These women were employed in administration (Valerie), evangelism (Julie), home-keeping (Alice), nursing (Ethel), teaching assistance (Glenda), or retired (Helen).

Six testimonies illustrate the nature and theology of this experience.

Valerie: I got baptised in the Holy Spirit about six months after I became a Christian ... I think it was the first time that anybody had asked me if I wanted to be filled with the Holy Spirit. I probably would [have] agreed earlier if anybody had asked me before then, but they hadn't done ... Actually it was an evangelistic, a few evangelistic meetings that I'd gone to anyway, although I was already a Christian, and the pastor asked if people wanted to be filled with the Holy Spirit and speak in tongues. And I really wanted to speak in tongues and so I went forward and he laid hands on me and prayed for me. And the thing that I remember most of all was I felt like my legs went from under me, particularly, I just felt that my muscles had kind of gone weak. And I know he prayed for me twice, for various reasons and I can't remember if it was the first night or the second night or both nights ... I didn't actually collapse onto the floor, but I didn't really feel that, you know, that I really had the strength to stay standing up. And I did speak in tongues but only a tiny bit the first night and then he prayed for me again the next night and then I spoke more in tongues. But what I remember most was I really felt that I loved God after it had happened. And I'd not felt that before. I felt grateful, you know, when I'd become a Christian. But after I was filled with the Spirit, I felt like I loved God and I'd kind of been waiting for that. 'Cos other people had talked about it and I hadn't really felt it myself. So that was the main thing that I remember.

Julie: For me, when I become born again I was in a church where they used to put emphasis on being filled, almost in every service they would ask people to get ..., ask the Holy Spirit to come into their lives. But I remember I could see people being filled but I was not filled in the service. So one time when I was at home I was praying. All of a sudden I just heard my tongue changing. I had my, my eyes were closed. I couldn't open them. I couldn't even get out of my [chair], I prayed for a very long time when I was praying. And I was praying in a language that I don't even understand. I felt the power of God coming upon my life. I started to shake. I was in the room alone. And I was shaking, I was praying, I was shaking. So since that time I started to speak in tongues, that I was speaking in my bedroom back home.

Mark: Okay. Was this back in your home country or ... ?

Julie: Yes, in my home country. It was about two months, maybe three months, when I accepted Jesus.

Mark: So three months after your conversion [agreement] you had this experience [agreement].

Harry My experience was slightly a bit different. I'd heard about being filled with the Holy Spirit and of course the church from time to time did invite people to come down for prayers to be filled with [the] Holy Spirit, so I went down. But nothing never happened. And then we used to have the Bright Hour when Maria was alive, and they invited me up to the front to pray. They were praying for a long time and they were praying in tongues. And I was thinking, well, what's wrong, but I was just a new Christian. I didn't really understand and I was a bit offended, to be quite honest. So anyway I was just sort of leaving and I was walking home and I was just talking to the Lord. If anybody [heard me] they'd think I was crazy [laughter]. But first of all, I didn't really like what I did, you know, and I was just venting my feelings. And I just thought, and I believe it was the Lord, and he said, 'Why don't you just go and speak in tongues?' But on the night I went to sleep and I had this experience and I felt that my stomach was pushing out and my head was being lifted back and I just cried out, I didn't speak in tongues. But I realised that was the baptism of the Holy Spirit. That was my experience.

Joseph: We used to have revival that people used to go to the altar. We used to call it tarrying. And you would tarry there for the Holy Spirit and you would go and you would praise. One night I was there, down on my knees and I was praising the Lord, praising the Lord. After so long I found that the words were coming out quite different. My whole entire body was changed. It was like I [was] lifted up [agreement] out of my natural body, you know. There was power, there was liberty, there was everything. I was a changed person. I knew that something had happened. I knew I'd been filled with the Holy Spirit. It's, when you're filled with the Holy Spirit, you meet Christ. You'll never be the same again [agreement]. And you know when it happened.

Mark: So was this in your home country?

Joseph: This was in England here … The church when I go tarrying …

Mark: Oh, okay. This is the Church of God of Prophecy …

Joseph: … of Prophecy, yea.

Alice: I went to T.L. Osborn at Cambridge Street and I used to go on Friday nights to the showing films. And I got saved up there. But I didn't really understand and a couple there came to this church. They invited me down one Saturday night and I've been coming here ever since. I backslid for about two years. But something just, it must have been the Holy Spirit drew me back again, which was [when] I had a bad Asian flu and all over Christmas I could not move. And I kept speaking to Jesus and he kept speaking to me. He says go back, you know, to where you first found me, where I found you. And then I came back to Hockley and the person that invited me here was standing on the steps and he ran up the road and threw his arms around me and I've been coming back ever since. But I had the Holy Spirit about twelve months later, in the back hall, one Sunday night. It was an evangelist and this little old lady, I forget her name. She used to sit by me, but she was always sleeping. She'd pop off after the service started. But this night she kept awake and when he invited anybody who wanted the Holy Spirit to come up and she got me and she said, come on, Alice, and she went up and put her hands on my head. I went, I fell on the floor. The power came flooding over my head down to the bottom to my feet. And it was [a] wonderful, wonderful experience.

Mark: Did you speak in tongues?

Alice: Yes, yes.

Glenda: I had several experiences when I was much younger. The first experience I remember was quite young, probably eight or nine, something like that ... It was one of the Sunday night meetings and I remember everybody went down to the front for prayer. I just remember, I mean I was very young and it was this just complete motion just sort of took over my whole being and I remember it now so vividly. I just couldn't stop crying and I was only little and everyone was probably thinking, 'Oh what's the matter with you?', you know. But I cried for absolutely ages and I didn't really understand what it was. And obviously not understanding but I could feel this power and I don't know whether because I was so young and I couldn't fully understand what was happening to me. I just knew it was some sort of emotion and that something had happened to me [agreement]. And obviously, you know, I accepted God and I was very young being brought up in the church. But this was the first sort of experience I remember having. So that was one of crying when I don't really understand it ... I remember just crying, ha, I can't explain it. But then the second experience I had was completely the opposite and I was probably about eleven then, eleven, twelve, and that was just of complete joy. I was so happy and we were singing some really uplifting songs at the end of the service and God, just the presence was amazing. I just remember it and I was just filled with this joy and I just couldn't stand still and I was dancing in the Spirit. It was just amazing. And you know, the meeting went on so late because everybody was just praising God and I didn't speak in tongues but I had that feeling inside of me that I get now when I do speak in tongues, if you know what I mean. So it's the same emotion, same feeling but at the time I didn't speak in tongues, and that was probably, I'd probably be about twelve then when I did probably speak in tongues.

Summary of the Testimonies

For most of the participants, there was a gap between their conversion and their baptism in the Spirit, suggesting a two-stage process, either explicitly (Valerie, Julie, Alice and Ethel) or implicitly because they were already involved in church life (Harry and Joseph), although one participant had not received this experience (Helen). Many experiences were dramatic and included things like: feeling that one's legs were going to collapse and feeling weak (Valerie), feeling a sense of power and shaking (Julie), feeling one's whole body changing as if being lifted up, as well as feeling power and liberty (Joseph), or falling to the floor and sensing power filling one's body (Alice). One person received his baptism in the Spirit in a dream, and felt his stomach push out, his head being lifted back and so he cried out (Harry). Another person experienced multiple fillings with the Spirit as a child, so it was difficult to pinpoint a second, post-conversion experience. She experienced a sense of power at the age of 8 years old, joy and dancing at 11 years old and speaking in tongues at 12 years old (Glenda). A number of the testimonies stated that the person had spoken in tongues at their baptism in the Spirit (Valerie, Alice, Julie and Joseph), although only one person stated explicitly that he has not, and does not, speak in tongues, even though he believes he has been baptised in the Spirit (Harry). The effects of these experiences were understood as giving a greater sense of love for God (Valerie) and of changing the person (Joseph).

Further Analysis

A number of biblical texts were used to assist the participants in their understanding of baptism in the Spirit, starting with the Great Commission of Matthew 28 (Joseph), Harry's very personal appropriation of John 7.37 and the idea of 'streams of living water' flowing out from inside of the person. Valerie remembered Acts 19 and the baptism in the Spirit of the Ephesian disciples of John the Baptist. The promise of Acts 1.8 was mentioned by Julie and the association of power with the coming of the Spirit. The day of Pentecost itself was noted, as was the Joel prophecy cited there (Joel 2.28–32; Acts 2.17–21) (Ethel). Julie also remembered Matthew 7 and the promise that God would give good things, even the Holy Spirit to those who ask (Mt 7.9–11; it is the Lukan version that mentions the Holy Spirit, Lk 11.13).

The participants associate baptism in the Spirit with the church practice of laying hands on people and prayer for the experience to occur (Valerie). This can be done in a general context when prayer is offered as part of the usual worship service, or more specifically when baptism in the Spirit is being offered (Joseph). Sometimes visiting preachers are invited to come and speak on the subject of receiving the baptism in the Spirit and it on these occasions that some people have the experience (Ethel).

Symbolically, baptism in the Spirit is associated with speaking with tongues, as Joseph explains from his experience at the Church of God of Prophecy:

> [Y]ou're praising God in a different language, then your speech automatically changes and you start to say things that you know nothing about what you are saying, you know. And sometimes [for] some people they interpret it, but at the end they always put their hand on you and say, 'You are filled with the Holy Spirit'. So they confirm it because they hear you, although you don't understand what you are saying. But they understand it and they know that you're filled with the Holy Spirit.

For Harry the sign was trembling because it is associated with the power of God. This was echoed by Valerie, who said:

> For me I associate [it] most with a sense of power, I just call it a sense of anointing
> ..., like a sense of fullness [agreement] and of peace and strength and often
> happiness as well, often liberation, those kinds of things [agreement]. That's
> to me more associated [with] being filled with the Holy Spirit than tongues is,
> because you can feel like you can speak in tongues at any time. But sometimes
> you sense that strength and ... those feelings of anointing, particularly when you
> like, you know, [have a] kind of fresh touch of God.

However, this was qualified by Joseph who said that some people actually feel
'godly sorrows' rather than joy and happiness.

Baptism in the Spirit and British Pentecostalism

As has been indicated earlier, the roots of the Assemblies of God denomination in
the UK can be traced back to the Sunderland revival, the impact of the Conventions
and the publication of *Confidence* magazine, edited by Alexander A. Boddy
(Cartledge, 2008a; Wakefield, 2007). The early British Pentecostals adopted a
three-stage Wesleyan paradigm – namely, an experience of conversion is followed
by a distinct event of inner or spiritual cleansing, which, in turn, is followed by
an experience of power for witness, called baptism in the Spirit (cf. Anderson,
2004: 187–191). However, the Wesleyan emphasis is less obvious from the mid-
1920s, perhaps under the influence of American evangelists such as Aimee Semple
McPhearson (Foursquare Gospel), who visited the UK in 1926 (Blumhofer, 1993:
280). The explicit three-stage paradigm was dropped from *Confidence* magazine
from 1917 and this is perhaps reflected in its demise elsewhere around the UK.
For example, William O. Hutchinson's statement of faith in *Showers of Blessing*
omitted reference to sanctification from 1914 (Hathaway, 1996: 43, 56). In any
case, since the time of the formation of the Assemblies of God in 1924, there has
been a general move away from a Wesleyan paradigm and what is taught appears
to be in predominantly two-stage territory: conversion followed by a second crisis
experience called baptism in the Spirit. However, different understandings of
sanctification are maintained, and this is demonstrated by T.B. Barratt who points
to the variety of accounts of spiritual cleansing: before, with and after the baptism
in the Spirit (Barratt, 1929: 4). This is supported by Garfield Vale's suggestion
that both 'instantaneous' and 'progressive' versions of sanctification are being
experienced by Christians (Vale, 1934: 12). Donald Gee, interestingly, uses the
five-fold gospel categories, but he configures them in a four-fold gospel manner:

> The Lord Jesus Christ is our Saviour, but real salvation makes men sanctified too
> (1 Cor 6.11). He is our Healer, but healing and holiness, physical and spiritual
> health, go together (Jn 5.14). He is our Baptizer in the Holy Spirit, but how
> deeply the baptized need to be sanctified also (1 Cor 13.1). He is our Coming
> King, but if this is our hope then holiness has become our chief necessity (1

Jn 3.3). Thank God that the Saviour, Healer, Baptizer and Coming King is the SANCTIFIER also. (Gee, 1931: 3)

As the tradition develops it becomes clear that sanctification is understood as largely denoting separation from the world and consecration unto God and that it is progressive by nature, having its roots in conversion, with a clear demarcation from the Holiness movement being stated (Carter, 1937; Sherlock, 1937a; Cooper, 1939).

Alexander A. Boddy had initially advocated speaking in tongues as the sign of having received one's 'Pentecost' (baptism in the Spirit), but this was modified after about 1912 to include other signs, especially divine love (Kay, 2000a: 14–15). J. Nelson Parr, the main leader of the emerging denomination from 1924, had been influenced by the Sunderland Convention (1910 and 1911), but from 1914 had probably been influenced by the formation of the American Assemblies of God denomination and the debates surrounding its emergence (Kay, 2000a: 28). On the day that the denomination was initiated in 1924 Nelson Parr was elected chairperson and certain Fundamental Truths were affirmed, including: 'the baptism in the Holy Spirit, the initial evidence of which is the speaking with other tongues', thus adopting the earlier theology of Boddy (Kay, 2000a: 29). This was maintained up to the 1960s, as recorded by Hollenweger, although set within the following context:

We believe ...
in the fall of man;
in salvation through faith in Christ;
in baptism by immersion in water;
in the baptism in the Holy Spirit with the initial evidence of speaking with other tongues;
in holiness of life and conduct. (Short version, Hollenweger, 1972: 520)

Tom W. Walker, although from the Elim denomination, represents the British movement as a whole when he writes that the Acts of the Apostles provides a template for understanding the Christian *ordo salutis* as containing salvation, baptism by immersion in water followed by baptism in the Holy Spirit 'as separate and distinct experiences' (Walker, 1976a: 27). Salvation is understood as the new birth following the repentance for sin and the acceptance of Christ as saviour, while baptism is the outward public confession of faith following the experience that has happened inwardly. Baptism in the Holy Spirit bestows upon the Christian 'galvanic power from on high, that energy-full endowment of the Holy Spirit' for the purpose of power for mission (28). These stages may not necessarily be separated by any length of time, but they are definitely regarded as theologically distinct and chronologically expected in that order. The doctrines of subsequence (baptism in the Spirit as an event subsequent to conversion) and initial evidence (the sign of glossolalia accompanying baptism in the Spirit), are clearly argued by the former principal of Mattersey Hall, David Petts, based upon a reading of the narrative of the Acts of the Apostles (Petts, 1998). He defends this Pentecostal position against the various critiques that have been used to undermine its validity, namely the hermeneutics of Acts in general, the exegetical challenges of key texts (Acts 8.4–25; 1 Cor 12.13; 12.30) and pastoral issues surrounding the practice.

More recently, the doctrinal statement has been revised and the corresponding statements from the Assemblies of God 'Statement of Faith' (2004) now read as follows:

> 6. We believe that all who have truly repented and believed in Christ as Lord and Saviour are commanded to be baptised by immersion in water (Matt. 28:19; Acts 10:47–48; Acts 2:38–39).

> 7. We believe in the baptism in the Holy Spirit as an enduement of the believer with power for service, the essential, biblical evidence of which is the speaking with other tongues as the Spirit gives utterance (Acts 1:4–5, 8, 2:4, 10:44–46, 11:14–16, 19:6).

> 8. We believe in the operation of the gifts of the Holy Spirit and the gifts of Christ in the Church today (1 Cor. 12:4–11, 28; Eph. 4:7–16).

> 9. We believe in holiness of life and conduct in obedience to the command of God. 1 Peter 1.14, 15, 16; Heb 12.14; 1 Thess 5.23; 1 John 2.6.[1]

It is clear that the same *ordo salutis* is conversion by faith in Christ and the experience of new birth, expressed through the sacrament of baptism by immersion, followed by a subsequent baptism in the Spirit as empowerment for service, the essential biblical evidence of which is speaking in tongues as inspired by the Spirit. From these flow the operation of the gifts of the Spirit and an expectation of godly living.

It is instructive to consider how religious experience is conceptualised using other academic disciplines. In this study specific contributions from philosophy and sociology are considered useful in explicating the nature of this central Pentecostal experience.

---

[1] http://www.aog.org.uk/church_interest.asp; accessed on 3 January 2008.

Religious Experience

A Philosophical Typology

Caroline Franks Davis in her important book, *The Evidential Force of Religious Experience*, offers philosophical insight into how to understand the nature of religious experience (1989). She observes that there have been 'non-cognitive' and 'cognitive' views of religious experience. The 'non-cognitive' views have assumed that there is such a thing as 'raw experience' that lacks any form of interpretive content, which must be added at a later stage. By contrast, the 'cognitive' view is a critical realist position that understands experience as being mediated via models and metaphors, which in themselves have essential cognitive functions (5–10). The strength of these models and metaphors as 'reality-depicting' is increased where they are grounded in communal histories and experiences over time (13). Indeed, she argues that there is a reciprocal interaction between concepts, beliefs, events, reflection, creative imagination and other cognitive and perceptual factors (147). In terms of strictly religious experience, namely ones that subjects themselves describe as religious or are intrinsically religious (31), she offers an interesting and useful six-fold typology. She acknowledges that the categories are not exclusive because an experience may exhibit several characteristics at the same time.

First, *interpretive experiences* are those which are viewed within a prior religious interpretive framework. This is especially the case for fervent believers. They see everything that they do or experience as religiously significant. Many ordinary everyday happenings can be attributed to an answer to prayer or divine intervention of some kind (33–35).

Second, *quasi-sensory experiences* are ones in which the key element is a physical sensation, or an association with one or more of the five senses, for example visions or pictures, voices or sounds, smells, tastes or physical sensation of touch. The most common is a vision of a spiritual being or some spiritual representation. She regards the post-resurrection appearances of Christ as falling into this category; and she suggests that these types of experiences acquire their form from the subject's own resources of religious ideas (37–39).

Third, *revelatory experiences* are ones in which the person acquires sudden convictions, inspiration, revelation, enlightenment or flashes of insight. These may be received 'out of the blue' and without any other signs marking the experience as religious. The religious feature is therefore defined as the 'revelatory' content. More frequently these types of experiences are part of a more complex kind that combines a number of difference features. They are usually sudden and of short duration; the knowledge acquired appears to be immediate, and is 'poured into' or 'showered upon' the person by an external agent, which is received with strong conviction but which cannot be put fully into words (39–44).

Fourth, *regenerative experiences* are regarded as the most frequent type of experience among ordinary people who are not mystics, ecstatics or prophets. These experiences renew the person's faith and improve spiritual health and well-being. They make a religion live rather than it being a set of doctrines or religious rituals. Experiences can be of new hope, strength, peace, security and joy which, because they are located within prayer or worship, are attributed to divine power or presence and are thereby religious. Experiences may also be of forgiveness, guidance, salvation (being 'saved' or converted), vocation, healing, moral virtues, love for others and the discovery of meaning and purpose to life. They can vary in intensity and duration, being regular, or simply sporadic (44–48)

Fifth, *numinous experiences* make the person aware of his or her 'creature-consciousness', which is despicable in the face of the *mysterium tremendum*. This sense of mortality carries connotations of awe and dread, being over-powered yet having intense energy, viewing the numen as transcendent and sensing 'rapture' upon contact. A 'numinous experience' may display only one of these features or a combination of a number of them. This sense of the numinous and our response to it can be triggered by the people around us, or by our own personal piety, or via the liturgies of religion and the atmosphere that surrounds ancient buildings. Again, the intensity of these experiences can vary from very mild to overwhelming. They are often regarded as ineffable – that is, surpassing ordinary categories of thought and therefore difficult to describe (48–54).

Sixth, *mystical experiences* give a sense of having apprehended an ultimate reality, offering an awareness of freedom from the limitations of time, space and the self, that is co-ordinate with a sense of 'oneness' (either with the divine or human other) and bliss or serenity. They are usually regarded as the pinnacle of the spiritual journey; the closest one may come in this life to meeting with the divine 'face to face'. The insights gained through such an experience are regarded as 'ultimate', eternal and universally true. The person appears to transcend space and time, losing a concern for the things of the world. Even though such experiences last only seconds, there is the sense that the person has stepped outside of time and into eternity. The person senses that the divine presence has penetrated him or her, allowing surrender to the transcendent, the renunciation of worldly ways and union with the divine and others (54–65).

Obviously, it can be seen from these very brief descriptions of the six types that there is a certain degree of overlap. Nevertheless, this typology seems a useful way of categorising experience in general terms in order to compare different kinds of data across a variety of religious traditions. It also has the advantage of allowing experiences to be shaped and expressed by implicit, as well as explicit, theological content, since how these experiences are articulated will inevitably reflect a particular religious tradition (159–161). This does mean, however, that there is no dichotomy between concepts derived from experience and concepts brought to experience, or between 'experience' and 'interpretation', since these are intertwined (165).

In summary, these Pentecostal experiences can be classified in Franks Davis' terms as interpretive, quasi-sensory, regenerative and mystical. It is with these categories in mind that we turn to sociology and the work of Margaret M. Poloma in particular.

A Sociological Interpretation

Margaret M. Poloma's study of the Assemblies of God denomination in the USA notes a discrepancy between the official position of the church, where baptism in the Spirit is 'witnessed by the initial physical sign of speaking with other tongues', and the extent to which it is accepted 'on the ground' (Poloma, 1989: 39). In her study 75% of the congregational sample claimed to be baptised in the Holy Spirit, while only 89% of those had ever spoken in tongues. She observed a difference between clergy and laity on the acceptance of the doctrine of 'initial physical evidence' because 39% of the laity agreed with the statement that 'baptism in the Holy Spirit may be experienced without tongues', with only 54% of the sample explicitly agreeing with the proposition that speaking in tongues was the 'initial physical evidence' of baptism in the Holy Spirit (40). This contrasts with Assemblies of God pastors, who must have had the experience to be ordained and are in agreement with this denominational doctrinal statement (only 2% disagreed).

William Kay's survey of 401 Assemblies of God ministers in 1996–1997 revealed that 99.8% of ministers regarded themselves as having been baptised in the Spirit. Of this sample, 81% believed that speaking in tongues is necessary as an initial evidence of baptism in the Spirit. There were 30% who believed that baptism in the Spirit could occur without speaking in tongues (Kay, 2000a: 73–74). These data suggest that while there is a certain expectation upon ministers they are less demanding generally with regard to their expectations of others. The fact that there are a number of pastors who believe that baptism in the Spirit could occur without the sign of tongues suggests that the doctrine of initial evidence is under some pressure from within the denomination and not just from the outside.

Poloma classifies baptism in the Spirit experiences as either collective or solitude behaviour. The collective behaviour is the most common one, especially during a special meeting or camp. The majority of the people she interviewed had such experiences in a revival meeting of some kind or in a regular church service. Although experiences varied for collective behaviour, Poloma identifies a change in the attitude towards the older practice of 'tarrying' among Assemblies of God pastors. Older pastors remembered the days when people would 'tarry' for the blessing for days, weeks and months, spending much of the time on their knees in prayer. This practice has now fallen into abeyance. People are now simply asked to come forward, to stand and receive the Spirit as others pray; and they are advised to let the language of tongues come by not speaking in their native language, whilst trying to speak in tongues (Poloma, 1989: 42). Some interviewees recalled feelings of 'ecstasy', spiritual purity, or physical behaviour, such as rolling on the ground, and healing (44–45). However, a significant minority experienced Spirit baptism in solitude and this is more likely for converts to the Assemblies of God, especially for pastors from other denominations becoming Pentecostal (46). The effect of baptism in the Spirit is reported in terms of improved prayer, boldness to proclaim the gospel and, for some, the power to give up alcohol, smoking or drugs (47).

Building on her earlier work, Poloma's book on the Toronto Blessing and Pentecostal revivalism makes a significant contribution to the understanding of charismatic experience (Poloma, 2003). Although this book focuses on the Toronto Airport Christian Fellowship (hereafter TACF) and the concept of revivalism, it considers these phenomena via the conceptual lenses of the 'mystical self' and the corporate 'mystical body'. For our purposes, it is the mystical self which is in view and is pertinent to our analysis.

Poloma notes that at the TACF a number of different physical phenomena can be observed and these have some resonance with the testimonies above. They include laughing, rolling, falling, jerking, shaking and grunting, accompanied by the interpretation that 'God is playing with his kids'. However, her observation also suggests that not all were laughing and that uncontrollable weeping and violent shaking were in evidence, providing support for the mixed metaphors of play and power (63–64). The TACF leadership used 'testimonial narratives' to explain what was happening, and in particular understood that physical manifestations and strange behaviour should be 'judged by their fruit', which can only be accessed via personal testimony. The testimonies arising from these experiences interpret the phenomena as signals of the presence of God: a flash sign saying 'Spirit at work … Spirit at work … Spirit at work' (65). In a survey conducted by Poloma the majority of respondents were already Pentecostal or Charismatic, having spoken in tongues (87%) and/or experienced being 'slain in the Spirit' (70%). In the TACF meetings 34% experienced 'dancing in the Spirit' and 24% experienced being 'drunk in the Spirit' (67).

These experiences are interpreted by Poloma using the dynamic ritual theory of Victor Turner that recognises societal groups as moving between the relatively fixed structures of 'normal' routine and the spheres of action that can be described as 'floating', 'antistructural' or 'liminal'. This liminality is part of the ritual process that operates on the edge of 'normal' society, a state of 'betwixt and between' that makes space for something else to occur (68). In revival rituals, such as the Toronto Blessing or baptism in the Spirit, a space has been made for that something else to happen. Poloma notes that in the TACF the ritual behaviour occurs in accompaniment to Christian rock music, which work together to produce a fluid antistructure ritual. It is in this context that the mystical self is revived via 'prophetic mime' (roaring, crowing/clucking and barking) and 'spirit drunkenness'. How the noises were interpreted by the congregation depended on the person's own evaluation of the experience expressed through the medium of the testimony, so that '[i]f the outcome was judged good, the story was accepted not so much for the animal sounds as for the message being imparted' (71). These noises are often made in the context of receiving prophetic revelation and visions, and therefore the sounds and gestures are understood as a means of God communicating. Spirit drunkenness, or being inebriated with the divine, is interpreted variously as receiving joy, prophecy, forgiveness and healing.

Poloma suggests that Turner's description of ritual with reference to antistructure as playful and 'carnivalesque' fits in well with TACF behaviour (74). It creates a 'betwixt and between' space for 'spontaneous communitas', which functions as a threshold of 'a storehouse of possibilities' (74; Turner, 1969: 94–130; cf. 1987: 101–104). Testimonies suggest that the ritual process allows for catharsis and transformations of self-identity. This fits in well with the ritual theory of Turner as it is associated with inward transformation or reordering as the outward behaviour displays chaos, although exact interpretations vary according to personal circumstances. It is this juxtaposition of the outward and the inward that resonates with the theory of Turner as the person negotiates change from the structure of the past to the structure of the future through an experiential 'no-man's land'. Open and emotional experiences are thus opportunities for personal identity transformation. It is through these personal revival experiences, according to Poloma, that fragmented selves and broken relationships are mended as 'building blocks for *communitas*' (Poloma, 2003: 81).

Reflection

Reflecting on the HPC testimonies in the light of these philosophical and sociological analyses, there are a number of interesting issues that can be considered.

Regarding the philosophical typology, several observations can be made. First, it could be said that all of the testimonies can be regarded as 'interpretive experiences'. This is because the experiences narrated all appear within a church context after the person has spent some time in a Pentecostal church of some kind, if not HPC. A number confess that the pastors and leaders of the church have talked about the experience and given the members some understanding and a set of expectations. Therefore, a *framework* is already in place in order to interpret what it is they will experience, even if there is some diversity of understanding. Second, all of the experiences are 'quasi-sensory experiences', in the sense that one or more senses are obviously involved in the experience. This is seen in descriptions of weak legs, shaking, a sensation of body elevation, falling to the floor, crying (noise and tears), dancing, and, of course, sound and speech through speaking in tongues. Third, the effect of these types of experiences moves them into another category, namely 'regenerative experiences'. This is because participants feel a greater love for God, the power of God in them, liberty and personal transformation and a sense of joy. Fourth, in all of the accounts there is the assumption that these experiences have in some way enabled the participants to apprehend ultimate reality, through the person of the Holy Spirit, and that they are therefore also 'mystical experiences'. There is a real sense of unity with the divine. It is understood as a significant meeting with the Spirit of God, through which their lives could now move forward in a new way. It is an experience of the Spirit of God which transcends the limitations of the natural body and puts them in touch with the risen Christ (Joseph).

The sociological analysis allows three further points to be made. The first is the nature of how baptism in the Spirit is acquired. Four of the testimonies describe how the experience was received within a corporate setting, either at a special meeting (Valerie and Alice) or at a regular church service (Joseph and Glenda). Two testimonies recall how the experience happened in solitude (Julie and Harry). Interestingly, both of them were involved in contexts where people were being regularly prayed for in church services, but for some reason they failed to receive the baptism. It was only on their own, in private, that they received the experience. It shows that the community of the church is the most important context and influence and that the ritual is part and parcel of Pentecostal practice, but that occasionally there are individuals who simply do not access the benefits of the ritual in a corporate context; therefore they appropriate them in solitude. Whether they could have appropriated these benefits without belonging to a corporate context is a moot point.

The second is the discrepancy between the official position of the denomination, as mediated by the pastors, and the views of the laity. It was noted above that only four explicitly stated that they spoke in tongues at their baptism in the Spirit (Valerie, Alice, Julie and Joseph), which means that the other four people did not do so. Glossolalia was obviously acquired at a subsequent stage by three of the participants, thus suggesting a disjunction between the official position and the experience of individuals. One person stated that although he believed he had been baptised in the Spirit, he still does not speak in tongues (Harry). The view that one does not necessarily have to speak in tongues as a sign of being baptised in the Spirit was one that occurred in another focus group. The official view was reiterated in this other focus group dialogue, which proved illuminating. Therefore, a full extract from this other discussion is worth presenting here.

Brian (from the focus group discussing worship) explains his understanding as someone who listened to the debate at the General Conference.

> Maybe I can give you the official position very easily, which I do actually basically go with [...]. What we would say is that biblically everyone that got filled with the Holy Spirit, where it specifically says in the Bible they got filled with the Spirit, people saw a difference. Instantly there was something that happened such that other people around said, 'What's just happened to them?' [agreement]. And in most of those cases it specifically says speaks in tongues, and in a couple of places speaks in tongues and prophesied. So that's why we wouldn't say prophecy is not an evidence of being filled with the Holy Spirit but, you know, the Bible says sometimes people speak in tongues, sometimes people speak in tongues and prophesy [agreement]. Now whether that meant there was a group of people, in that case some of them spoke in tongues and some of them prophesied, who knows? We would say that speaking in tongues is available for every believer, 'cos Paul spoke about, you know, I would that you all spoke in tongues and this is how you speak in tongues. And he talks about that one in a

way that he doesn't necessarily talk about a lot of the others in terms of the fact that [it] is available for everyone.

And then the other thing is this idea of evidence, the evidence of being filled with the Holy Spirit. Now personal experience is I did not speak with tongues on the day that I believe I got filled with the Spirit. It was three or four weeks later. Now, there to me is a crucial point about this. It is talking about the evidence of being filled with the Spirit. I could tell people that I was filled with the Spirit. But what evidence did they have [agreement]? Do you see what I mean? There wasn't, they couldn't say 'Oh, well, yes, you know, we see that evidence there'. Obviously when I began to speak with tongues then that was an evidence the people could see. And it was very linked, as I say, it was only a few weeks later and considering I'd literally been saved about 30 minutes after I got or even less when I got filled with the Spirit, it was quite practically, then, you know, you can understand there are problems. Nobody was explaining to me what [it] was all about. So, what it's kind of talking about is the essential evidence. If you want to see if someone is filled with the Spirit or not, scripturally people who got filled with the Spirit spoke with tongues, so we would say that [is] the essential evidence. It doesn't mean to say that someone is not filled with the Spirit if they don't speak with tongues. But we've got no essential evidence and, you know, maybe they are or maybe they're not. Maybe they've got to start moving out in the gifts. Maybe they're filled with the Spirit but actually [agreement] they don't understand or they're bottling the whole thing up [agreement], so that they're not using the gifts, in which case you're kind of missing a rather big point of being filled with the Holy Spirit. Because these gifts are distributed as the Spirit chooses.

Hannah (also from the focus group discussing worship) engaged in a dialogue with Brian on the subject:

Hannah: Would you not think, though, sometimes that some people could have, 'cos there's nine gifts of the Spirit, there's not [just] speaking in tongues [agreement]? Would you not think that maybe it's possible sometimes somebody might just impart of the gift of faith, before they speak in, you know, would God not maybe give you the faith, you know?

Brian: Well, it depends on what your understanding of the gift of faith is …

Hannah: Or he can give your a word of knowledge, do you know what I mean?

Brian: Yes, yes.

Hannah: Would, I mean I know we've always from the year dot said the proof of the Spirit is the speaking in tongues. But, you know, would it not be that sometimes that God could give them any one of the other nine gifts, surely he could [agreement] ...

Brian: Well, the official position, which I also believe is yes, in essence, I agree with you. Of course, God can give any gifts. But we can go through the scriptures at some point which indicate that tongues is available to everybody. Not all the gifts are available to everybody [agreement]. But tongues is, so that's why tongues is a standard thing. You know, that's why, it's because of the origins of the movement that it's there. And some people wonder if it really is absolute statement of faith it needs to be there. But basically and scripturally people who got filled with the Spirit spoke in tongues and ... for everybody. It doesn't mean they're not filled with the Spirit otherwise but that's basically it.

This discussion is very illuminating and suggests that different interpretations exist side by side and that there is some differentiation between the official denominational understanding and its ordinary appropriation.

The third is the nature of the experience as a threshold experience that allows for a change in self-identity and greater incorporation into the community of the church. There is a clear sense in some of the testimonies that physical and chaotic physical behaviour occurred (legs collapsing, feelings of bodily change and elevation, falling to the floor, tears and dance) or experienced in a dream (stomach being pushed out). These types of behaviour, although not exhibiting the animal noises associated with Poloma's idea of prophetic mime, nevertheless suggest an antistructure ritual enabling a reordering of identity structure through liminal experiences. The results of these experiences are understood as empowerment (Joseph and Glenda), love for God (Valerie) and transformation of the person (Joseph). Again, this suggests that there has been some significant personal change as a result of the reordering facilitated by the ritual. The strong sense that their experiences are part and parcel of the community means that once the threshold has been crossed a new level of Pentecostal identity has been gained. They are accepted as members of the *communitas* and are able to function at a new level within a congregational fellowship. They have moved closer to the centre of the group and ties have been forged and strengthened.

I now turn to the work of leading Pentecostal theologian Frank Macchia, who has offered a significant proposal centred on the theological distinctive of baptism in the Spirit. It provides a Pentecostal contribution towards a theological reflection on these testimonies in the light of the philosophical and sociological analyses.

Pentecostal Theology of Baptism in the Spirit

Frank Macchia proposes a Pentecostal theology using the metaphor of baptism in the Spirit, which he aims to apply more broadly in order to overcome the criticisms of Pentecostal pneumatology (Macchia, 2006). Rather than separating the work of the Spirit into neat distinct categories, he wishes to see it as an integrated whole (18). As part of this project he considers the way in which recent Pentecostal scholars, such as Steven J. Land (1993), and commentators, such as Walter J. Hollenweger (1997) and Harvey Cox (1996), have managed to give an account of Pentecostalism and its spirituality without recourse to this distinctive theological marker. In particular he notes how Hollenweger considers Pentecostalism to be fundamentally experiential and culturally constructed, and therefore how theology is conceived in that framework, thereby focusing on the oral and performative dimensions (Macchia, 2006: 50). Doctrinal statements are therefore considered to be very secondary to how Pentecostals do theology, and it is this experiential and intercultural approach which allows for greater possibilities in terms of diversity and global ecumenism. But Macchia contends that this appreciation of the oral, narrative and dramatic features of Pentecostal theology need not leave the doctrine of baptism in the Spirit behind: it is not an either/or but a both/and. This is because '[t]he church has lived for centuries with both narrative and doctrinal expressions of the faith, and Spirit baptism as a biblical metaphor can function well as our chief distinctive on both levels' (56). Therefore, he wishes to see the metaphor used in both kinds of theology because such a disjunction is foreign to the biblical accounts and to Pentecostal preaching. Macchia argues that:

> Spirit baptism implies a 'baptism' in or with the very breath or Spirit of God, indicating a participatory metaphor of our relationship with God that is to have a significant experiential effect. This experiential dimension of Spirit baptism tends to be lacking in the formal definitions of the metaphor among other Christian families in the world. Furthermore, the Pentecostal connection of Spirit baptism with charismatic experience says something profound about the diverse and polyphonic way the Spirit makes Christ present in and through the church. (Macchia, 2006: 32)

He constructs a Pentecostal theology around this central metaphor by expanding its boundaries: he places it within an eschatological framework and a trinitarian perspective before applying it to ecclesiology and Christian vocation in the world. Engaging with the seminal work of James D.G. Dunn (1970, 1975), he agrees that Spirit baptism is a decisive event that establishes Christian identity. The gift of the Holy Spirit is 'dramatically experiential' in the New Testament (Macchia, 2006: 67). But for Macchia, Spirit baptism is not just received as part of general conversion-initiation (as for Dunn); rather, given Luke's distinctive witness, it signifies a 'prophetic calling and empowerment for service' (68). It has an important vocational element to it. Increasingly the reception of the Spirit in conversion-initiation (including baptism) is understood by Pentecostals as further 'released' in subsequent Spirit baptism for empowerment for witness (77). But it would be quite wrong to construe Macchia as simply reiterating classical Pentecostal doctrine at this point. Rather, he contends that an empowerment for witness is Luke's umbrella concept, under which other features are contained.

> The powerful presence of the Spirit in Spirit baptism was not only felt in
> proclamation and spiritual gifts. In Acts, powerful moments in the Spirit enriched
> praise and *koinōnia*, created devotion to the teaching of the apostles, inspired the
> common meal, and broke down barriers between estranged people (cf. 2.42).
> (Macchia, 2006: 79)

Thus, the conception represents the fairly broad contours of Luke's theology.
Indeed this expansion of the metaphor allows Macchia to relocate Spirit baptism
primarily in relation to the kingdom of God, and only subsequently in relation to
the church (Mt 3.1–2; Acts 1.3). By locating Spirit baptism within the kingdom of
God, one essentially frames it by means of inaugurated eschatology. This means
that Spirit baptism in the here and now (with faith, hope and love) is an anticipation
of the Spirit baptism that is yet to come (Macchia, 2006: 87). It is always a now
and not yet, present and yet coming, experience. It is both a divine action and a
human experience that produces a variety of gifts and abilities. It 'constitutes' the
church and empowers it to witness to the world, but it also transcends the church:
it cannot be contained or constrained by the church because it inaugurates the
kingdom of God (106).

There is also a trinitarian structure to Spirit baptism that means there is both a
movement from the Father through the Son in the Spirit and from the Spirit through
the Son to the Father. '[T]he triune life of God is not closed but involved in the
openness of self-giving love. Spirit baptism thus corresponds to the metaphor of
outpouring (Acts 2.33; Rom 5.5)' (116). This means that the trinitarian *koinōnia*
is expanded to include the whole of creation. All three persons of the Godhead
are involved in the experience as the God of Spirit baptism fills and surrounds
Pentecostals (117). The eschatological goal is that Christ will fill all things (Eph
4.10), anticipated in the metaphor of baptism as deluge and the *telos* that 'creation
becomes the temple of God's presence' (Macchia, 2006: 117). It is Christ who is
the Spirit baptiser, as he pours out the Spirit from the Father in order to inaugurate,
and then to fulfil, the kingdom of God (118–119). Pentecostal Spirit baptism is
distinct from Christian initiation, although intimately connected to it and follows
on from it; and it involves 'a release of the Spirit in life for power in witness'
(153).

Macchia argues that Spirit baptism is '*the very substance of the church's life in
the Spirit, including its charismatic life and mission*' (155, italics in original). His
central ideas are captured in the following statement:

> The Spirit is the Spirit of communion. Spirit baptism implies communion.
> This is why it leads to a shared love, a shared meal, a shared mission, and the
> proliferation/enhancement of an interactive charismatic life. Spirit baptism
> thus implies a relationship of unity between the Lord and the church that is
> not fundamentally one of identity but rather communion. Solidarity between
> Jesus or the Spirit and the church is then a quality of communion. This insight
> prevents the church from an overly realized eschatology that simply identifies

the kingdom with the church or its hierarchy without an appropriate dialectic
or eschatological reservation ... Communion implies participation by faith in
God's love in the midst of weakness. The unity it offers is a gift but also a life
and a mission to be pursued ... (John 17.21). (Macchia, 2006: 156–157)

The bestowal of the Spirit by Christ the baptiser means that the *communio* of the
divine life is given as well (159). The perichoretic nature of the Trinity offers a
relational context in which self-giving love is both received and offered back in
doxology. Thus, the church's *koinōnia* is rooted in pneumatology as the *communion*
of the Trinity mediated by the Spirit and forms the basis of the *koinōnia* of the
church. For Macchia, '... the love and *koinōnia* at the heart of the kingdom both
constitute the church and are embodied and proclaimed through the church to the
world by the baptism in the Spirit' (161).

Finally, in the context of the Christian life, Macchia suggests that baptism in
the Spirit is love's 'second conversion' (280–282). Experience of the 'ecstasy'
of love can function to enable Pentecostals to transcend themselves and give of
themselves to God and to others. Spirit baptism can so fill Pentecostals with the
love of God that they transcend their own boundaries and limitations. In so doing,
there is fulfilment as personalities are Spirit baptised and the divine life flows
through them (Jn 7.38). Speaking in tongues was a sign in Acts (2.4) that the early
Christians had becomes bridges of 'empowered ministry' to those from different
languages and cultures (Macchia, 2006: 281). Glossolalia is as much a sign of
weakness as it is a sign of power; it is 'a broken speech for the broken body of
Christ till perfection comes' (Spittler, 2002: 675; Macchia, 2006: 281). But it is not
the only sign and other symbols can include addressing one another with psalms,
hymns and spiritual songs (Eph 5.18–19) or speaking the truth in love (Eph 4.15).
Self-transcendence begins when we are members of the community of the church
(1 Cor 12.13). Macchia contends that:

> The experience of the baptism in the Holy Spirit can be a renewal of faith, hope,
> and love as well as an enhancement of power for mission. It is an enhancement
> of our conversion to Christ but also a 'second conversion' that turns us in Christ's
> love toward the world in prayer for its renewal and in our participation in God's
> mission. We groan in the Spirit with sighs too deep for words (glossolalic
> utterances) for the liberty of the Spirit to come, and we rejoice in signs of
> the new creation already among us through acts of love and signs of healing.
> (Macchia, 2006: 282)

It is interesting to consider the testimony material in the light of Macchia's
contribution. There are several themes that can be identified from his discussion:
eschatology (the now and not yet of present experience), the Trinity as a way of
framing the divine-human encounter, the experience being linked but subsequent
to conversion, bringing communion with God and others, which is exhibited in

love that transcends boundaries as well as signs and symbols such as glossolalia or healing.

Rescripting Ordinary Theology

It is clear that while participants did experience something of the forthcoming kingdom, it was noted in a number of cases that the experience was not straightforward. Julie and Harry stated that the reception of the experience was not according to Pentecostal expectation and both of them initially felt that they had missed out because they had not received it in the context of worship. This suggests that something of the eschatological tension is also demonstrated in the reception of the Spirit. The Holy Spirit is sovereign and cannot be manipulated by human desires. The accounts offered by Valerie, Joseph, Alice and Glenda, however, suggest that when the presence of the Holy Spirit comes then the person experiences the power of the age to come in transformative ways. These accounts suggest that the very experience of Spirit baptism is marked by the 'now and not yet' of the eschatological age and cannot be neatly packaged for religious consumption.

Macchia argues that the experience should be a divine-human encounter that is framed in a trinitarian manner. The language of the participants suggests that they lacked an explicit trinitarian grammar to do this. They talked of the Holy Spirit coming upon them and a relationship with God (Valerie, Julie and Glenda), the Lord (Harry), Christ (Joseph) or Jesus (Alice). Again, this suggests that the overall sense of theism with a focus on Christology dominates (Warrington, 2008: 34). There is not a natural trinitarian way in which experience is framed by the participants and this suggests that perhaps the very experience as trinitarian event needs further attention. The focus group was asked about the doctrine of the Trinity and the following interview excerpt throws an interesting beam of light on this discussion.

> *Mark*: When you think of the Holy Spirit, how do you think of the Spirit in relation to the Father and the Son?

> *Joseph*: Three persons in one. The three persons are different. All of them work in unison together. The Trinity is the powerhouse, for God so loved the world. When Jesus come in the flesh and he was both man and God. Angel speak to Mary and said Jesus would come. When Jesus was going around, they invited him to stay. Jesus said he had to go and 'When I go I pray the Father to send the Holy Spirit'. So Jesus was talking about the Father at the same time and he was talking about the Holy Spirit at the same. Jesus confirmed that he had a Father and he had the Holy Spirit. Approach the throne in the Spirit, the Father is in the middle, the Spirit on the left hand and the Son on the right. And then you have the fountain before the throne of God and the fountain has the word...

Harry: I've found that with the experiences I've had primarily I've associated that with the Holy Spirit but when I do pray I always acknowledge the Father and I always pray in the name of Jesus [agreement]. I do view them as distinct, one God in three persons. But I do view them as having distinct offices or operations in the way that they interact with people I do find them distinct [...]. In the day to day things when I feel the presence of the Holy Spirit.

Mark: Do you ever pray to the Holy Spirit ...?

Glenda: I never thought of it in that way, to tell you the truth. I've always felt that I have a relationship with God and God has given me the Holy Spirit. I don't always think of him as a person, it's more an emotional feeling, empowerment, comforting side. It's not, I don't think of him as a person. I don't accept the Holy Spirit in the way that I feel that I have accepted Jesus or God into my life. I don't know if that's right or wrong but [laughs]. I also felt that the Holy Spirit was always something that comes after that, like a precious thing that comes upon me and so I've never really thought of it as a person that you could pray to ...

Julie: I pray to the Holy Spirit in times of prayer to strengthen us. In Romans 8.26 it says that we don't know how to pray but the Holy Spirit helps us. So we invite him as our strength to help us to pray effectively.

Mark: So would you pray the words, 'Come, Holy Spirit'?

Julie: Yea, when you are beginning to pray ... We invite the Holy Spirit, but we pray through Jesus' name [agreement] ...

Helen: I pray to God the Father ...

Alice: I was looking at the Word this afternoon and about half way through I started to speaking in tongues and I couldn't stop for about 10 to 15 minutes and started weeping for 10 to 15 minutes.

Mark: So who were you praying to?

Alice: To the Holy Spirit ...

Helen: I pray to the Father. I invite the Holy Spirit but I pray to the Father.

Mark: Do you ever pray to Jesus as well?

Helen: Yes to Jesus, but the Bible says, our Father ...

Glenda: I think sometimes it depends on what you are praying about. In some circumstances you know Jesus went through, then I think sometimes you say, Jesus, this happened to you. Do you see what I mean, I could pray to God but because Jesus was on the earth and he was human and he experienced everything that we go through but now I think it's more of a personal relationship in that way.

Harry: I mean in warfare when I'm praying and sometimes when I'm praying and I want to see something broken in the work place or at home and I will say, Lord, I just pray by the power of your Holy Spirit let you make this or that or stop this or whatever or give me wisdom. And I do most definitely associate the Holy Spirit as a person and that goes back to once again experiences that I've had where I've felt embraced and it's physical and I've associated that experience with the Holy Spirit but I still thank the Lord, I thank Jesus and I thank the Holy Spirit.

Valerie: I was going to say that I tend to just think of God mostly. I think that when I begin to pray I often do relate to the Father because I think that you should pray to the Father. I do on occasion speak to the Holy Spirit or I speak to Jesus. But generally speaking I feel that I'm relating to God and to the Father. But when I sense an experience and if I were to examine it intellectually I would ascribe it to the Holy Spirit because I believe it's the Holy Spirit, 'cos I believe that it's the Holy Spirit who [is] present with me now. I still just think of him as God, generally and that's what I'm thinking of ...

Joseph: ... When I pray I pray to the Father. I always start my prayer time with 'Jesus, instruct us when we pray, "Our Father who art in heaven"' [agreement]. And I always find myself praying to the Father. When I look in my spirit I go before the Father and I know that the Son is there and the Holy Spirit is there, when I pray to the Father. And when I finish my prayer I say in Jesus' name. And I feel justified that I pray then because I need all three.

Harry: Thank you for the question about praying because sometimes I just talk to the Lord and to me that [is] still praying. Sometimes, it's Father, and sometimes it's Jesus and whatever mood I'm in I'll say that. I'll always acknowledge Jesus, in the name of Jesus, it just depends on the prayer [...]. There are times when I'm praying in my mind because it's not appropriate [...] so praying in my mind and I will acknowledge it as well because I feel the presence of the Holy Spirit but I'm praying in my mind [agreement].

This exchange suggests that there is definitely a trinitarian grammar in place but that it does not necessarily inform every aspect of the ordinary theology. One area where it does not frame experience is baptism in the Spirit.

It is clear from the narratives that baptism in the Spirit is a subsequent experience to conversion (Valerie, Julie, Harry, Joseph and Alice). However, the link that Macchia suggests as part of the theology of baptism in the Spirit appears to be lacking in these narratives. In many cases there is *both* a chronological *and* a theological disjunction. It is regarded as theologically distinct, not just chronologically distinct. But if Spirit baptism is a manifestation of the kingdom of God, not just the practices of the church, one would expect it to be integral to the whole of the Christian life. As such it is rooted in the proclamation and reception of the gospel of Jesus Christ. Given the close connection with the sequences displayed in the conversion narratives, it would be worth giving emphasis to the nature of Spirit baptism as not just distinct but also as a release of that which was given in regeneration.

It is certainly the case that the experience of baptism in the Spirit immerses the person into a communion with God. This is indicated by descriptors such as: praying for a very long time (Julie), crying out (Harry), experiencing power and liberty (Joseph), power flooding over her head (Alice) and a general feeling of power and joy (Glenda). Such experiences of communion with God flow out into relationships with others in the community of the church. Thus, there is a real sense in which individual experiences with God are situated within a context that both informs and is informed by a communion with God and with others. Therefore, a theology of baptism in the Spirit could be understood as primarily corporate communion rather than inherently individualistic piety. Just as the sacrament of baptism symbolises the union with Christ and his church, so baptism in the Spirit is also symbolic of that same union. Both are prior to an individual's personal faith and can nurture them in their journey of faith.

There are clearly theological symbols associated with this experience, most notably speaking in tongues (Valerie, Julie, Joseph, Alice and Glenda), but it is also noticeable that other symbols are in evidence. Valerie had an experience of profound love: 'I felt like I loved God and I'd kind of been waiting for that': what Macchia might call love's second conversion (cf. Poloma and Hood, 2008). Others experience personal transformation – for example, Joseph: 'I was a changed person. I know that something had happened.' Harry felt that he had experienced the Spirit so profoundly that the words of John 7.37 were being fulfilled in him: 'streams of living water' were flowing through him to others. This suggests that there is a tension between official denominational theology and the experiences of church members. Therefore, the script of baptism in the Spirit should allow for a certain degree of diversity of experience, which reflects personal differences and different workings of the Spirit.

Summary

The doctrine of baptism in the Spirit is probably the most distinctive Pentecostal experience and practice, especially when allied to the sign of glossolalia. Other Charismatic churches would advocate dramatic experiences of the Spirit and the use of glossolalia, but would not necessarily place them together as an empowering post-conversion experience available to all believers. Most of the participants experienced baptism in the Spirit in an Assemblies of God context in corporate worship, although some did not and there was some variation in experience and consequently a degree of dissension from the denominational orthodoxy. This was especially the case with regard to glossolalia as a sign of having been baptised in the Spirit, with the other gifts of the Spirit seen as possible signs as well. Not everyone in the group spoke in tongues. The experiences of the members were certainly 'interpreted experiences' in the sense of being aligned to an existing framework of understanding, despite the variation. They were 'quasi-sensory' and 'regenerative' events for most people, leading to experiences of love, power, liberty, joy and transformation. It could be said that they enabled participants to apprehend ultimate reality and could therefore be described as 'mystical' experiences. Following Poloma's (2003) adaptation of Turner's notion of ritual liminality, baptism in the Spirit can certainly be understood as a threshold experience that allows the member to move closer to the centre of the community. Pentecostal theology stresses the experience as an empowerment for service, but, following Macchia, it can be seen that this experience has consequences for worship, fellowship and hospitality. It is an eschatological experience of the future that constitutes the church, also having a trinitarian structure to it. This experience of trinitarian communion leads the members of the church to love both one another and those outside the boundaries of the church for the sake of the kingdom of God. Yet the experience of the members suggests that not all experience the coming of the kingdom in the same way: there is also some disappointment and frustration. Participants demonstrated a limited trinitarian grammar, but it did not inform their experience of baptism in the Spirit. Nevertheless, the experience did bring a sense of communion with God and others in the congregation and did appear to empower their witness in the world.

Chapter 6

Healing

Healing is a central aspect to Pentecostal and Charismatic Christianity. It is a feature that receives a lot of attention and it is also one that causes a certain amount of controversy. This is because claims to healing inevitably attract media attention as 'sensational' and newsworthy. In some cases it is because healing evangelists are considered to have used dubious 'techniques'. It is also unclear in the minds of many people as to whether any real healing has actually occured or is just being claimed. The issue of those who are unhealed remains an important theological and pastoral consideration. Indeed, how ordinary Pentecostal theology deals with the kind of dissonance that the lack of healing brings in a specific community is also significant. In order to explore these kinds of issues, this chapter considers a number of testimonies of healing and describes the theology that undergirds them. It attempts not only to connect the ordinary theology to the official statements but also to engage with the debates that exist in the Pentecostal world. In so doing, it allows the scholarly debates to inform the ordinary theology and the ordinary theology to illustrate the main concepts in use. Social science discourse on charismatic and religious healing is used to interpret the narratives before being developed in turn by theology, allowing theology once again to rescript the narratives, expanded by insights from the social sciences.

Testimonies

The Focus Group

The focus group contained four men and six women. The men originated from Nigeria (Martin), Uganda (Tom) and the UK (Benjamin and Charlie). Two were relatively young men (Charlie and Tom), while the other two were middle-aged (Benjamin and Martin). Their occupations were domestic cleaner (Charlie), cleaner (Benjamin), administrator (Tom) and business adviser (Martin). The women originated from Barbados (Alisa), Jamaica (Isabel and Eileen), Ghana (Gemma), Nigeria (Sarah) and the UK (Beverley). They were mostly middle-aged (Sarah, Beverley, Isabel, Gemma and Eileen) and one was elderly (Alisa). Their occupations included nursing (Sarah), administrative executive (Beverley), home care assistant (Isabel), secretary (Gemma), cleaner (Eileen) and retired (Alisa).

Pentecostals believe not only that God is able to heal but that he does actually heal today. They believe that Jesus is the great healer and the signs and wonders that he accomplished during his earthly ministry, and which were performed by the apostles in the book of the Acts, continue today. Therefore, it is very easy to get Pentecostals to talk about their healing experiences because it supports their worldview that God is active in their world today. Their very own experiences testify to the fact of God's presence and power in their lives. I have selected four testimonies in order to illustrate the kinds of healing that are recalled.

> *Beverley*: Well, some years ago I was diagnosed with the very early stages of cancer and, to make this short, we went to [the] Minehead conference and there was an altar appeal and I went forward but it wasn't full healing as such. It was a different altar appeal for service, but I went forward and there were many pastors praying over a huge number of people. And my husband and I, we got prayed for and then this pastor walked away but he came back; and he prayed over me again. Now because there was such a noise around, I couldn't hear a single word of what he prayed. And then we went home and I'd had two tests about cancer and they said you're going to go for a third one and then if this proves positive I've got to go in for the operation. Anyway I phone up the doctors and my husband was standing at the side of me and he was praying over me and they said Mrs Jones we've wonderful news for you. You're clear, it's all gone ['Praise God', affirmation by the group]. And they sent me the documentation and I've still got that documentation to state that I am clear … That's two years ago and nothing's ever come back.

> *Isabel*: I've got [an] experience, it's been some years ago now. I was suffering from very severe sciatica in the lower back and I'd [been] prayed over a period of time and nothing happened. And we had a prayer session and that's where I received my healing. The power of God came down on me and the word of God came forth and the Lord said: 'As I went on he would just heal me gradually', and that's how I received my healing.

> *Sarah*: Well, quickly, I can give a testimony about two years ago or even three. All of a sudden I had this skin disease, disorder and I started to bleed all over. It was like a baby's skin and it was dreadful. I don't go to doctors, to be honest, but I went to four doctors and they couldn't put a finger [on it]. Everybody kept diagnosing this and that. They did tests for all sorts of things and I just [kept going] to the hospital, to the skin hospital and I didn't know what it was. All over my skin [it] was and because of close covering you wouldn't see it. And I started to say to the Lord, 'What's happening?' Suddenly I woke up and said: 'Lord, you [have] got to heal me'. I had to believe God. All of a sudden it just went. Look, I've got scars of this thing that came suddenly but I knew the doctors didn't know what it was but God did heal me. It was a miraculous thing because it was awful, dreadful, it just came suddenly all over. I just felt as I was praying, you know, a lot of people went in the night, in the middle of the night. I always wake up between twelve and three to pray. Then the Lord

said: 'If you believe me, I can heal you'. And it just went, miraculous, four doctors couldn't know what it was but God did.

Tom: Well, I can say two weeks ago I was having a pain in my back, one side, I don't know if the back or ... I couldn't bend properly and I was like 'What's happening?' I took paracetamol. I was not feeling well but said, 'I will be healed in the name of Jesus' and we had, that week, we had the ... [African choir visit] ... and ... before the choir [sang] Angela, she gave a testimony about her leg and then when she said she decided to forget about it, just saying the pain is not there. And that's what I also said, 'Let me forget about it, leave me up to now', and I'm not feeling any pain. Any[way], even this morning I can't, but I'm feeling good. I can bend and I was, even I woke up in the morning like this [does some movements]. I'm like this, 'Let me feel, maybe the pain is still somewhere else' [laughter]. I really enjoyed [it] after I prayed I said, 'God is good, is great and is really ...'

Mark: Did you pray in a service or just by yourself?

Tom: Yea, I prayed in the service, I prayed at home and I was praying, I was thinking of what Pastor Angela said, the same thing. I decided to forget about it and do my things the normal way. I should not keep my mind on the pain, and that's how the pain went.

Summary of the Testimonies

These testimonies illustrate a number of important attitudes towards health and healing. First, the health of these Christians is regarded as important to God. All of them prayed about their health and their need. Second, faith in God and believing not only that God could heal, but that he would heal them in particular, is an important aspect. In some cases healing is supported by experiences of power from God and words of prophecy attributed to God about the nature of the healing. Third, healing can be instantaneous or gradual and both are attributed to God. Fourth, prayer for healing is not a private matter but part of the corporate ethos of the church and the Assemblies of God denomination. Prayer for healing occurs in a variety of settings. Fifth, God is the healer but prayer is offered 'in the name of Jesus', thereby illustrating a general theism and Christological focus associated with Pentecostalism. Sixth, medicine is not totally rejected but it appears to have a secondary role in relation to religious practices. Seventh, there is a pragmatism at work as well, illustrated by the testimony of ignoring the pain in the belief that it will go away.

Further Analysis

Participants identified specific key biblical texts as helpful in their understanding
of healing in general. The healing of the lame man at the Beautiful Gate and the
woman with the issue of blood were mentioned (Acts 3.1–10; Lk 8.43–48). Sarah
said that she always thought about Isaiah 53.4–6, the passage on which the 1 Peter
text (2.24) is based, as well as Matthew 8.17 (see chapter 2). She explained the
meaning of these texts for her, and a dialogue developed with others contributing
to the discussion.

> *Sarah*: To me it's like Christ has taken on board, you know, carried my illnesses, my
> sicknesses [agreement] so I don't have to carry it because he [has] taken over my
> illnesses and infirmities in his own body on the cross ... and he suffered for me and
> he's taking it all away, so I claimed to say, by his stripes, you know, I am healed.

> *Mark*: So you claim it, it's almost like, you ask him or claim it, how does that
> [work]?

> *Sarah*: I claim it because it's in the Bible. The word of God is truth. It says he took my
> infirmities, my sicknesses on his body. It's been done in the past tense. Two thousand
> years ago Christ went on that cross of Calvary, took all my illnesses and diseases on
> his own body. I don't have to bear it any longer because it's been taken ..., all my
> illness ...

> *Isabel*: And by the stripes ['I am healed': Sarah] that he received, by the stripes that
> Christ received, we can claim healing because it's there in the atonement.

> *Mark*: Okay. Does this mean that every single person? What? Can be healed or should
> be healed? How would you phrase that?

> *Isabel*: Can be healed ... because it takes belief ..., belief in what Christ has done.

> *Mark*: So is it a matter of faith?

> *Isabel*: Yes [agreement].

> *Mark*: So, the person who has no faith can't receive?

> *Isabel*: No, you can't.

> *Mark*: What happens if you have no faith? You, people might, because there's levels
> of faith, aren't there?

> *All*: Yes.

Mark: Some have strong faith and [others have] weak faith. So, if you've got strong faith you can receive [agreement] and if your faith is weak you don't. How does that work?

Isabel: It works this way, how you communicate to God ... That's why, my faith, I may be not good in reading the Bible but I can be good in praying ... and I can be healed if I put my faith in God. It's all about putting your faith and believing that God can heal you because he sent his only son, Jesus Christ, to die for my sins, so I don't need to carry my sins any more. I just, God listens, I have a pain in the head and if you pray with faith ...

Mark: Okay. So would you say people who are not healed just don't have the faith?

All: [Noise (too many people spoke at the same time)]

Alisa: He said he will have mercy on whom he will have [mercy] [agreement] ... and it isn't everyone who prays for healing that will get healing at the same time. Because if you remember that when he said to Peter, I think it was, no Paul, Paul had an affliction and he called out to God and he said my faith is sufficient for you [agreement]. So it is said that he carried his affliction right through his lifetime. So it doesn't mean that everyone will get healed at the request of healing but God will carry you through because he says, I will be with you ... and you'll go through the waters and it will not overpower you. You'll go through the fire and it won't burn you. So you may not get healed but have faith and confidence in him day by day, he will carry you through the difficulty.

This sense of God being with them and giving them security while also allowing certain difficulties and challenges to remain was also expressed by one person citing Psalm 91.1–2:

He who dwells in the shelter of the Most High will rest in the shadow of the Almighty. I will say of the LORD, 'He is my refuge and my fortress, my God, in whom I trust. (NIV)

Martin expressed this view and suggested that sickness and illness might also be ways of the Lord preparing the person for something else. Beverley suggested that there have been people of great faith who have not been healed, for example one of the founders of the church, Miss Fisher, who died because of cancer and despite much prayer. Alisa commented that it is not up to us to tell God what to do, but that we should live day by day 'believing and trusting in him'. Sarah said that she knew a pastor in Nigeria who was blind and through whom God heals thousands of people, but he has never been healed. She agreed that this might be for some hidden purpose, although she reiterated her concern about the role of faith for healing based on the letter to the Hebrews and the statement that without faith it is impossible to please God (Heb 11.6). Isabel reminded Sarah that Paul had a thorn in the flesh and that God told him to wait on him (2 Cor 12.7). Sarah reiterated her belief that if a person believes and lays hands on another who is sick and prays then they can be healed, even if they are not a Christian but from another religious faith, such as Islam, provided that the person praying has faith.

The church also practises the anointing with olive oil upon the sick to symbolise the Holy Spirit's anointing with prayer. Hands are laid on individuals, which is also regarded as symbolic of anointing. Just as Christ laid his hands on the sick for their healing, symbolising his anointing touch, so members today lay hands on others in prayer. It is regarded as being similar to the apostles' use of hankerchiefs to convey their anointing. Today, members can lay hands on others and pray because of the anointing of the Holy Spirit on all, which gives them authority to pray for the sick. The church has also set up a prayer chain so that needs can be prayed for over the telephone, or indeed via email. Prayer for the sick is also offered by the pastors when they visit people at home or in hospital. Sarah remembered that the pastors of her former Nigerian church, the Christ Apostolic Church, would bring water to the sick, which they would prayer over and invite the sick person to drink (Olubunmi, 1981: 390–391). She found it to have healing power if drunk in faith. Sarah continues to believe in this practice and uses such blessed water personally, but acknowledges that this is not a normal HPC practice. The place where healing is shared with other members of the church is through testimonies in the worship services. It is here that the symbols associated with healing are regarded as similar to the rite of Holy Communion, as Beverley comments:

> It always reminds me of Christ's suffering but also my salvation and my healing ... Because, as we say, by his stripes we are healed and it's the shedding of his blood [That's true]. So when we take the communion, when we come to that table, we know that everything we need is provided there and especially the blood [agreement]. And if we apply the blood to our lives we can accept the healing.

Healing in British Pentecostalism

The Assemblies of God denomination stands in the earliest tradition of British Pentecostalism that expects healing to be part of the 'full' gospel offered to humankind (Cartledge, 2008a). Alexander Boddy focused on the use of the practice described in James 5.13–16, where the elders are called by the sick person, who is then anointed with oil in the name of the Lord and prayer offered in faith is expected to make the sick person well (*Confidence*, 1914). In another article Boddy argues that salvation should be understood in the sense of being made whole. In Christ, our representative human life, we can experience wholeness that includes health and healing. He is the one who has overcome the power of sin, disease and death and undoes the power of the Fall through the cross (Isa

53.4–5). Through our identification with Christ in his death and resurrection we can have faith to overcome the power of Satan. In Christ there is no disease, so if our lives are hidden in him we can experience his health and his healing, since all sickness comes from Satan whom he has defeated on the cross (Boddy, 1910a). The use of these biblical texts continued to be important, as can be seen in the 1924 statement of faith; and this statement, as noted earlier, has not changed since the denomination's inception, despite pressure from contemporary leaders. The current Assemblies of God *Statement of Faith* article on healing reads as follows:

> 10. We believe that deliverance from sickness, by Divine Healing is provided for in the Atonement (Isa. 53:4–5, Matt. 8:16–17, James 5:13–16).

This suggests that healing is in the same category as the forgiveness of sins. Pentecostal understanding has often tended to talk about 'healing in the atonement', meaning that not only are our sins borne by Christ but also our sickness (McAlister, 1937; Sherlock, 1937b; Comstock, 1938; Warrington, 1998: 169; Theron, 1999: 50–51). This has been an issue of debate in recent times, with an amendment to this statement suggested by a sub-committee chaired by David Petts (2001). The sub-committee proposed to the Executive Council of the Assemblies of God that an alternative article of faith be adopted, namely:

> We believe in the healing power of Christ bringing deliverance from sickness by the means of prayer, laying on of hands, the anointing of oil and the gifts of the Holy Spirit (Mk 16.17–18; Jam 5.13–16; 1 Cor 12.9–10). (Petts, 2001)

This was placed on the Provisional Agenda for the General Conference in 2001 but withdrawn from the Final Agenda because the Executive Council subsequently decided that the issue was too divisive to bring before the Fellowship at that time. A recommendation that the 2002 Agenda include a debate in which all sides would be represented and that any constitutional change be brought to the General Conference in 2003 was also withdrawn.[1] The older version was simply retained in 2004 when the revised *Statement of Faith* was endorsed by the General Conference.

Nevertheless, the question as to how healing is 'in' the atonement remains; and it goes to the heart of the matter for Pentecostals. As William Kay observes:

> Where all Pentecostals might agree that healing is a possibility dependent upon the grace that flows from Christ's atonement, the consolidation of this possibility into an appropriable right puts the entire matter on a completely different basis. If physical healing follows faith in the merits of Christ's death, then any disease, like any sin, can at any time be removed by proper belief. Thus the onus for

---

[1] This factual detail was provided by David Petts, who chaired the Executive Council during this period (personal email dated 10 November 2009).

> healing, like the Arminian onus for salvation, falls firmly on the supplicant and
> God may be depersonalised and transformed into a mechanism by which human
> needs are met. (Kay, 2000a: 88)

Kay notes how there are two poles in Pentecostal belief: a covenant right in the face of the devil's lies, on the one hand, and the gracious divine provision, on the other; both have been alternatives espoused by dominant personalities in Pentecostalism. Knight's typology (1993) addresses this polarity and maps out alternatives between the pole of God's faithfulness to his promises (Copeland, Price and Hagin) and his freedom to act mysteriously (Kuhlman and Farah), showing that there are positions in between (MacNutt, Wimber and Blue).

David Petts (1993) has argued against the popular understanding on the basis of his exegesis of key texts (Mt 8.17; 1 Pet 2.24). For Petts, '[i]t was because of man's (sic) sin that atonement … was necessary. No atonement was needed for sickness. Sickness is not a misdemeanour which attracts a penalty' (282). However, given (1) the inclusion of sickness within Paul's thinking regarding suffering (*pathēmata*) in Romans 8.18, (2) the transformed nature of resurrection bodies, incorruptible and therefore sickness-free, (1 Cor 15.35–57) and (3) the gift of the eschatological Spirit (Rom 8.22–23), he proposes that healing may be understood to be 'in the atonement' in two senses. First, it can be understood in an ultimate sense: the ultimate victory over sin and death is the result of Christ's work on the cross. Second, it can be understood in an indirect sense because the gift of the Spirit is a result of the atonement and healing today (1 Cor 12.9): it is an eschatological blessing (Petts, 1993: 332–355).

Keith Warrington follows a similar line and argues against 'a doctrine of unconditional healing in the atonement' on the basis of 2 Corinthians 12.7, Galatians 4.13, Philippians 2.17, 1 Timothy 5.23 and 2 Timothy 4.20 (Warrington, 1998: 169–170; 2003: 79–84). He suggests that for most Pentecostals healing is understood as an indirect result of the atonement which is 'not necessarily realised in this life' (Warrington, 1998: 170). However, the popular Assemblies of God understanding has been given recent scholarly support by a number of American scholars. Robert Menzies argues that a narrow understanding of atonement simply in terms of sin misses the broader semantic range of meaning (Menzies and Menzies, 2000: 160). He suggests that the forensic metaphor needs to be supplemented by the classic view of *Christus Victor*, which understands that through the cross the powers (devil, death and sin) are defeated, thus offering liberation (161). Christopher Thomas (2005) supports the position of Menzies from his study of John's Gospel (focusing on Jn 3.14–15) that 'physical healing is grounded in the atoning life of Jesus' (Thomas, 2005: 38). This is given further support by Kimberly Alexander (2006) in her analysis of early Pentecostal periodical literature across the Pentecostal spectrum. She summarises her findings when she states: '… the doctrine of Divine Healing in the Atonement was understood as part and parcel of salvation. As a provision of the Atonement, and as part of Christ's "two-fold" ministry, healing is a necessary ingredient of what it means to be holy and whole' (53.). Nevertheless,

British charismatic theologian Max Turner contends that although all the benefits of salvation in Christ are rooted in the atonement this does not mean that everyone can merely claim their healing by faith (Turner, 2007: 330). This is because the Christian life is just as much marked by suffering as it is by liberation and thus it mirrors the cross as well as the resurrection (334–335).

It is certainly the case that the language of 'by his stripes we are healed', which is a synonym for 'healing is in the atonement' in Pentecostal discourse, is used much more widely than merely praying for the sick. Indeed, the healing metaphor appears to govern the ordinary soteriology: 'as his [the Suffering Servant] body was wounded so the people were healed' (Marshall, 1991: 95). It becomes the dominant metaphor and other soteriological metaphors (e.g. ransom, satisfaction, reconciliation and fellowship) appear to be subsumed within it. Therefore, the metaphor both expands and contracts. It expands to include these other features but it also contracts so that it becomes individualistic (my burdens/healing), and church focused ('come to us' mission). This soteriology could easily become therapeutically driven: Christ solves my problems each week associated with burdens or health issues. But the question of how this healing is appropriated 'by faith' continues to be a problem.

Warrington (1999) also addresses the question of faith and healing. Faith is regarded as crucial for healing, but the question is whose faith? The person being prayed for, the pray-er and/or others witnessing the prayer have all been suggested. In many Pentecostal writings it is simply unclear whose faith is in view. Warrington suggests that when Jesus mentions faith in relation to healing he was referring to his own faith (34). Jesus neither used techniques to increase faith, nor did he encourage people to increase their faith, nor condemn them for their lack of faith. Warrington states:

> For many Pentecostals, faith is equated with belief in a promise; a promise that healing is the guaranteed right of the believer, proven by Jesus' ministry of healing. Thus, they assume that before God will heal them, they have to believe that he is going to do so. Anything less than this is deemed to result in rejection by God as far as receiving healing is concerned. It is, in effect, an anthropocentrically-initiated faith. (Warrington, 1999: 35)

Therefore, some have ignored the symptoms of sickness and thanked God for their healing even though it is not apparent. Warrington argues that such a praxis is very far removed from the ministry model of Christ. The question as to how widely this position is held by Pentecostals has been researched in the UK, and similar questions have been researched in the USA.

Gillian Allen and Roy Wallis, in a project conducted in the 1970s, researched a small Assemblies of God church located in a Scottish city (1976). They discovered that medicine and prayer for healing were understood as complementary – that is, medical diagnoses and cures were accepted and used in conjunction with expectations of divine healing through 'gifts of healing' within the congregational members. The basis of this view was the Assemblies of God doctrine that divine healing was provided for in the atonement of Christ and that it 'can, in theory, be obtained by anyone in the same way as salvation from sin, by faith in Christ' (119). This, as noted above, is based on James 5.14–16 and the statement that the 'prayer of faith' can save the sick. Failure to heal was explained by means of 'lack of faith' or God's will for some higher purpose (127).

Empirical research by Kay showed that Pentecostal ministers (N = 930) in the main British denominations (Apostolic Church [AC] 87.5%, Assemblies of God [AoG] 88.9%, Elim 80.9%, and the New Testament Church of God [NTCG] 98%) agreed with the proposition that 'physical healing is provided by Christ's atonement'. Kay deliberately attempted to test a different expression by using 'provided by' rather than 'in' the atonement, but it must be doubted whether the subtlety of this linguistic move was noticed by the respondents. There was a more mixed picture emerging when they were asked if they agreed with the statement: 'divine healing will always occur if a person's faith is great enough'. It is noticeable that 55.1% of AC pastors and 60.8% of NTCG pastors agreed with this statement, compared to only 13.5% of Elim pastors and 19.7% of AoG pastors (Kay, 2000a: 101–102). Furthermore, Kay suggested that a preference to affirm this statement is linked to age, with older ministers more likely to affirm it; and that it is also linked to a lack of formal theological education (102). This hypothesis was tested by me (Cartledge, 2003) in a survey of Pentecostal and Charismatic churches in the UK. I discovered that only 24.6% of congregation members (N = 633) believed that healing would always occur if a person's faith was great enough. Those at the lower end of the socio-economic scale, those with lesser educational qualifications and those youngest in the faith tended to affirm this proposition (Cartledge, 2003: 205–207). Interestingly, Margaret M. Poloma's (1989) research in the USA showed that 61% of her respondents (N = 1,275) in the Assemblies of God believed that they had experienced 'miraculous healing'. Of these, 50% believed that they had received their healing during a worship service. Only a third, however, believed that 'divine healing will always occur if a person's faith is great enough'. This means that '[t]hose who believed strongly in the availability of healing in contemporary times were more likely to experience it than those who doubted (r = .16). The "positive confession" approach ['believe it and receive it'], however, was not significantly related to the experience of healing' (Poloma, 1989: 62). Those recording a greater frequency of prayer and Bible reading were more likely to report an experience of healing (Poloma, 1989: 63).

Theories of the Self and Charismatic Healing

In order to understand this social and contextual theology better, I shall engage with three social scientists who have studied Pentecostal and Charismatic healing rituals within the North American context.

Thomas J. Csordas (1997) offers a cultural phenomenology of charismatic healing as displayed within the Roman Catholic Charismatic Renewal movement. He links the notion of healing within this context to the idea of the sacred self. He defines the self in the following way.

> Self is neither substance nor entity, but an indeterminate capacity to engage or become oriented in the world, characterised by effort and reflexivity. In this sense self occurs as a conjunction of prereflective bodily experience, culturally constituted world or milieu, and situational specificity or habitus. Self processes are orientational processes in which aspects of the world are thematized, with the result that the self is objectified, most often as 'person' with a cultural identity or set of identities. (Csordas, 1997: 5)

Roman Catholic charismatic identity of the self as sacred is derived from 'a unique spiritual experience' (Spirit Baptism) that promises a renewal of the church, based on a 'personal relationship' with Jesus and direct access to divine power and inspiration through the use of 'spiritual gifts'. This relationship with the divine offers a template for orientation to the world and spiritual gifts enable a means of processing self-identity that brings about that orientation (18). Thus, healing experiences are understood as enabling the true self to be known in and through Christ. 'This self is sacred insofar as it is oriented in the world and defines what it means to be human in terms of the wholly "other" than human' (24).

Allied to this notion of the sacred self is an analysis of the cultural context of North America, where the cultural values of spontaneity, control and intimacy are mirrored against the ritual practices themselves. For North Americans positive mental health is often associated with the possibility of acting spontaneously through 'impromptu gatherings' or events. Similarly, positive health is associated with 'being in control' of one's self, one's body, one's mind, when 'life is not out of control'. The theme of intimacy is demonstrated in the romantic love of the Disney variety and close social friendship [e.g. the TV show *Friends*] and family [e.g. the TV show *Diff'rent Strokes*]. Csordas argues that 'health' is an idealization of the self in these terms and healing is a part of the process of growing towards this ideal (19). Therefore, 'the ideal sacred self is inherently healthy' (26). Not only can the wounded or broken be cured but spiritual growth can be advanced so that the sacred self is both whole and holy (26). Thus, the sacred self is constantly involved in a process of transformation.

The different genres of healing are associated with a tripartite anthropology: body, mind and spirit, rather than a dualistic one (mind/body) (39). For Roman Catholic charismatics the spiritual realm is simultaneously ineffable and empirical, such that participants are understood to experience the very presence of the divine or, occasionally, evil spirits. In other words, they are experienced as real in their own domain and associated with the healing ritual (39). Thus, healing corresponds to these three domains: physical healing is bodily, inner healing is emotional and deliverance is spiritual, although sometimes a fourth is added, namely repentance for personal sin (MacNutt, 1974: 163).

Csordas makes two important observations regarding the therapeutic process (Csordas, 1997: 71–72). First, he observes that ritual healing operates on a 'margin of disability' present in many conditions. By this he means the way in which some people with impairment withdraw from certain activity. He illustrates this point by reference to the person who is classified as 'legally blind' but who is nevertheless able to engage in a wide variety of activities, where others with the same impairment retreat into a posture of near incapacity. Similarly, people with chronic pain in a limb may be able to move the limb but refrain from doing so because of insufficient motivation.

> Disability is thus constituted as a habitual mode of engaging the world. The process of healing is an existential process of exploring the margin of disability, motivated by the conviction of divine power and the committed participant's desire to demonstrate it in himself as well as by the support of the assembly and its acclamation for a supplicant's testimony of healing. To be convinced of this interpretation one need only consider the hesitant, faltering steps of the supplicant who at the healer's request rises from her wheelchair and shuffles slowly up and down a church aisle ... (Csordas, 1997: 71)

The ritual of healing therefore challenges 'the sensory commitment to a habitual posture' and removes inhibitions 'toward normal postural tone' (71).

Second, he suggests that ritual healing is best characterised by an 'incremental efficacy'. Occasionally, spontaneous miracles are claimed, but, more commonly, partial and everyday healings are declared. This means that the engagement with the margin of disability is only initiated, but never completed, by the ritual event of healing. Therefore, the degree of experiential engagement with the ritual process is crucial to the incremental efficacy. He concludes that '[b]ecause of the fundamental indeterminacy of the self, there is no guarantee that the creative products of ritual performance will be permanently integrated into a person's life'(72). It is therefore an 'open-ended process' with no guarantees of permanent effects.

One area that was not mentioned by the focus group is inner healing. Debra-L. Sequeira's research on a charismatic Episcopal church in the USA discusses both inner or soul healing as well as physical healing (1994). Inner healing focuses on painful memories that inhibit members from experiencing the love of God. Those engaged in ministry claim that God loves members unconditionally and that he desires that they be 'emotionally free and whole' (Sequeira, 1994: 135). Eight interviewees said that they had been healed from childhood traumas concerning parental abuse, painful relationships or generally negative childhood memories carried into adulthood. This is accomplished through a ritual of visualisation, described by someone called Sheila:

The Scripture indicates that he [Jesus] is there or he was there with us; he is omnipresent. When we picture Jesus with us in a past event, we are not putting him there. The Holy Spirit simply shows us that he was there. In other words, the Spirit assists our faith to see what God's word has already declared. I do not claim the past can be recreated through visualization. I teach that our personal past is recorded in our memories and emotions, and that since Jesus is omnipresent, with his guidance we can recall those memories, and know and experience him there with us. It's our resurrected Lord Jesus's healing presence which brings a healing balm to our souls. Jesus is the Lord of our yesterdays just as surely he is the Lord of our todays. (Sequeira, 1994: 136)

Sequeira observed that inner healing remains controversial in the church because of its 'psychological' nature, not being as obvious as physical healing.

An example of physical healing is also discussed by Sequeira. Michael, a man suffering from arthritis, could not lift his right arm and was experiencing extreme pain. On a particular Sunday the priest asked if there was anyone in the congregation experiencing 'hot hands', referring to the fire of Pentecost for healing, and five people indicated that they had hands for healing and were invited to come to the altar. Then the priest asked if there was anyone present with a healing need and Michael came forward and explained his need. Those nearest to Michael were also invited up to the front to pray for him, and he was encircled by people praying with their eyes closed, praying in English and in tongues. Sequeira was a member of this group and had her eyes open, watching the others pray. After about five minutes she stated that she 'felt a tremendous amount of heat, like an electric current, shoot through my upper body' (137). She described how others in the circle also felt this heat and that Michael exclaimed: 'I feel the heat; it's wonderful!'. After another five minutes of prayer they returned to their seats, feeling shaken and giddy. Michael claimed a miraculous healing of his arthritis and never showed any signs of relapse for the remaining months of Sequeira's research. His testimony of healing became part of the healing ritual of these particular services for a number of weeks following. Thus, it contributed to the performance of the 'renewal' at the church.

Sequeira interprets this healing ritual in the context of other public *charismata*, such as glossolalia, and regards these performances as expressions of greater intimacy with God, articulated Christologically in familiar terms, such as 'my Jesus'. This language reveals their sense of personal knowledge of God, which is strengthened by their engagement in specific healing rituals. For Sequeira it is the sharing of this commitment to renewal through common ritual performance that provides a sense of unity and purpose. '[R]enewal entails intimacy or personal closeness with God and between close friends, and a commitment to community; a commitment based on the performance of charismatic renewal which is essential to members' ethos and worldview' (141). It is through this dual commitment (intimacy with God and a community in renewal) that members are empowered by ritual performance for their lives in the world. Therefore, the self becomes emotionally fulfilled and empowered to engage with the challenges of life.

Meredith B. McGuire (1998) reported that American middle-class Christians considered the ultimate purpose of healing to be the transformation of the self, 'in "proper" (i.e., subordinate) relationship to a transcendent deity' (238). For McGuire, the human self has a 'unitary quality' (McGuire, 1990: 285). She expresses her approach by stating:

> Let us assume that the human body is both a biological and a cultural product, physical and symbolic, always framed in a specific social and environmental context in which the body / mind is both active agent and yet influenced by each social moment and its cultural history ... Let us appreciate that a person's subjective sense of self is intimately linked with body / mind. We experience things done to our bodies as done to ourselves. In continually revised biographical memories, we accomplish narratives which give subjective meaning to our bodily and emotional experiences. Through our body / minds we experience our world – experiences of illness, pain, chronic disabilities and death, experiences of hunger and cold, experiences of childbearing, birth, nursing, experiences of aesthetic pleasures, sexual pleasures, and sensuous pleasures (such as the taste of 'comfort food', the sound of a lullaby, a friend's supportive caress). (McGuire, 1996: 102)

She further defines the body in relation to the whole self and away from Cartesian dualism (mind/body, nature/culture and individual/society); and she identifies three levels of engagement by the human body: lived or experiential, political and social.

First, the lived body is 'our vehicle' for knowing and interpreting our world and any understanding of healing must take account of pain, suffering and illness as experienced, as dis-eased.

> The lived body is not the same as the body-as-object. Thus, the objective character of a body that a doctor labels 'diseased' bears little resemblance to the person's subjective, lived-body experience of being ill. Through the lived body, we know our bodies as subject, as intimately experienced; by contrast, social bodies and political bodies tend to transform bodies into objects – objects of power, objects of scientific analysis, objects of medical intervention, objects of social control, objects of commodification, and so on. (McGuire, 1996: 104)

The second level is the political, 'through which the body is linked to relations of power' (104). The body is both an instrument of power and a site of struggles concerning power. Religious traditions have sought to control the body through moral codes and spiritual practices. They have regulated diet, hygiene, posture, exercise and sleep. McGuire cites Bryan Turner's observation that social body regulation has affected reproduction, spatial norms, internal restraint and appearances or body representations (Turner, 1992). Illness can be used as a means of dissent or resistance, a way of communicating that the person will not or cannnot cope any longer. However, for many, being ill is like letting out a scream: it may or may not be heard. Nevertheless, the scream may have therapeutic value and, if heard, alert others to the pain and the political cause.

The third level is the social body, in the sense in which society uses the body to symbolise meaning.

> [S]ociety uses body parts, postures and functions, not only to *represent* meanings
> but also to reproduce or transform them. Furthermore, for the individual member
> of society, these body images and meanings are linked with conceptions of one's
> self and one's relationship with the larger material and social environment
> (McGuire, 1996: 107).

In some cultures emotions are identified with body parts – for example, in China anger is represented by the liver and anxiety by the heart. Illness is often understood to be a metaphorical expression of 'somatic, emotional and social concerns', expressed via experiences of pain, suffering or disability. For example, suffering from 'nerves' can be understood as an 'embodiment of socially adverse existential conditions and disorder', as found in a comparative study of descriptions from Kentucky, Newfoundland, Costa Rica, Guatemala and Puerto Rico. These feelings are experienced somatically (107). 'Nerves embodiment ... can communicate the disintegration and breakdown of the self / society contract in explicitly bodily terms with the body disturbances reflecting the nature of that disturbance' (107).

All three levels are obviously connected and McGuire contends that it is through ritual action, such as healing rites, that the three levels are reconfigured in such a way that transformation, or healing, occurs. That is, the lived, political and social are reinterpreted or resolved in a new way. The healing experience empowers the person to challenge or reinterpret the political or social forces. In other words, the ritual performance is intended to accomplish what it represents (McGuire, 1988: 232; McGuire, 1996: 107, 109). A theologian might say that it has sacramental efficacy!

Reflection

In an attempt to use the theoretical perspective of Csordas, we have to note the obvious sub-cultural differences between American Roman Catholic Charismatic Renewal and British classical Pentecostalism that is largely comprised of West Indian and African members. Clearly not everything from America travels to Britain easily. However, there are also a number of interesting connections.

First, spirituality in both cases provides a worldview through which to orientate oneself in relation to the world. It is not only spiritual gifts, but the whole plausibility structure of the Pentecostal worship experience that delivers and sustains an orientation towards the world in which the kingdom of God takes precedence.

Like the Roman Catholic charismatics, the self is defined primarily by means of a relationship with God, made possible not because of *imago dei* but *Spiritus dei*. Second, the themes of spontaneity, control and intimacy are replicated in British Pentecostalism and the sacred self involved in the healing rituals experiences all of these features. It is probably true that health is idealised, but this idealisation for Pentecostals is elevated to a macro level, whereby the rhetoric of healing dominates all other and is interpreted as lifting the burden of physical ailments. None of the focus group members offered narratives about emotional healing, but rather focused on the physical ailments. Third, the tripartite anthropology is missing from these narratives, so the clear connection with these other healing genres cannot be made in the same way. In effect, the 'physical' eclipses the emotional and the spiritual, or rather they are understood as being fundamentally present in and through the physical. Fourth, the insight that the therapeutic process functions at the margin of disability is an interesting and important insight (also noted by McGuire, 1988: 241). It is certainly the case that Pentecostals engage in healing ritual fairly routinely, but it is not necessarily the case that one can dismiss their experiences as all fairly minor. Regarding Beverley's testimony of being healed from cancer, her ailment could not be viewed as minor, even if its severity is in a minority. Nevertheless, there is probably an 'incremental efficacy' for the majority of participants insofar as they are engaged in low-level healings routinely, which are framed in terms of the 'burden' of sickness being lifted (e.g. Isabel).

Turning to the work of Sequeira, the sub-culture of an American Episcopal church involved in Charismatic Renewal is certainly very different to this British classical Pentecostal church. The difference is marked once again by the absence of inner healing mentioned in the Pentecostal narratives. As noted above, healing for these Pentecostals is largely conceived as physical, although the conversion narratives noted elsewhere suggest that the process of conversion deals, to some extent, with psychological issues. This may be a feature of socio-economics, in that largely middle-class Christians are less concerned with physical ailments because of the greater access to quality health care. However, in Britain with the National Health Service this should be less of a problem, even if recent research has suggested that there is still a significant discrepancy between the social classes and the health care outcomes of life expectancy and morbidity (Wanless, 2003). Three similarities stand out. (1) There is a focus on Christology: Jesus is the healer, even if it is expressed differently. The visualization technique is not practised as a mode of healing at HPC. Nevertheless, prophecies may contain such visualization focusing on the person of Jesus, intimacy with whom it is assumed is a sign of being a Christian. (2) There is also a commitment to friendship and community which mirrors the intimacy with God through Jesus. Both churches exhibit a strong sense of communal unity resourced by common ritual. (3) Both sets of Christians in this context of intimacy and community find the healing rituals empowering. This empowerment is renewed weekly through the mechanism of testimony, as others within the community hear the stories told of God's work in their lives. This enables those who are not healed to share in the experience of others indirectly and supports the plausibility of the worldview to be maintained.

Finally, with respect to the interpretation of McGuire, it is certainly the case that HPC members would view themselves holistically and not just dichotomised as mind/body, but also as spirit. First, the lived human reality is multi-dimensional yet united in a whole person. Listening to individual accounts of suffering and healing clearly allows very personal narratives to be shaped by each other. The sharing of narratives is very much part and parcel of the church culture and occurs regularly in public worship and private conversation. But in all of the narratives there is a unity of experience rather than any form of compartmentalisation. Second, the body as a site of a power struggle is also something that Pentecostals understand and it is interesting to observe that a number of these people are from the lower socio-economic strands of society, living in a deprived inner-city area. Many of them experience the disempowerment of migration and are rebuilding their sense of esteem by tapping into spiritual power. Of course, they recognise this is a struggle, and that is why faith is important. It is also the case in Pentecostal discourse that there are spiritual forces to be fought against for the sake of health, even if these testimonies do not make much of this dimension. The devil does not seem to be made a scapegoat in these narratives (cf. Percy, 1996: 55). What might be suggested is that illness can function to alert church members to the political issue of social integration. The needs of the socially marginal bodies are being heard and have begun to be integrated into a largely White British Pentecostal denomination. However, there is also a sense in which the White working-class members (mostly older) are now in the minority, yet they do not seem to be marginalised: a delicate balance seems to have been struck! Third, society at large can place burdens on people of limited resources. Again, this reflects the socio-economic status of many of the members of the church. Since the idea of carrying burdens can be associated with back pain or sciatica, it may well be that social burdens are represented by physical strains and stresses such as these. At the beginning of each worship service, Pastor Angela invites the congregation to give their burdens to the Lord, in order to be free to worship him. At the end of the service, during the altar calls, again burdens and sicknesses can be given to the Lord. This theme of giving one's burdens to Jesus is also reflected in the atonement discourse, as he is regarded as the one who has 'taken our infirmities and carried our sorrows'(Isa 53.4), so that by his wounds we are healed, made whole and able to carry on. Empowerment through physical healing, therefore, enables members to overcome 'socially adverse existential conditions'.

Evangelical and Pentecostal Theology

In order to theologically rescript the ordinary healing soteriology, two dialogue partners will be used to provide material with which to interact. These two interlocutors are Bruce R. Reichenback, an Evangelical theologian, and Amos Yong, a Pentecostal theologian, respectively.

In a recent Evangelical discussion of the atonement edited by Beilby and Eddy (2006) there is a proposal that there is such a perspective as a 'healing view'. That is, an argument can be advanced that prioritises the metaphor of healing in order to explain the notion of the atonement. This is the view advocated by Bruce R. Reichenback (2006).

The Healing Model of Atonement

Reichenback begins with a discussion of Old Testament material and, specifically, the idea that *shalom* as well-being, wholeness and peace is what Yhwh offers his people but that humans clearly lack it (Jer 6.13–14). Restoration occurs when their rebellion ends (Isa 58.8). This means that well-being was provided through the Day of Atonement ritual in acts of forgiveness and restoration, which is now provided once and for all through the atoning sacrifice of Christ upon the cross. As a physician Jesus takes up this task (Lk 4.23) to proclaim good news to the poor, freedom for prisoners, recovery of sight to the blind, release of the oppressed and proclamation of the year of the Lord's favour (Lk 4.18–19; Isa 61.1).

The problem to be solved by our healing is the state of the human condition: the desire to be like God, determining what is good and evil (Gen 3.1–6); inclining to do evil (Gen 6.5); and in disobedience to God (Isa 1.2–4; Rom 3.10–11). Humanity cannot rectify the situation, it is helpless and sin-sick. Sickness describes not only our spiritual condition but our physical, economic, social and environmental circumstances (Isa 1.5–7). Therefore, healing and restoration is required of the people (Isa 10.21), the land (2 Chron 7.14), the institutions (Hos 6.6–7.1) and health (Ps 41.3–4, 8). The necessary requirement is to turn to the Lord the healer (Ex 15.26; Jer 14.19–20). The close connection between sin, sickness and well-being suggests the importance of the healing motif. The idea that God brings about calamities and punishes sin through sickness is a strand throughout the Old Testament (1 Sam 5.6–12; 2 Sam 12.13–18; 2 Sam 24.13; 1 Kings 13.4; 2 Kings 6.18–20; Num 12.20–16); the link between sin and sickness is made in the New Testament as well (Mt 8.4; Lk 11.14; Jn 5.14; Mt 9.18; Acts 5.1–10; Jas 5.13–16), even if there is not a one-to-one correspondence (Job 23.10–12; Jn 9.1–3).

In Israelite religion there appears to have been no class or group of people designated 'healers', which was unusual for ancient societies. The exceptional texts appear to be Job 13.4 and Jeremiah 8.22. The priests, of course, were concerned for the health of the people but via the cult and its rituals and ceremonies (Lev 13–14). Prophets occasionally healed (1 Kings 17; 2 Kings 5) but it was not necessarily regarded as a normal prophetic function. In Old Testament thought God was the source of everything, including sickness, therefore it was God who was primarily the healer upon the condition of repentance (Hos 6.1–2), rather than looking to others (Hos 5.13). Sickness was not only physical but spiritual, involving the forgiveness of sins (Ps 103.2–3; Hos 14.4); and indeed, trust and obedience were required for ongoing health (Ps 91.3,6). Therefore, sin is the condition and sickness is the result. The healing of both is required for *shalom*, well-being.

In the Old Testament the priests did not heal but inspected people in order to exclude them from the cult. Sacrifice atoned for sin but did not cure the ailment. The Old Testament text that announces a permanent solution to the problem of sin is Isaiah 52.13–53.12. Isaiah 52.15 recalls the sprinkling of the blood on and in front of the atonement cover and on the horns of the altar (Lev 16.19). The human predicament of sickness (pain) and sorrows (mental and physical) is brought on us by sins and transgressions. We are sinners who need to be made well (53.5), with sin being removed and our sickness healed. The Suffering Servant takes on the burden of sin and its results, sickness and pain, even though the Servant was innocent (53.9). He was pierced for our transgressions, crushed for our iniquities, cut off from the land of the living (killed) for the transgression of the people (53.5,8). The effect of this act is healing: his punishment brought us peace, justifying many (53.11). The Suffering Servant is a substitutionary guilt offering, so that the suffering, death and resurrection (he will see the light of life, 53.11) address sin and sickness. In other words, the Messiah is the healer (Mal 4.2). Atonement as healing means that the relationship is restored through an action of God's Servant who personally takes on our sin and its punishment, granting forgiveness and bringing reconciliation, restoration and *shalom*: 'No one living in Zion will say "I am ill"; and the sins of those who dwell there will be forgiven' (Isa 33.24, NIV).

The New Testament addresses both the healing of sickness and the healing of our broken relationship with God. Jesus is the physical healer (Lk 4.23), whose ministry is characterised by healings (Mt 9.35). He heals directly and immediately. The healer of the Old Testament has come to earth via the incarnation. Matthew cites Isaiah 54.3: 'He took up our infirmities and carried our diseases' (Mt 8.17, NIV). For Matthew sin and sickness are connected, as displayed in the narrative of the paralytic (9.1–8). The power to heal is linked to the authority to forgive sins. Luke also connects healing and atonement as the means of addressing our sinfulness (Lk 22.37). 'Christ's atonement heals our fundamental human predicament, that is our alienation from God due to our disobedience and attempts to displace him' (Reichenback, 2006: 132). In the New Testament worldview, Christ is the saviour from sickness (Lk 8.48), from death (Lk 8.49), from demons (Lk 8.26–28) and from sin (Lk 7.50), which is at the root of all the others. Christ both cures the human predicament of sin, removing it, and restores us to wholeness in relation to God and others.

The Christian tradition has identified Jesus Christ with the Suffering Servant of Isaiah 53. 1 Peter 2.24–25 states that: 'He himself bore our sins in his body on the tree, so that we might die to sins and live for righteousness; by his wounds you have been healed. For you were like sheep going astray, but now you have returned to the Shepherd and Overseer of your souls' (NIV). Both Paul and Luke appear to identify the Servant with Jesus in the context of explaining the good news of the kingdom of God (Rom 10.16; Acts 8.34; Isa 52.7, 10). 'Christ's suffering and death cleanses those who have strayed from the covenant, and being made "to be sin for us" (2 Cor 5.21) he personally bears away the sins (Isa 53.11), as the goat takes them into the desert. In this he restores us as cured (righteous) to God and to the community' (Reichenback, 2006: 136).

The objection that sin and disease belong to different categories, with disease the consequence of sin, needs to be addressed. It is claimed that disease does not carry a penalty that requires atonement. Whereas people can be forgiven and remain forgiven, not everyone is healed and those who are do not remain well but succumb to illness again. Isaiah must therefore be using the language figuratively and so must the author of 1 Peter. Reichenback argues that although the spiritual and physical differ, physical healing is intrinsically linked to the atonement. This is because the nature of the atonement is multi-dimensional, therefore the nature of restoration is multi-dimensional: it is holistic and includes physical healing. Salvation and blessing are linked in Old Testament thought and both can be regarded as part of the restoration with God, and therefore located in relation to Christ's atonement. Furthermore, he contends that because people have been forgiven does not mean that they stop sinning; similarly, just because people have been healed does not mean that they will not experience further illness and ultimately death. At the end of the Isaiah passage the Servant intercedes for the sinners, and similarly in James the model is of the church anointing the sick with oil and interceding for their healing. Of course, enquiring of God as to why people are not healed is also important, but it also parallels the discussion as to why people do not respond to the good news of forgiveness through Christ.

Soteriology as Healing

Amos Yong is a Pentecostal theologian who has produced what is, arguably, one of the most profoundly Christian theological accounts of disability (Yong, 2007). It is a book that connects with some of the emerging themes of this ordinary theology, such as: the community of the church as fellow travellers, who share each others' burdens and especially with the great physician, Jesus Christ; who experience healings in an incremental manner; and who are often positioned at the margin of disability. In order to explicate these themes and rescript them theologically the work of Yong is both relevant and useful. But first I need to explain the important features of Yong's thesis in relation to our topic.

Yong offers a theological engagement with disability issues and in particular allows the concerns of disability discourse to help shape a constructive theological vision. A theological anthropology is proposed that suggests the *imago dei* should be conceived in embodied, interdependent and relational terms. An ecclesiology is suggested that is inclusive of disability as members of the broken body of Christ participate in catechism, sacraments, liturgies and fellowship in the Holy Spirit, which empowers all for ministry within and beyond the boundary of the church. Traditional categories of soteriology are reviewed in the light of disability, including justification and healing. He concludes by reconsidering eschatology in the light of disability and challenges aspects of this doctrine that erase the effect of disability both in the eschaton and now.

It is in the context of anthropology that a healing soteriology is situated. Yong proposes an emergent anthroplogy that is embodied, relational and transcendent (248). He describes the relationship between the spiritual and the physical in the following terms:

> In this framework, human souls are emergent from and constituted by human bodies and brains without being reducible to the sum of these biological parts. Similarly, human communities are emergent from and constituted by human persons without being reducible to the sum of these individuals. Finally, I am suggesting, the relationship between God and human beings is a further but definitive emergent level of reality that involves and is fundamentally constituted by our embodiment and our interactions with others and the world, but is irreducible to the sum of these parts as well. (Yong, 2007: 188–189)

His understanding of the human spirit is based on the biblical passage of Genesis 2.7, where the breath (*ruach*) of God forms the human living being, and accounts for human consciousness. Human beings are therefore 'subjective objects', able to know themselves as both subject (knowing) and object (material). Human persons know each other through a relational space mediated via embodiment (183). Therefore, anthropology is inextricably interrelational, intersubjective and interdependent, with friendship as a key means of sustaining what it means to be human (187).

Yong builds on this anthropology in order to propose a healing soteriology. '[S]alvation is the transformative work of the Spirit of God that converts human hearts from lives of sin, estrangement, and inauthenticity to lives of peace, wholeness, and reconciliation between human beings and God' (229). He makes the distinction between curing and healing. A cure relates to a physical ailment of one kind or another, while healing is holistic and is not restricted to the physical need (245). Salvation may include physical cures but cannot be limited to curing, even if 'there is cause to celebrate small miracles' (247).

A holistic soteriology contains three important foci. (1) It begins with the body. It takes seriously the illness and healing narratives of individuals, not merely 'the medical model' and its account of reality. In this context, 'religious rituals mediate healing at least in the sense of enabling people with disabilities to adapt to and exist with their condition' (250). Furthermore, the Holy Spirit can give 'joy in weakness' (250). For Yong, love is the deepest expression of the presence of God's Spirit, to renew and heal our hearts and minds. (2) Salvation is about the healing of relationships through which God sustains human life and nurtures human flourishing (251). This begins with the natural family but, for Christians, it is sustained by the Christian family, the church. The people of God should be formed into a welcoming, inclusive community of healing. The good news is that 'we belong' and God declares his acceptance of our lives through the welcome and embrace of others. Thus, the church offers 'subjective experiences, encounters, and engagements with God's saving work' (252). In its life the church not only witnesses to the power of the Spirit (Acts 1.8), the importance of friendship, but ultimately to self-sacrifice in costly love for others. (3) He argues that soteriology also addresses socio-political structures. It is concerned with issues of injustice in their concrete particularities, the economics of global capitalism and the politics of individualism. In response, he argues that soteriology offers a socio-politics of interdependence and interrelationality. The church subverts dominant ideologies by inspiring alternative normative Christian practices (Yong, 2007: 255–257). Of course in all these dimensions, there is the reality that we live in, what might be called the reality of 'Holy Saturday', betwix and between the now and not yet of the consummation of the reign of God. We are saved, we are being saved and we shall be saved. It is a *via salutis*, which envisions Yong and provides a resource for rescripting ordinary soteriology informed by pneumatology.

Rescripting Ordinary Theology

This discussion has led to the point where we can now, utilising the theoretical perspectives above, offer a rescription of ordinary theological discourse.

The dominant healing motif is intimately connected to Christ's work on the cross as a saviour who carries our burdens of sin and sickness. It is an act of transference, whereby that which afflicts us was historically in a once-for-all act carried by Christ for us, on our behalf. As a consequence of this salvific act, the burdens of sin and sickness can be carried away. For Pentecostals, the means by which this transference takes place is twofold: by the power of the Holy Spirit and as appropriated by faith. Christ, who is the saviour and the baptiser in the Spirit, sends his Holy Spirit to give relief from the burdens of this life. The burden of sickness is the focus of salvation but it extends to anything that might worry us, such as family issues, financial matters and employment concerns. In this way, by means of pneumatology, the benefits of Christ on the cross are made real to these Pentecostals. It is through the rhetoric of physical healing that a wider realised soteriology is expressed.

The Christological focus of this theology can be further strengthened, and in this sense rescripted, by emphasising not only the work of Christ upon the cross but also the assumption of humanity in the incarnation. Christ is the healer not just because of his act of atonement but because he embodied in himself the one who is the healer of Israel (Yhwh). As Gregory of Nazianzus famously stated: 'what is not assumed is not healed; but that which is united to God is saved' (Gallay with Jourjon, 1974: 50). Christ by his act of incarnation made possible the union of humanity with God, by healing human nature. The resurrection of this new humanity, once and for all, points to the possibility of a renewed humanity despite the reality of death. This soteriology displaces the dominant forensic metaphor, and subsumes it under a broader notion of healing as salvation, with a Christological focus rooted in the incarnation, ministry, cross and resurrection of Christ, emphasising the Saviour who is the great physician (Lk 4.23), who both proclaimed and demonstrated in his own life his concern for the whole of humanity and its salvation (Lk 4.18–19).

The salvation that has been inaugurated by Christ is holistic and includes the forgiveness of sins, the healing of the whole person: body, mind and spirit, and the reconciliation of individuals and communities alienated from each other. In Yong's terms it is embodied, relational and socio-political. The ordinary theology of HPC focuses almost exclusively on physical healing, even if other narratives such as the conversion testimonies clearly point to emotional and spiritual healing. Although the category is expanded to include burdens of all kinds, it could be rescripted to include the four categories mentioned by MacNutt (1974): sin, physical, emotional and spiritual. In this way the overarching biblical concept of *shalom* might be used to designate the nature of the salvation being offered. The release of burdens does not just allow for a sense of relief – that is, the absence of something, namely a load to bear – but it makes room for a new experience of one-ness with God and with others, including people in the wider community and with the whole of creation as the theatre of God's glory. This sense of unity, harmony and fulfilment through Christ is what the Christian tradition, drawing from its Jewish roots, has termed *shalom* or peace.

The community of the church is essential for the support that members need in order to share in this narrative world. This is because healing is not only expressed through a discourse of testimony, but it is also enacted, embodied and performed within the ritual of the church. It has a sacramental quality to it. People might indeed pray for their needs on their own, but they will also pray for each other's needs in the worship services and the prayer meetings. Healing soteriology in this context is deeply relational. In the worship services, members experience spontaneity as the Holy Spirit meets with them through prophetic words, the laying on of hands and prayer, praise and worship. Others mediate the presence of Christ. By trusting others and letting go of one's burdens there is a symbolic transference of burdens to others in the church who represent Christ to them. This leads both to intimacy with others and with Christ by the Spirit. As a consequence, greater control is restored through 'incremental efficacy'. It becomes a ritual site for empowerment. Thus, a sense of peace, wholeness and reconciliation in the church is a mirror of the overall soteriology mediated via a theology of healing as atonement. In other words, the power of the cross is made real by the power of the Holy Spirit and this sense of empowerment is captured in the rhetoric of the ordinary discourse.

Health is clearly idealised as an obvious signifier of salvation and as a demonstration of faith. In worship services, testimonies of physical healing act as 'auditory icons' denoting the saving act of Christ, by his Spirit, in the lives of his people (Albrecht, 1999: 143). It is symbolic of physical healing and spiritual wholeness. The struggle to be healed and the issues of faith, persistance and hope are all part of what it means to be human in a Pentecostal worldview.

To be whole and holy means to participate in the journey of salvation, the *via salutis*, and to struggle against the margin of disability by means of 'incremental efficacy'. At times there are major experiences of healing within the church and these are celebrated. But most often there are smaller experiences, what might be called 'minor miracles', and experiences of 'relief' from the burden of sin and sickness empower the members to carry on and to be joyful amidst the strains and stresses of life. Of course, the problem of the unhealed remains. The tension in the group discussion between those emphasising the appropriation of healing by faith and those emphasising the fact that not all are healed but that God gives the strength to carry on is maintained by this theology. The weight of the burden, in fact, might be more to do with anxiety over sickness than the sickness itself. In other words, the margin of disability might be more psychological than physical. Nevertheless, a holistic approach means that one can still experience healing, because the burden of anxiety is shared by others through prayer, given over to Christ, who takes it away and thus empowers the believer to carry on, perhaps limping, but with a renewed vision that Christ is with him or her by his Spirit, and that makes all the difference in the world.

Summary

The practice of praying for healing is a central feature of Pentecostalism and it reflects the language of the 'full' gospel as it relates to the physical welfare of Christians, not just spiritual salvation through conversion. Participants affirmed their faith in God's power and his willingness to heal today. Testimonies of personal healing formed the basis of the chapter's discussion. Faith is often regarded as essential in the appropriation of healing and it is used through prayer 'in Jesus' name'. Healing may occur either spontaneously or gradually and sometimes with the assistance of medicine. Occasionally members pray and ignore the pain in the belief that it will go away. It is acknowledged that God does not heal all illness and that sometimes he may use sickness for his higher purposes, but if this is the case then he offers support and courage to face the difficulty (Ps 91.1–2). In this congregation healing was elevated to become the dominant soteriological metaphor (based upon Isa 53.4–6; Mt 8.17 and 1 Pet 2.24), whereby Christ is the one who relieves people from their burdens, which includes their sicknesses, in an act of transference. Emotional healing was not mentioned by the participants (or the visualisation technique). This is because physical healing is the dominant category and other categories are subsumed within it, so it is symbolic of healing more generally. Although there were accounts of major healings, it is probably the case that most examples of healing were of a minor kind. This suggests that healing functions at the level of 'incremental efficacy' (Csordas), as low-level healings are experienced routinely within the context of a friendly and supportive community. This community is a means of social integration, as migrant members can find a 'home from home' and are able to overcome 'socially adverse existential conditions' through the empowerment that incremental healing brings. Therefore, salvation can be theologised in terms of holistic healing, as Christ is the great physician, and other metaphors can be subsumed within it.

Chapter 7

Life and Witness

This chapter aims to investigate Pentecostal attitudes to Christian life and witness, as understood in relation to the work of the Holy Spirit in the context of contemporary British society. It does so by exploring the focus group material, especially the narratives that discuss the experience of evangelism in the lives of participants and the issues these experiences raise. There are three overlapping contexts for the placement of this material within larger theoretical accounts. The first context is the nature of Pentecostal theological identity with its commitment to witnessing to others concerning its life in Christ by and through the Spirit. The motivation that this identity gives each participant is important because it is a key dimension in understanding what is taking place. The second is the wider British society and the relationship of Christianity to the broader cultural issues. Britain has a Christian heritage and this is still to be seen with a state church (the Church of England) and representation in government (bishops sit in the House of Lords). But measures of public religious practice consistently record the decline in church attendance, especially since the end of World War II, often associated with the notion of secularisation. How contemporary Pentecostalism understands itself with regard to this social context is important for an analysis of its life and witness. Third is the specific context of multi-cultural and multi-faith Birmingham. This melting pot of cultures and religious traditions provides an important context for understanding the kinds of ordinary theologies that are espoused by the respondents. All three contexts provide important features in which to locate and understand ordinary discourse.

Testimonies

The Focus Group

The focus group contains four men and three women. The women spanned the age range from young (Yasmin) to middle-aged (Patricia) and elderly (Lilian). They originated from Jamaica (Lilian), Nigeria (Patricia) and the UK (Yasmin) and their occupations were student (Yasmin), support worker (Patricia) and retired nurse (Lilian). The men were relative young, with three under 40 years (Desmond, Scott and Denzil), and one man was elderly (Richard). They originated from Jamaica (Richard), India (Denzil), Nigeria (Scott) and the UK (Desmond). Their occupations were student (Desmond), engineer (Scott), photographer (Denzil) and retired (Richard).

The conversation began with an invitation to the participants to discuss their experiences of evangelism in the British context and the role of the Holy Spirit. Three participants made interesting contributions.

Desmond: I was sleeping one night and I had a dream of someone in college who for some reason was injured somehow and I went and prayed over them in front of everyone and they were healed instantly. What happened, it was kind of like saying to me that I had to get over that people [are] looking at what you do. You have to basically just go for it, kind of thing. And what happened is when I went into the college the next day or two days later ... my friend, her name's Lesley, she came in with crutches and I thought this is unusual 'cos I had a dream about her, like, two days ago. And then she was talking about coming to the church and everything. Then I was saying, 'cos I must have brought it up in the conversation or something. Sometimes the Lord opens doors for stuff like that. And I said: 'So how did that happen?' She said, 'playing football', which she normally does every week. She landed in a pot-hole or something like that. It twisted her ankle or her knee out of place. So she was on crutches. The doctors said a minimum [of] eight weeks for her to get back to, without crutches, but still injured. And I said, it's like the Holy Spirit prompted me to, you know, speak. I said 'well, that can be healed for you, that's not a problem'. And she said, 'cos I was talking about it to her before about stuff like that can happen. But she didn't really believe it kind of thing until it happens to her. I said: 'Well, it can happen to you. Alright, next week Monday, you'll be healed of it.' And I was praying all over the weekend and stuff like that that. She came in Monday, I was kept in contact with her, she came in Monday and I was just waiting, you know, waiting to see if she comes in with crutches or not. 'Cos that's times when faith is tested, if the Holy Spirit was helping me, you know, speaking to people and stuff like that. And she came in and she just walked in like playing football. 'Cos I take a sports course and that's what we do in the mornings on a Monday. She just came and started kicking [a ball] around, so I said, 'so you haven't got your crutches any more then?' And she was like, 'Oh yes, it got healed'. She believed it totally.

Mark: So did she become a Christian as a consequence of this at all?

Desmond: The only thing that's stopping her is what she has to give up, kind of thing. But I said to her that it's nothing compared to what you'll have with God, kind of thing. So, like what Jesus said about the seed, dropping has to die and then the crop will grow, you know. She just needs, it's not for me to make someone turn a Christian, it's just I was just doing what God said really and that's made a really big step from total unbelief, atheist, to there's God out there but I don't know when and I am ready or ... and that was 'cos of the Holy Spirit that was.

Another participant, Denzil, spoke about his own family circumstances. He came from an Indian background but was now a British citizen.

Denzil: One of my mother's sisters, she was from, she lives in the Netherlands. And she wasn't really a Christian or anything like that. She wasn't really a believer but she fell ill. This is going back ten years in 1998 and to cut the story short and get more to the point …, she had some sort of bacterial infection, which came up to her brain, inside her brain. And my mum was there, she went there. My mum being a strong Christian she was praying every single day and, you know, and 'Give me a sign' and … her sister, she became brain dead in hospital. She was like, literally, her body cut off. It was almost like as if she was dead. But her eyes were wide open, and this was for three days, this was. And she was [like] that for three days. On the third day she got up again. And to my mother this was like something very significant, like, you know, Christ rising up, back up. Not that she was Christ, but maybe it was a sign for her. But, yes, sometimes I knew it would [be] hard as a Christian. God can work, the Holy Spirit can work in other people's lives as well, whether they're a Christian or not, for your sake as well … For the sake of other Christians as well, the Holy Spirit is at work as well, maybe in secular communities and other religious ones. But I don't believe that they'll be the same way as it would work, as we know the Holy Spirit.

Mark: So what's the real differences, would you say then, between people's experiences [of] the Spirit, you know, colleagues at work that experience something of the Spirit in their lives and then Christians, who experience the Spirit? What would be the difference?

Denzil: The way I look at it is in my experience I've seen somethings happen. Okay, I know what the Holy Spirit is 'cos I read the Bible and come to church and so forth. But when I see somebody else at the work place or something. See, I believe God knows everybody, every, each individual and I believe that sometimes God wants this person to live, or he wants it to die in a certain way, which will bring him to him, to bring him to God. So I believe that the Holy Spirit is working in everybody and God is looking at peoples of all religions to see who he can bring to himself. That's the way I look at it but I don't expect someone who's … to say, 'Oh I've got the Holy Spirit', you know, and stuff like that because they don't know, they don't know.

The idea that the Holy Spirit was at work in very different communities and, indeed, in every person was echoed by Yasmin, although in relation to what might be called secular society.

Yasmin: Talking about the Holy Spirit in the secular world, I mean we all know what Holy Spirit is and God sent it down to help us guide and for us to do the right things and lead us in a certain direction. And I believe that a lot of people might not know about God or reject him but I still believe the Holy Spirit will help people because it's here to help everyone. God loves everybody, not just Christians or Pentecostals, Romans Catholics, he loves everybody, so I believe that the Holy Spirit was sent down here to guide us. He wasn't sent to guide a certain type of people. I believe that he guides a lot [of] people and the fact that people might not know about it. Like, say, one day someone's having a really really bad day and, like, say, they're running for the bus and the Holy Spirit could say to the bus driver, 'Stop for this lady today' and it stops. And she's … going to be grateful that the bus stops. They might not … like … I want to say, like, people think things are coincidence, like … might of lost their wedding ring or something and they've been panicked, they might not be Christians or any kind of, have no faith at all, but they might be panicking, 'Oh, where's this'? And find it in like the weirdest place or something. I believe that he guides in the smallest thing, and he guides us in the biggest [agreement], so what people don't, might not, believe per se is the Holy Spirit. I believe he is still there to guide us and help us [agreement] through whatever we do. So, like, even, like, if we're just having a little bit of headache and I wish this headache would go and it's go and, ah yea, they might not think it's the Holy Spirit. I just think it does help in the secular world. I mean, like, with the things like the tornadoes and things, tsunamis, I think they could be much worse [agreement] than what they could have been [agreement], you know, like, not houses and things just destroyed and stuff, 'cos when it comes to like hurricanes, there does … Like for it to pass in a certain way and leave biggest cities alone, you can't just think that's just coincidence and stuff. I believe that it helps.

She believed that the Holy Spirit was sent to guide us and even though people reject God he still guides them by his Spirit. She reflected further on her experience of a friendship with a person from the Hindu faith.

My friend's still currrently a Hindu but she has come to church, thank the Lord. [I] pray for her … because she's hasn't found anything when she goes to temple with her family. But she went to a service in [the] church, just up the road and she felt like the power of God there and, like, during the service, and if this was, like, her first encounter with God. And although, you know, that, like, God is always loving and keeping his arms open for people who want to come to him because he is very gentleman-like, you know, he'll wait until you say, 'Hey, here I am, look, here I am, I want to know you'. And I think she had that experience for the first time and never forgotten it. And I think she's still on a journey 'cos … everybody's on a journey. And certain things happened, other things have happened and it's like a knock-on effect, isn't it? 'Cos you start off with one thing and then your mind's open a bit more or you feel a bit secure in what you know or you get some more knowledge and then you might want to know another bit and then something else happens and it's just. And then it makes you grow 'cos everybody's got to grow and grow. So I think the Holy Spirit does work in the world.

At this point in the conversation, I asked the group about whether the church engaged in interfaith dialogue. I was told that there was no direct engagement by the church, although individuals from the church conducted street evangelism. A number of the participants felt that it was not easy to express their Christian identity in other contexts because in Britain there was the problem of 'political correctness'. 'Political correctness' refers to language, ideas, policies and behaviour that intend to minimise social offence. In this context, they expressed the concern that by proclaiming the gospel they would offend their non-Christian neighbours. This was illustrated by a discussion of how the signs in Birmingham city centre around Christmas time no longer seemed to include the explicitly Christian traditional greeting 'Merry Christmas'. One person suggested that perhaps this change came as a result of certain religious pressure groups. Another person expressed concern about religious violence, especially terrorism. The view that Christianity appeared to be denigrated in the media was also expressed by a different person, whereas it was considered that other religious traditions were seldom treated in the same manner. The same person also felt that the government did not listen to the concerns of ordinary Christians when formulating policy that affected them directly.

Summary of the Testimonies

In summary, these narratives indicate the struggle of witnessing in a secular and multi-faith world within an overall Pentecostal spirituality. For example, inspiration via a dream can be allied to prayer for healing as a means of witness, and the choice of the person not to convert is respected (Desmond). Prayer is regarded as powerful to heal people who are not Christians and this can be a means of them considering the Christian faith more deeply (Desmond and Denzil). It is believed that the Holy Spirit is active in non-Christian lives because God is sovereign over all and influences all. He is interested in all people, including people of other religions, to see if he can bring them to himself (Denzil) by giving them experiences of his power (Yasmin). The view was expressed that the Holy Spirit guides everyone, even in small matters, and even minimises the impact of natural disasters (Yasmin). However, it was felt that the secular context of Britain did not assist Christians in their witness and that political correctness certainly inhibited their freedom because of concerns not to offend people of other religious traditions. It was also felt that the media were unfair towards Christianity, and that the government was also culpable in this regard. The focus group generally felt that other religious traditions did not always respect the Christian heritage of Britain.

It is important to contextualise these beliefs and values within the history of the denomination and recent religious changes in Britain. Therefore, I shall engage with the work of William K. Kay (1989) who has attempted to describe this history accompanied by sociological analysis.

British Society and the Assemblies of God

It was observed earlier that the doctine of sanctification had framed the Assemblies of God's approach to wider society: separation from the world and consecration unto God (Carter, 1937; Sherlock, 1937a; Cooper, 1939). This dual orientation can be seen in the denomination's relationship with British society over the course of the twentieth century. In his doctoral thesis, Kay charts the history of the Assemblies of God from its inception in 1924 to the time of his writing (1989). He observed how the Assemblies of God in Britain provided hope to the poor and unemployed in the Great Depression of the late 1920s and early 1930s. Many churches had been established in industrial working-class regions where the need was greatest. 'The lively singing, often setting catchy spiritual songs to music hall tunes, and the powerful preaching coupled with an expectation in divine healing, gave hope to the hopeless' (Kay, 1989: 105). In this period of the 1930s, Pentecostalism had to contend with the changes in cultural expectations that came with such things as 'contraception, an increased divorced rate, holiday camps, the appearance of the family motor car, Sunday sport, greyhound racing, the BBC, cinemas and building societies' (107). On the whole they attempted to separate themselves from the values of the world around them in order to maintain their identity. In this regard, the Assemblies of God denomination could be classified as a conversionist sect because of its 'anti-world and otherwordly' stance and its emphasis on recruitment by conversionist means, even if those who formed the denomination rejected the notion of 'sectarianism', seeing themselves as related to other communities of Christian believers (99–100; Wilson, 1966: 179–198; 1982: 89–120).

In the 1940s the Assemblies of God purchased property for the sake of a General Office. This was prudent at the time, given the government building programme and the fact that the cost to rent or purchase was approximately the same. This suggests that the denomination was moving towards a more institutionalised state, adopting bureaucracy, even if hierarchy was (theoretically) denied. Bureaucratic models from the Houses of Parliament at Westminster were also adopted during this period, for example use of the term 'Select Committee'. As Kay suggests, the situation was complex.

> In their rejection of certain forms of 'worldly' entertainment and leisure, pentecostals deemed themselves holy, and might be deemed sociologically sectarian. In apparently accepting certain 'worldly' forms of governmental procedures, Assemblies of God deemed themselves as acting to prevent exploitation by overbearing individuals. (Kay, 1989: 205)

By the 1950s, Pentecostals, like every other church, faced a society in which church attendance was in decline and it also began to struggle against the rise of the secular tide, even as new church buildings were being opened. This was assisted by an alliance with Evangelicals in other denominations, as preparations were made in the 1950s for the arrival and ministry of Billy Graham. This acceptance was reinforced at a greater level when the BBC broadcast a Pentecostal worship service, thus bringing Pentecostalism into mainstream television viewing and compromising its stance towards 'worldly' media (248). Thus, it can be seen that the anti-worldly attitude changed over time and the move towards denominationalism within the mainstream world of Evangelicalism and publicly sanctioned religion began to be established. This was aligned to a general withdrawal from social action, even if pronouncements on the moral degeneration of the country were often made from the pulpit (Gilpin, 1976: 119). Over the course of this period, the Assemblies of God built up relationships with different Pentecostal groups from around the world via the World Pentecostal Conferences. Even in these years the beginning of globalised and transnational Pentecostalism can be seen.

The 1960s brought greater secularisation and the development of 'pop culture' through music and lifestyle choices. It also brought religious innovation as Pentecostal spirituality was embraced by the mainstream churches in the Charismatic movement. This created identity issues, as the type of Christianity associated with classical Pentecostalism was seen outside this domain and thus, to some extent, reconfigured (Kay, 1989: 288). This loss of spiritual territory, in the sense of a distinct spirituality managed by classical Pentecostal denominations, was now the focus of competition from outside (Massey, 1992). Donald Gee, the key Assemblies of God leader of the period, argued that the denomination must reform, but this reform was expressed by means of pietist language: a greater waiting on God and a slower pace of activity, with fewer committees and a simpler constitution. These identity issues were also exacerbated by concerns with authority and the status of church leaders in an increasingly secular society, where there was the need to claim authority either by expertise or by means of charismatic gifting. Of course, in an increasingly educated society members of the congregation might be better educated than the pastor and, in a Pentecostal setting, even more charismatically gifted as well.

In the 1970s once again economic problems dominated, with rising unemployment reaching 2 million by 1980. Racial tension in multi-cultural Britain was fuelled by the arrival in 1972 of Uganda's Asians, escaping the terror of Idi Amin. Nevertheless, over the course of the decade living standards did rise, especially for those in work. The churches engaged in ecumenism, which is one response in the face of declining numbers. However, Pentecostals on the whole remained outside of such ecumenical gatherings and continue to do so. The affirmation at Nottingham in 1977 by evangelical Anglicans, which would have included a significant number of charismatics, to stay in the Church of England probably made greater contact with Pentecostals more difficult (Kay, 1989: 294). Another group, however, made its presence known at this time: the House Church movement (hereafter HCM), otherwise known as the Restoration movement. The common charismatic spirituality was expressed in very different ways, with the HCM showing a greater degree of accommodation to secular cultural values, especially in relation to leisure and fashion (Walker, 1988).

By the 1980s the crisis facing the Assemblies of God deepened, with the New Churches (formerly the HCM) and the mainstream charismatics growing and reconfiguring. A new generation of leaders was able to offer reflection on the reasons for their problems (Kay, 1989: 335). For example, Pentecostalism was understood as a form of Evangelicalism, adding a different perspective and tradition, rather than being very distinct. This meant that the Students' Pentecostal Fellowship could be disbanded as, increasingly, university Christian Unions became influenced by the Charismatic movement. The influence of the Restorationists' desire for community churches and their resistance to central administration also influenced the Assemblies of God. Church buildings began to cater for community interests such as sport, childcare, bookshops and accommodation. In an impersonal technological and bureaucratic age, the desire for meaningful personal relationships was provided by means of small groups as well as large church meetings (337). This supported the family as meetings were often held in the home, thus encouraging a more relaxed approach to piety that eventually found its way back into the main Sunday church services as well.

Kay's doctoral study, given its time period, does not deal with one of the most important factors that has influenced the nature of Pentecostalism in Britain since the 1980s, namely migration and transnational Pentecostalism. Especially since the 1990s, Pentecostals from all over the world have migrated to the West, looking for a better life and fulfilling the call to reverse mission (Kalu, 2008: 271–291; cf. Kay, 2007: 221–222). Many of them come believing that God has called them to live in Britain, to contribute to the re-evangelisation of a once-great Christian nation. In this context, new Pentecostal churches have become established. However, the study of HPC also indicates that many immigrants decided to join existing churches that have sufficient resemblance to the Christianity they know from their homeland. That is why churches like HPC have a very sizable number of Africans and West Indian immigrants, many of whom have made a permanent home in Britain. This means that attitudes towards British society are varied, intercultural and complex, with identity issues arising from both ethnic and religious convictions (ter Haar, 2001: 125–128). But it also means that attitudes to other religious traditions, which connect both their old and new worlds, exist together in British Pentecostal contexts.

For members of the focus group, five of whom originated outside of the UK (from India, Jamaica and Nigeria), the notion of transnational Pentecostalism is strongly represented. From the narratives it is clear that they have adapted, or are in the process of adapting, to a modern (perhaps postmodern?) liberal western democracy. This suggests that the accommodation described by Kay has continued. However, there are clear tensions, and the causes of these tensions are not necessarily cultural, although cultural differences obviously play a part. Rather, they are theological. It is the difference of values exhibited between Pentecostal spirituality and secular society that is deemed to be hostile to Christianity. The two main avenues of this hostility are the national government and the media, for both are regarded as responsible for undermining the Christian character of the nation. It is perceived that the government does not respect the rights of Christians to exercise their beliefs and values in the public sphere, while the media denigrate Christianity through their promotion of controversial shows. They are also perceived to be discriminatory because other religious traditions would not be treated in such a manner.

British Society, Secularisation and Religious Pluralism

The sociology of religion has charted quite successfully the decline in formal religious institutional affiliation of the British population, especially since the end of World War II (Davie, 1994: 49). It has been stated that: 'Evidence of long-term decline in formal religious participation in Britain is overwhelming' (Gill, 2003: 280). Callum Brown even traces the key date to 1963 and a cultural shift precipitated by the 'swinging sixties', when the inter-generational ties with church life were ruptured (Brown, 2009: 1). Grace Davie has also described the paradox that goes alongside this analysis, namely that British people continue to believe in God, even if they no longer attend churches on a regular basis: they believe without belonging (Davie, 1994; 2007: 138–140). However, the 2001 census data suggest that the majority of British people (42,079,417; 71.6%) make some form of connection with Christianity (belonging) in relation to religious identity, even if it is unclear what it is that they actually believe (Weller, 2008: 25; cf. Davie, 2007: 114–116).[1] It has been suggested in the light of this and other research that perhaps 'belonging without believing' or 'believing without practising' better characterise the attitude of the general British public (Francis and Robbins, 2004; also see the reply by Davie, 2004). However these religious changes are described, they have been accompanied by changes in society as a whole during this period: from an industrial model to a predominantly consumption model (Davie, 1994: 19–20). Even religious affiliation can now be considered through the lens of consumerism (Aldridge, 2000: 186-190). There have been significant changes in demography and the nature of the household during this period, with shifts in gender roles. As mentioned above, during this period there has been increased migration to the UK from Commonwealth countries, in particular, as well as by persecuted minorities. In urban centres, such as Birmingham, this has contributed to ethnic and religious pluralism. West Indian Christians and, more recently, African Christians have arrived in the UK. Indeed, the rise of urban Pentecostalism bucks the trend in the decline of mainline denominations (Davie, 1994: 63). The influence of these

---

[1]   http://www.statistics.gov.uk/census2001/profiles/commentaries/ethnicity.asp; accessed on 23 September 2009.

Christians on HPC is reasonably evident. There is an older generation of White working-class members, an older generation of working- to middle-class West Indians (cf. Hollenweger, 1972: 188), a recent generation of largely middle-class Africans, as well as a younger generation of British-born Black (West Indian) and mixed race members who are socially mixed.

Migration is an important factor in this context, and with immigration come beliefs and values that are both in continuity with the existing belief system and, to some extent, in discontinuity. Obviously this is linked to globalisation – that is, 'the increasing speed of movement as people, ideas, images and capital take advantage of modern means of communication' (Martin, 2005: 26). This includes the greater movement of Pentecostals from the south to the north of the globe, which is generally classified under the notion of 'transnationalism' (Corten and Marshall-Fratani, 2001; Davie, 2007: 215). David Martin (2005) suggests that for those on the move, Pentecostalism has provided 'an internal compass and a portable identity' (151). In order to appreciate this portable identity, and to gain a broader set of insights into intercultural Pentecostal attitudes more generally, recent research into Pentecostal beliefs and values can be considered. The research by The Pew Forum on Religion & Public Life (2006) surveyed attitudes among Pentecostals from ten different countries (USA, Brazil, Chile, Guatemala, Kenya, Nigeria, South Africa, India, the Philippines and South Korea). Unfortunately, it did not survey British Pentecostal atttitudes. Nevertheless, in relation to an intercultural congregational context, such as HPC, it does provide some interesting and useful information.

The research discovered that Pentecostals are committed to proclaiming the belief that Jesus Christ is the 'exclusive path' to eternal salvation and therefore this obliges them to evangelise. With the exception of South Korea, 70% of Pentecostals believe that having faith in Jesus is the only way to be 'saved from eternal damnation' (The Pew Forum on Religion & Public Life, 2006: 27). Unsurprisingly, the research found that the majority of Pentecostals make an effort to share their faith with non-believers at least once a week (6–7, 21). Many Pentecostals believe there is a role for religion within the political sphere and argue that their views on political matters should be expressed publicly. The exceptions are in India and South Korea, where the majority of Pentecostals think that religious groups should stay out of politics (57). It is important to Pentecostals that state leaders have strong Christian beliefs (75% from seven countries; 66% from the remaining three countries). There is a mixed view as to whether God actually fulfils his purposes through politics, even though most believe that God is active in the world, including politics (59). The majority of Pentecostals believe in a clear separation between church and state (seven countries), although a sizable minority in each of these seven countries would like to see their governments take steps to make their country a Christian one, especially African Pentecostals, and most especially in Nigeria (7–8, 60). This means that for Pentecostals as a whole their religious identity is more important to them than their nationality, continent or ethnicity (61). Consequently, there is 'broad-based' support for civil rights, an independent judiciary and freedom of religious expression, especially for themselves (62–63).

This leads on to the nature of religious pluralism as a social reality in the UK context. It is clear that religions other than Christianity have migrated to, and found a home within, Britain. Not only is there pluralism within Christianity, but there is also significant pluralism with regard to different faiths (Davie, 1994: 63). The largest and most significant minority in Britain is Islam, although in Birmingham it can be a significant majority in certain localities, and wields considerable influence in the shaping of local communities and on the city as a whole. In 2004 there were 158 mosques recorded in the West Midlands compared to 9 synagogues, 51 gurdwaras and 57 other (Eastern) religious bodies. Of course, this is dwarfed by 3,123 trinitarian, 138 non-trinitarian and 644 'other' Christian places of worship, but it does signify the importance of the Muslim presence in the county (Weller, 2008: 65). In 2003 it was estimated that in Birmingham there were 120,000 Muslims (12% of the city population), 45,000 Sikhs, 40,000 Hindus, 5,000+ Buddhists, 2,600 Jews and about 200 Jain families. The same study also estimated that there were approximately 60,000 people with their origin in Africa or the African Caribbean. In addition, there are now second and third generation immigrants from the 1950s and 1960s, who form an integral part of the local community. This socio-religious situation is also dynamic, for example, with the recent influx of eastern Europeans, especially Polish immigrants. 'The City Council already accepts that Birmingham will become a Black and Asian majority city before the year 2020' (Hewer, 2003: 68). However, this Black and Asian population is largely concentrated within a 2 mile radius of the city centre. In some districts 83% of primary school children are Muslim, with some schools having 100% Muslim pupils (69).

It is clear that Pentecostals do not just engage with the social reality of religious pluralism but also with the idea of the 'secular' state as irreligious. It is here that we need to define the concept of a much contested word: secularisation (cf. Davie, 2007: 46–66). José Casanova's definition includes three features: (1) a differentiation between distinct spheres of life, with the secular being denoted as distinct from 'religious institutions and norms'; (2) a decline in religious beliefs and practices; and (3) the marginalisation of religion to the private sphere (Casanova, 1994: 211). It is a concept that is now much debated by sociologists of religion and theologians where once it was accepted as normative (Martin, 2005; Gräb and Charbonier, 2009). It has been called into question as an inevitable product of modernisation (Davie, 2007: 64). Nevertheless, for the purposes of this analysis, Casanova's desciption is useful. In his terms, it can be seen that Pentecostals are not just concerned with the decline in religious affiliation, which they seek to address through evangelism, but also with the accompanying 'demoralisation' – that is, the loss of a shared set of moral values in the public sphere that are based on the Christian tradition (Wilson, 2003). They combine this concern for 'traditional values' with the freedom to make personal affirmations of faith (Plüss, 1999: 178). As noted above, Pentecostals, on the whole, accept differentiation (separation between church and state) but reject decline in religiosity as inevitable and the marginalisation of Christian faith to the private sphere.

In an update to his previous work, Kay considers the accommodation of Pentecostal and Charismatic Christianity in the face of secularisation (2008). In secularisation theory, not only is society becoming less religious in general terms, but smaller religious sects are turning into accommodating groups or denominations, such that they are less anti-worldly and become willing to compromise on exclusive truth claims. He argues that Pentecostals have resisted secularisation by (1) being *isolated* through rejection and ostracism, by their own evaulation of the world as an evil place, their holiness teaching which forbade them to participate in leisure pursuits, and a lack of educated leadership (Allen, 1990: 240); (2) using strong *organisation* that specified beliefs, clarified relationships and established leadership; (3) managing *growth*, despite the decline of other churches, thus validating their beliefs, combined with a clear and authoritative message; (4) offering a *worldview* that expects the Holy Spirit to intervene and God to provide, enchanted by both the wonders of technology and the wonders of God; and (5) providing a *social utility*, where people could find supportive relationships through large or small gatherings, and purpose in life.

Reflection

An early sociological study of religion in Birmingham suggested that 'the sectarian Churches, whose membership is generally increasing, appear to be uninvolved in community relations and activities beyond the sphere of evangelism' (Jarvis and Fielding, 1971: 97). While this may have been accurate in 1971, it would certainly be untrue for HPC today, with a number of different community orientated activities, even if evangelism remains paramount for the church (Weaver, 1972: 16). Although HPC members would tend to be exclusivist in relation to soteriology (the words of John 14.6 form a huge text on the side of the church and it is visible to the passing traffic), there is a distinct openness to the Spirit working in the world and in the lives of non-Christians, based on, but nevertheless enlarging, its existing worldview. This suggests it is accompanied by a more inclusivist pneumatology, even if this would not be regarded as salvific in itself. They would also align themselves with the majority of global Pentecostals who regard their faith as a public matter and therefore reject the public/private dichotomy of secular thinking. The open and public demonstration of faith is regarded as a fundamental human right (Article 18 of *The Universal Declaration of Human Rights*),[2] an act of freedom befitting a once Christian nation, even if the nation is perhaps now 'post-Christian', hence the need for reverse mission. The numerical strength of Pentecostals globally means that it no longer could be regarded as strictly isolationist, although individual communities may still be so.

---

2   http://www.un.org/en/documents/udhr/index.shtml#a1; accessed on 23 September 2009.

However, HPC seems to rest on the edge of engagement and isolation, involved in some community action and co-operation with other Evangelical Christians, but lacking a wider ecumenical involvement (characteristic of the denomination as a whole in the UK and Pentecostals globally) and disinterested in interreligious dialogue or co-operative interreligious community action. The feeling is of wider societal antipathy towards Christianity in general, rather than Pentecostalism in particular. They are no longer a small, persecuted sect (cf. Wilson, 1961). Rather, the Assemblies of God denomination in general, and HPC in particular, is part of an established, mainstream Evangelical Christianity in the UK.

Pentecostal Theology of Religions

There are two contributors to theology in the context of religious pluralism from a Pentecostal perspective that are able to inform this discussion.

Amos Yong is probably the leading Pentecostal theologian attempting to wrestle with a theology of religions (1999, 2000, 2003, 2005, 2008a, 2008b). He argues that Pentecostal missiology should emphasise *both* the proclamation of the Christian message *and* interreligious dialogue (Yong, 2000: 214). A Pentecostal theology of religions should be used alongside the attempt to understand religious traditions in their own terms and in their concrete expressions. The Holy Spirit is understood as being active in creation, humanity generally and in all cultures, which includes religions, and this specifically informs his thinking (311–312). Indeed, he argues that the world's religions are providentially sustained by the Spirit of God for divine purposes (Yong, 2003: 46). This can assist us to appreciate the positive aspects of religion, while the category of the demonic enables an account of destructive forces to be given. This pneumatic approach means that Pentecostals can adopt an open posture, allowing the Spirit to give greater, if provisional, understanding of truth. Openness is best displayed in a dialogical attitude, a willingess to work with those who appear to bear the marks of the Spirit (in terms of fruit: love, joy, peace, etc.), while at the same time giving a freedom to proclaim the truth of the gospel of Jesus Christ (Yong, 2000: 313).

Therefore, a pneumatologically-driven approach has great potential for a positive engagement with other religious traditions, even for Pentecostals (Yong, 2005: 235–236). This is because there is an assumption that the Spirit has been poured out on all flesh and this includes all cultures, and part of culture is religious expression. In short: the Spirit of God is everywhere and this experience should lead us to be genuinely open to difference (cf. Solivan, 1998: 40). He expresses his concern that fellow Pentecostals should engage positively when he says:

> In many ways, pentecostals are still at the very beginning of this process. We have contented ourselves so far with dialoguing only with languages closest to ours – evangelical and fundamentalist forms of Christianity – and have either ignored the rest or warned our pentecostal faithful against consorting with these

'enemies' of the faith. Yet vital pentecostal faith in the late modern world requires
that we open things up. If a sectarian attitude that withdraws from the world is
motivated by fear, a dialogical attitude that engages the world is motivated by
the truth that sets people free. (Yong, 2005: 237)

Yong argues that the gospel always comes in cultural dress, just as Jesus of
Nazareth was a first-century male Jewish carpenter (what has been called the scandal
of particularity), so the church in every time and place is culturally conditioned, as
is the message it proclaims. It cannot be any other way. Therefore, theology must
be open to different perspectives (multi-perspectival), different discourses (multi-
disciplinary) and different cultural expressions (multi-cultural) (240). But, as he
contends, to open the multi-cultural door means opening the multi-religious door,
at least in the sense of recognising the multi-cultural reality of religion. He insists
that, because Christian identity is still being formed, we see through a glass dimly.
Our knowledge is finite this side of the *eschaton*, therefore we should be open to
the insights from other religious traditions. He gives the example of the parable of
the Good Samaritan (Lk 10.25–37), which illustrates how a 'religious other' can
have an educational and illuminating impact on one's own faith tradition.

In order to provide a theological framework for a Pentecostal and therefore
pneumatological appoach to interfaith encounter, Yong posits three hypotheses
(Yong, 2005: 250–253). First, God is universally present by his Spirit, therefore
he sustains religions for his divine purposes. This, in effect, simply restates the
omnipresence of God. Second, the Spirit ushers in the kingdom of God and insofar
as the signs of the kingdom are made manifest then these are also signs of the
Spirit's presence. '[R]eligion is resolutely intertwined with the human condition
and with human hopes and aspirations and is only arbitrarily divorced from
individual and communal identities' (251). Third, given the universal presence
of the Spirit, he can be said to be absent from religions when there are signs of
resistance to and activity against the kingdom of God (cf. Solivan, 1998: 41). The
eschatological 'not yet' of the kingdom of God points to the hiddenness of God in
human experience. In order to discern the activity of the Spirit in other religious
traditions, Yong encourages Pentecostals to understand the various contextual
and background factors in such an encounter (geographical, historical, economic,
political and social) and to focus on the particularities of the faith communities in
question. This must be followed by a genuine encounter with the religious other.
'To enter relationships is to be transformed by them, as all genuine relationships
are dialogical. This transformation affects our Christian identity' (Yong, 2005:
255).

Yong builds on this earlier work in a more recent book, which explores the
nature of interreligious relations using the concept of hospitality (Yong, 2008a;
cf. 2008b). He considers the multi-cultural and multi-religious nature of American
society, which is also regarded as democratic and secular. He highlights the
fact that there are two competing agendas: one to guard the rights, plurality and
freedom of religion and conscience, the other to retrieve the Judeo-Christian legacy

for contemporary society. The debate is between the value of diversity, which is understood as an essential resource for a globalised society, and the value of a cohesive vision, upon which the American nation was built. It has been framed as a debate between the virtue of pluralism and the vice of political correctness and relativism (Yong, 2008a: 30–31). In the USA there is no state-sponsored religion, yet religion and politics are intertwined. This leads Yong to argue for the need to cultivate both religious particularity and interreligious understanding. He contends that 'a vision for a respectful mutuality that is able to engage in dialogue about ultimately meaningful (religious) convictions and yet at the same time is strong enough to sustain commitments to the public good' (31). He develops an approach to interreligious dialogue by means of a set of pneumatic practices presented in the form of four theses. These are as follows:

> *Thesis 1* – For Christians, Jesus Christ is not only the paradigmatic host representing and offering the redemptive hospitality of God, but he does so as the exemplary guest who went out into a far country …
>
> *Thesis 2* – For Christians, the gift of the Holy Spirit signifies the extension of God's economy of abundant hospitality into the whole world …
>
> *Thesis 3* – For Christians, the practices of hospitality therefore embody the trinitarian character of God's economy of redemption …
>
> *Thesis 4* – For Christians, then, the redemptive economy of the triune God invites our participation as guests and hosts in the divine hospitality revealed in Christ by the power of the Holy Spirit. (Yong, 2008a: 126–127)

Christian mission is participation in the hospitality of God, having received God's redemptive hospitality. Evangelism is nothing more than inviting others to experience the same (131). For Yong, it means participating in the trinitarian *missio dei*, which means seeing the presence of God throughout the created order and focusing on the kingdom of God, not merely the church. At the heart of this mission is reconciliation between God and humanity, but also between aliens and strangers (Volf, 1996). 'Christian mission is the embodiment of divine hospitality that loves strangers (*philoxenia*), to the point of giving up our lives on behalf of others as to be reconciled to them, that they might in turn be reconciled to God' (Yong, 2008a: 131). This means, for Yong, that hospitality becomes 'stranger-centred' rather than church-centred. In this approach the church aims to open up a 'free space' for encounter with the religious other in order to become friends. It also means entering into a reciprocal relationship whereby hospitality is received, not just given, and in such a scenario there is a vulnerability, which should be seen as a necessary part of the process of hospitality.

From an ecclesial perspective, it means 'a visible and welcoming public face, a dialogical posture, and a commitment to public servanthood' (134). It may be that the church can engage with other religious traditions through common causes, or neighbourhood projects or meals, which play an important role in hospitality. Yong suggests that the Wesleyan eucharistic tradition of an 'open table' fits best with such an approach to hospitality. He also avers that this could be extended, not necessarily in sacramental terms, but in fellowship terms with people of other faiths (136). Following Barth (1956: 414–425), he argues that the love of one's neighbour participates in the absoluteness of God's love and our response to that love (Yong, 2008a: 151). Indeed, the love of God to us is oftentimes mediated via the stranger (e.g. the Good Samaritan). The contribution of the stranger can be 'sacramental' in the sense of revealing something of the hospitality of God. For Yong, Christ is omnipresent, so that in such an interfaith encounter, it is possible not only for the religious other to witness Christ in Christians, but also the other way around. Christian hospitality is premised on the assumption that Christ may be present in guests: such a 'sacramental moment' is interpreted by Yong pneumatologically (Rom 5.5) (Yong, 2008a: 153).

Yong applies his approach to three types of religious others: the immigrant, the exile and the refugee. The issue of immigration is the most pertinent to this study. He suggests that a theology of immigration should attend to religious diversity. Following Alfred Ancel (1974), he suggests that immigrants should be considered as brothers (and sisters) rather than strangers. Friendship should be established in a brotherly or sisterly spirit, which can enrich church life, through its 'epistemological rupture', as perspectives from the margin are encountered. Although theology should consider the wider implications of globalisation and the reasons for immigration, it should include moments of dialogue when aliens and strangers come together as guests and hosts around a table of friendship and fellowship (Yong, 2008a: 156).

Fellow Pentecostal Tony Richie is also someone who has considered the question of Pentecostals and interfaith dialogue in his doctoral thesis (Richie, 2010). He observes that Pentecostalism has been usually regarded as exclusivist regarding its attitudes to other religions. He traces this theology to its historical connections in conservative Evangelicalism and Fundamentalism (Richie, 2010: 72). But he also suggests that there is an emerging inclusivist approach, which has been influenced by Jürgen Moltmann (1978) and Clark Pinnock (1992, 1996). He is especially appreciative of Pinnock, who sees other religious traditions not as vehicles of salvation but as nevertheless experiencing something of the Spirit of God and therefore open to the possibilities of salvation, being pre-Christian rather than non-Christian (Richie, 2010: 78). This strain, he contends, is also present in the early classical Pentecostal tradition, through the writings of Charles Fox Parham and J.H. King. It is picked up by Veli-Matti Kärkkäinen and his trinitarian approaches to other religions (2002: 229–239; 2004), as well as Amos Yong, noted above. Richie summarises the importance of the work of Kärkkäinen and Yong when he says:

> For Kärkkäinen and Yong, then, it is important that a Pentecostal theology of religions should help Pentecostal Christians engage the religions through discernment rather than through any *a priori* views about the religions. This means that people of other faiths need to be heard first on their own terms, even

while (Pentecostal) Christians would also be invited or even required to testify in their own tongues. The key here is to be able to comprehend other religions according to their own self-understanding, without prejudging or defining them according to our own Christian (or Pentecostal) theological categories (for example, in exclusivist, inclusivist, or pluralist terms). Such a Pentecostal approach thus sustains and motivates the inter-religious encounter, and does so as part of the Christian mission. (Richie, 2010: 83)

Richie argues for a distinctly Pentecostal approach to other religions that uses the work of Lesslie Newbigin as a launch pad (exclusive concerning the unique revelation in Jesus Christ, non-exclusive in allowing the possibility of the salvation of the non-Christian; inclusive in not limiting the saving grace of God to the church, but non-inclusive in rejecting other religions as vehicles of salvation; pluralist in acknowledging the work of God in the lives of all people, but rejecting a pluralism that denies the uniqueness and decisiveness of what has been done in Jesus Christ) (87; Newbigin, 1989: 182–183). Using the narrative of Acts 2 and the day of Pentecost to offer a Pentecostal perspective, he observes that the outpouring of the Spirit enabled a diversity of tongues: the many tongues retain their particularity even as they point to the unity of the one Spirit. These many tongues correspond to the many cultures of the Mediterranean world, which in turn relate to the many different religions (cf. Solivan, 1998: 42). Given this relationship between religion and culture, Richie suggests that these tongues represent, at least potentially, many religions, which in turn point to the redemption of religions (eschatologically) as well as languages and cultures (Richie, 2010: 89). But he also qualifies this statement by observing that this is not a baptism of cultures as a whole, rather it merely points to the freedom of God to work within different cultures. From a Pentecostal perspective it means that cultures (including their religious expressions) must be discerned via an *a posteriori* approach. Just as prophetic words are weighed after they have been spoken (1 Cor 14.29), so it is only after an interfaith encounter that judgments are made. The tongues or testimonies of the religious other must first be heard in their own terms before a theology of religion can be constructed. This will involve a critical analysis of religious beliefs and practices, using a 'hermeneutic of charity' (or perhaps one might say, following Yong, a hermeneutic of hospitality; cf. Richie, 2010: 113–115, and Yong, 2008a) that attempts first to understand before making a judgment, even if there will also be a hermeneutic of suspicion because of the urgency of the gospel. Judgments should be regarded as provisional and open to revision at any future moment (Richie, 2010: 91–92).

Given this background of Pentecostal approaches to the issue of the religious other, Richie proposes a model of Pentecostal engagement based on the notion of testimony. By testimony, in this context, Richie means telling others of what God has done in one's life in order to encourage them (165). These stories also 'illuminate, clarify and verify' God's work in people's lives (166; cf. Arrington, 2003). They remind others that God still works in today's world. They also hold out the possibility that God can do it for you too. It can be transformative for the testifier and hearer alike as new possibilities are opened up by the narrative. It is an important ritual in worship as it witnesses to the ongoing encounter with God (Boone, 1996). Therefore, it is regarded as a highly prized act and integral to Pentecostal spirituality, containing as it does significant autobiographical elements and doxological content. It is thus an expression of the 'orally based, narratively expressed tradition' (Ellington, 2000), as well as being a commitment mechanism (McGuire, 1977).

Applying testimony to interreligious dialogue, Richie contends, is the most obvious Pentecostal *modus operandi*. He suggests that it benefits Pentecostals for the reasons noted above and helps 'retain their original energy and vitality' (Richie, 2010: 195). Therefore, the dialogue with religious others should not be primarily a 'cognitive conversation' but rather an exercise in story-telling that illustrates and exemplifies their own identity. Discursive interactions may follow, as the religious others tell their own stories in turn, which may result in mutual understanding. He summarises this approach when he says:

> For Pentecostals, inter-religious testimony is still a telling in faith of how the Christian story as told in Scripture gets lived out in contemporary lives by the power of the Spirit. Religious others may be then expected and invited to respond according to their own perceptions. Here testimony contributes to dialogue as it involves genuine exchange between participants. Of course, discernment and judgment are necessary in evaluating testimonies offered around the dialogue table. From the Pentecostal perspective, Scripture and the anointing of the Holy Spirit give reliable and worthy guidance. The contextual environment of the historical or traditional community of faith and the input of rational thought are also helpful aids. Presumably, the rich traditions of religious others will also provide them with tradition specific standards by which to hear and evaluate testimonies. (Richie, 2010: 198–199)

Participation is essential for this form of dialogue to be successful. However, Richie is ambivalent about the goal of such testimony/dialogue being conversion. He prefers to leave the outcome as open, allowing the Holy Spirit to work in unpredictable ways, and allowing for transformation to be two-way. Rather, Pentecostals should see this form of testimony as also a form of worship, a form of doxology. Indeed, Richie would place it within a triad of practices: prayer, testimony and dialogue. That is, prayer precedes the activity and hopefully dialogue emerges afterwards, thus the three become inseparable (2010: 205–206).

Reflection

In many ways there is a clear resonance between the pneumatological reading of Yong and the openness recorded in the testimonies. However, I suspect that HPC members would not follow his apparent Christological inclusivity. The open posture of the members suggests that Pentecostal pneumatology can include the providential working of the Spirit in creation, humanity and culture. This point should be qualified by noting a conversation with Scott from Nigeria, who spoke to me a few days after the focus group meeting and distanced himself from some of the ideas that had been expressed. This perhaps expresses some of the intercultural and theological tensions that exist within the church but also within wider Pentecostalism. Nigeria is a country that has a terrible record of interreligious violence, even if in the south of the country Christians and Muslims live together relatively peacefully (at least this was my experience of living there in 1992–1993). A Nigerian Christian might be suspicious of other religious traditions, especially Islam, and therefore it is not surprising that a different attitude was expressed (Ukah, 2009; Kalu, 2008: 225–246).

Yong's point that sectarianism is motivated by fear is apposite, but in the context of a multi-faith city in the UK it needs further nuance. After the bombings in London on 7 July 2005, resulting in 52 deaths and over 700 injuries (Weller, 2008: 195), there is some degree of fear within large urban areas where there is a sizable Muslim community. The UK security services currently deal with a number of terrorist plots on a daily basis, which fuels the concern of ordinary members of the public. This context of the fear of terrorism inevitably shapes non-Muslim perceptions of Muslims in the UK and inhibits interreligious engagement on the ground. A recent Gallup survey of attitudes within the British public (1,001 telephone interviews) and British Muslims (504 face-to-face interviews) found that 49% of the British public do not consider British Muslims to be loyal to the UK as their country; and only 44% of the British public consider British Muslims to be respectful of other religions (Gallup, 2009: 20, 24). By contrast, 99% of British Muslims consider violent attacks on civilians as morally unjustified, with 89% stating that it is totally unjustified (39). Only 48% of British Muslims, however, consider the use of violence for a noble cause as unjustified at all, compared to 80% of German and 75% of French Muslims. The report concludes that '[s]ince 9/11 and the terrorist attacks in Madrid and London, mistrust toward European Muslims has become palpable. Significant segments of European societies openly express doubts that Muslim fellow nationals are loyal citizens' (45). Given the suspicions that most Pentecostals have towards Muslims in general (Gerloff, 2008: 216), it is no surpise that this attitude appears to be reinforced at this current time. Therefore, the concrete realities of the UK would perhaps suggest that there are forces at work which mean that religious traditions are starting from a point further back than perhaps could be expected before 2005.

Yong's analysis of American society certainly finds resonance with the HPC members and could be translated to the UK, although the religious histories are different. The two competing agendas – rights and plurality, on the one hand, versus the role of the Christian tradition, on the other – are also being played out here. But, of course, the situation is somewhat different because of the smaller number of practising Christians compared to the USA, even as the state church gives a certain kind of public Christian presence. It is here that the political correctness and relativism noted by Yong has relevance. It is precisely this rhetoric in the public domains of the nation that has added to the sense of the marginalisation of Christian discourse. For Yong, the way to address the situation is not overtly political, but rather by means of hospitality, as guests and host sit around a meal table. But is this approach really going to change attitudes within the media? Indeed, even getting a seat at the table without conforming to stereotypical expectations appears to be a tall order.

Richie is concerned that Pentecostals learn to listen to religious others – that is, they hear them on their own terms, before labelling and dismissing them. The diversity of the many religious traditions mirrors the many tongues of Pentecost, thus enabling Pentecostals to at least be open to the possibility of the Spirit working beyond the boundaries of the church. God is free to work through the diversity of cultures and therefore his work must be discerned *a posteriori*, using a hermeneutic of charity, which is virtually identical to Yong's concept of hospitality. Some of the HPC members would, I think, be open to an engagement with other religious traditions, but bracketing out presuppositions in order to discern what the Spirit is doing through the other *a posteriori* is a significant shift. Indeed, it requires a lot of groundwork to be done in order to reach this place of openness, which, as I have noted above, the current social and political context makes more challenging.

Richie suggests that the mechanism for a distinctly Pentecostal approach is testimony itself, telling the story of what God has done and is doing in one's life. From this can flow a conversation about details of doctrine, values and practice, with an openness to the outcome of such an encounter. Certainly my experience of facilitating the story-telling of Pentecostals at HPC would suggest that Richie is certainly on to something and this is a very real mode of engagement. However, I suspect that most of the Pentecostals involved in this kind of meeting would not see it as merely dialogue or a conversation but as an act of evangelism. To tell one's story of God's operative grace is to proclaim the gospel through the medium of testimony. One of the observations from my own research is to note the rhetorical force of testimony: it aims to persuade listeners. If there is a degree of openness to other religious traditions, then there is also a strong commitment to evangelism (cf. Lord, 2003). Is this inherently problematic? Not necessarily. However, on Richie's account it inhibits dialogue *a priori* because the other becomes merely objectified as 'conversion fodder'. Again, there is a significant point of tension, but this is not new and has been observed in other European contexts (Westerlund, 2009).

Rescripting Ordinary Theology

An attempt at rescripting Pentecostal theology of life and witness would include a number of features, which could derive from one central theological belief, namely: the lordship of Jesus Christ.

HPC would not be expected to compromise its life and witness as based in a confession that Jesus Christ is Lord. This is a very basic creedal statement, and perhaps the earliest of all Christian confessions (1 Cor 12.3). Christians confess as an act of faith that he is the Lord of the whole of creation and this means society, cultures, including other religious traditions, as well as the life of the church. If Christ is Lord, there need be no fear of the other who is different, because all things are ultimately under his lordship. To affirm the work of the Spirit in the world does not mean that Pentecostals are advocates of religious pluralism in a prescriptive sense, far from it (Gallagher, 2006: 31), but it does mean that fear can be replaced by confidence and hope. This confidence and hope, together with humility (because it is fundamentally the work of God), can lead to openness and engagement rather than closure and withdrawal. The sectarian attitudes of the past can be reversed. The contexts in which these Pentecostals are located can therefore be approached in a different manner.

Given the fact that Pentecostals at HPC represent many countries from around the world, they are a symbol of what it means to live together in harmony despite the many differences of culture and language. In their faith they have found a unity that transcends cultural differences. They have discovered a theology of embrace, not of exclusion (Volf, 1996). Again, it is rooted in the lordship of Christ over the church. It is the Lord of the church, who calls people into a unity despite the multi-cultural differences that exist. This does not mean that there are no disagreements or even tensions. This can be seen in the dissenting Nigerian voice. But there is a genuine acceptance of the other Christian within a culturally pluralistic congregation. Of course, there is indeed some degree of tension between immigrants and the host culture, but the church provides a 'home from home' and allows for integration to be negotiated more easily. It provides a bridge community that is rooted in the host society.

The suspicion and hostility towards secular British culture, the government and the media can also be transformed. If Christ is Lord not just over the church but over the whole of creation, then the Spirit of the Lord will be active in all of the structures of creation. It is true that British society is less hospitable to Christian values than it used to be, and it is true that the government is less amenable to certain Christian beliefs than in previous generations (although perhaps this is a moot point); and it is certainly true that the media are more hostile in their representation of Christianity than they ever have been: chasing the sensational, setting up false alternatives and consciously ignoring nuances and subtleties. But, these attitudes can be only modified by engagement rather than withdrawal. The secularist dichotomy of public truth versus private values is being challenged by Christians who see the whole of creation as the arena for God's good purposes. A theology of engagement is required whereby Pentecostals seek to appreciate what God is already doing in the world by his Spirit and join in. This requires discernment and can mean both affirmation, where appropriate, and critique, where appropriate.

Any attempt by scholars of religion to turn classical Pentecostals into theological liberals should be resisted as ideologically motivated. Nevertheless, a modified conservative position could take its cue from Richie's appropriation of Newbigin.

It could be affirmed in its stance as exclusive in relation to the unique revelation in Jesus Christ, but allow the possibility of the salvation of the non-Christian, based upon the universal working of the Spirit of God beyond the boundaries of the church. It could be inclusive in not limiting the saving grace of God to the church, even as it is non-inclusive in rejecting other religions as vehicles of salvation. Of course, to be entirely consistent it would also have to affirm that religion *qua* religion does not save, and that includes expressions of Christianity, not just other religions (but most British Pentecostals would happily agree with this idea as they look at the quality of state religion!). It would acknowledge the work of God in the lives of *all* people, but reject a pluralism that denies the uniqueness or lordship of Jesus Christ. It would reject naive universalism. This theological statement is in continuity with Pentecostal theology, even if it has an openness to the possibility that God is operating salvifically outside of the church. Along the lines of Yong and Richie, it could be suggested that the proper theological posture is an openness to hospitality, charity and a willingness to negotiate, or at the very least begin a conversation (cf. Tan-Chow, 2007). To cite Yong again: '[i]f a sectarian attitude that withdraws from the world is motivated by fear, a dialogical attitude that engages with the world is motivated by the truth that sets people free' (Yong, 2005: 237).

Summary

Pentecostals, as part of the worldwide church, seek to live out the Christian message in the context in which they are situated. This means witnessing to those among whom they live in today's society based upon their own beliefs and values. In the context of Birmingham this brings together issues of Pentecostal identity, secular society and multi-culturalism. Multi-culturalism brings with it a multi-religious reality. The testimonies articulated the Pentecostal desire to witness to their Christian experience, the role of the Holy Spirit as guide in witnessing, and the tensions that the contexts bring, especially regarding political correctness, other religious traditions and the way in which Christianity is portrayed by the media and government. The transition from minority sect to respected denomination is charted by Kay (1989), who suggests that the Assemblies of God denomination is now part of the Evangelical mainstream in the UK. Pentecostal churches have grown over the course of the twentieth century and they have generally bucked the trend in the decline in religious attendance among mainstream denominations. Even though the majority of the population regard themselves, in some sense, as being Christian, they do not practise their religion through attendance at places of worship. This is in stark contrast to Pentecostal denominations in the UK. Against this background, it can be seen that HPC has grown in recent years, with its numbers being augmented through the acceptance of immigrants. The church is engaged with its community, yet also limited in its partnerships and thus displays a reservation towards other religious traditions. Members of the church expressed openness towards the Spirit at work in the world, including other religious cultures, although there was not a uniformity of understanding here. There is some concern about other religious traditions, which are perceived as potentially violent towards Christianity and the general population of the UK, which resonates with attitudes towards Islam reported in a recent Gallup survey (2009). It is suggested that a dialogical posture is a possible way forward based upon the notion of hospitality, which draws upon the most recent Pentecostal scholarship in the field of the theology of religion (Yong, 2008a; Richie, 2010).

Chapter 8
World Mission and the Second Coming

Eschatology is extremely important for Pentecostals. The early Pentecostals were motivated in their missionary endeavours because of their belief in the imminent return of Jesus Christ. For Pentecostals it is inextricably linked to the mission of the church and continues to be so today. However, even though this doctrine of the second coming of Christ is an important motivation to evangelise, it also appears as though there is a fair degree of uncertainty around the subject. On this topic it was difficult to start with a testimony or personal narrative because of the nature of the subject matter. Therefore, it was explored by means of a dialogue between the researcher and members of the focus group. The dialogue is described below and gives some important and interesting insights into the thinking and understanding of the members of HPC. The only time that the subject of eschatology was discussed publicly was when a visiting Pentecostal evangelist, David Hathaway, preached one Sunday morning. This public declaration of theology is juxtaposed with the ordinary beliefs of the members in order to raise some of the inherent tensions that are present in contemporary Pentecostalism. The chapter will contextualise the material in relation to early and classical Pentecostal theology, before considering recent discussions of Pentecostal millennialism and millenarian discourse. These perspectives will be used to interpret the ordinary eschatology before being rescripted with the use of theological resources from Pentecostal scholarship.

A Dialogue

The Focus Group

The focus group contained seven women and two men. The men were young and originated from Nigeria (Gerald) and the UK (Luke). Their occupations were in business (Gerald) and heavy goods driving (Luke). The women were mostly either middle-aged (Linda, Elinor and Louise) or relatively young (Philippa, Yvonne and Geraldine), with one elderly woman (Lois). They originated from Germany (Philippa), Nigeria (Yvonne and Elinor), Jamaica (Louise), Montserrat (Geraldine) and the UK (Lois and Linda). Their occupations included sales representative (Philippa), nurse and fitness instructor (Geraldine), legal practitioner (Elinor), cook (Louise), unspecified (Linda), unemployed (Yvonne) and retired (Lois).

The discussion elicited beliefs and opinions as to what will happen in the future regarding the second coming of Jesus Christ, world mission and the role of the

Holy Spirit. What follows is a transcript of the conversation in the group, which captures the contours of the dialogue.

> *Geraldine*: We were taught from the Bible that the Holy Spirit was sent after Jesus ascended into heaven, so basically [to] guide us so that when he comes he will take, he will guide us as to what we need to do while he's preparing a place for us. So that's the link between the second coming. It's … trying to get us all to work as one, to get us ready for Jesus' return, so that's how I see it anyway.

> *Mark*: Okay. Do you think the second coming is going to be soon or not?

> *Georgina*: Very soon.

> *Mark*: Very soon. How soon?

> *Gerald*: Very soon in the sense that, actually, it will be concerning the fact that the Holy Spirit is the one that will do most of the work. The gospel must be preached to all nations. Without the fact that all nations, all tribes, all different people must hear the gospel before the Lord Jesus Christ comes. That's one thing … there. And it is the Holy Spirit …

> *Mark*: So, you think that everybody will hear the gospel before Jesus returns or have the opportunity, do you think? And would you just clarify that one for me?

> *Gerald*: Actually everybody … I believe that it will be a privilege … but when one is preached to, the person gave his life to Christ but as far as he heard the gospel. Now whether to accept it or not now depends on [the] individual.

> *Mark*: Right, okay, but the gospel will be preached to all nations [agreement] and then Jesus will come. Anybody else have any thoughts on this?

> *Geraldine*: I think that we've got no excuse. In this time none of us have an excuse saying we haven't heard the gospel because we've got the internet, got the telephone, got the TV, we've got missionaries going out all around the world. So in that respect we've seen that the whole world has to hear the gospel before the coming. The whole world has heard the gospel, so … that's what I think.

> *Mark*: So are you saying that, is everybody else agreed, that Jesus is coming soon …?

> *Philippa*: I was always under the impression that there are preconditions, that a few other things that are mentioned in the Bible before he does come and relating to the Jews as well. I mean, as far as I know that hasn't happened as yet. No one knows when the Lord's coming because he announced it in a parable when Noah was preaching and

they said, like, the animals go in two by two and no one know when the Lord come but right now in the fulfilment of the Bible in the world going on now. 'Cos we're having nation fight against nation, brother killing brother, abusing, fathers abusing kids, so it's like the fulfilment is coming out to the end. But none of us know any time, 'cos I'm one of these people that we [are children] of God. That's when the Lord comes, we [are] on the right road ...

Elinor: Actually I can't really quote the Scriptures ... but when you hear of rumours of wars and all these things it's just the beginning of the end. Now I discovered with my husband a few days ago and I told him I was sick ... Especially in the middle list, it signifies that Christ is coming soon. It's just the beginning [agreement]. The real thing has not set in.

Mark: Do you want to put, I mean when you say Christ is coming soon, do you have a sense of what that timeframe might be or not? Soon: is that within 10 years, within 20 years ['no one knows' unidentified speaker], within 50 years ['nobody knows' unidentified speaker]? You don't know but you just think it's soon [agreement] ...?

Lois: I know the Lord said that when he went into heaven ..., he was sending the Holy Spirit and once they were filled with the Spirit they'd be able to go out to all the world, more or less to every nation to preach the gospel. And until every nation and every person's heard the gospel I don't think the Lord will return and plus the fact he said no man, only the Father, knows when he will return ...

Gerald: No one knows the exact day or the hour, no one know [unidentified speaker]. But as Christians what, you know, the Bible tell us is that there are signs [agreement] of what at least we will see that will signify the coming, the second coming of the Lord Jesus Christ. I've always said, now when we have rumours of war, you know, ... and all that, everything is [in] the Bible. So if we really, you know, we are taking time to monitor events, what is happening globally, we'll be able to know. But nobody can say the time or the date [of his] coming.

Summary of the Dialogue

In summary, we can describe the views of the group by saying that the Holy Spirit is understood to help Christians to prepare in unity for the return of Jesus, even as he empowers them to preach the gospel to all nations. It is only after the gospel has been preached to all nations that Christ will return (Mt 24.14). Everybody will have an opportunity to hear the gospel preached before Christ returns. But whether a person accepts Christ will be up to the individual. Today we have no excuse because of the media and electronic communication through the internet, telephone, TV and, of course, missionaries working around the world. There are preconditions to be fulfilled before the return of Jesus: the role of the Jews, the signs of wars, rumours of wars, and abuse of children are mentioned, even if these ideas are articulated imprecisely. At this time there is a need to monitor events globally to appreciate how these signs are being played out. However, the prediction of the date is impossible. The timing of the second coming is unknown. Only the Father knows when Jesus will return. But there is some degree of confidence in the fact that the second coming will be very soon, even if what that means cannot be defined in any meaningful timeframe.

A Sermon

On one Sunday morning a well-known Pentecostal preacher, David Hathaway, delivered a sermon in which he proposed a particular view of eschatology and commended it to the church. David Hathaway is the founder and president of Eurovision Mission to Europe and works as an evangelist in continental, and especially Eastern, Europe. He portrays himself as a person who has lived on the edge for God. He claims to have been 'miraculously released from a communist prison (in 1972), healed of cancer twice and almost killed on five occasions'.[1] Hathaway uses his Eurovision International TV Company to broadcast programmes to Europe, but especially targeted at Russia, the Ukraine and Germany. He also engages in public speaking at conventions and churches. Thirteen years ago he started a Christian magazine, *Prophetic Vision*, which now has three quarters of a million readers from 134 countries in six different languages. His stated vision is to evangelise Europe, especially Russia, and to exercise a ministry in Israel (he used to own an Israeli tour company called 'Crusader Tours' through which he also smuggled Bibles into communist Europe) via large campaigns and the use of the media; as well as exercising 'the power of a living God of miracles and healings'. But he also believes that by distributing the *Prophetic Vision* magazine worldwide he can 'prepare the whole church for the near return of Christ'.[2] For example, opening articles often contain references to biblical prophecy being fulfilled and the role that the magazine plays in preparing its readers for the second coming of Jesus Christ. Here is one extract from the magazine, illustrating the ways in which his views are expressed.

> The purpose and the vision of this magazine is not to simply bring a 'prophetic word' to individual 'believers' – but to demonstrate to believer and sceptic that the Prophetic Message of the Bible is literally being fulfilled in our world today – that in our life-time we are seeing the fulfilment of the final Biblical prophecies, which will see the Return of the Messiah, Jesus the Christ. However – because I believe that this is happening now, this magazine is intended to challenge you and me to renew the call of God and to stir you and me to action to fulfil the Great Commission now! Time is short – the Lord is coming – we

---

[1] www.propheticvision.org.uk/david.html; accessed on 22 April 2009.

[2] www.propheticvision.org.uk/eurovision.html; accessed on 22 April 2009.

must show the lost that Christ will rule the world very soon – we must win them and save them from the fires of hell! This is why I cannot retire but must re-FIRE and do everything within my power, and with your help, to evangelise now!!! (Hathaway, 2008: 2)

The magazine also contains accounts of evangelistic rallies and numerous short testimonies of healing, which support the idea that the Spirit is being poured out in preparation for the coming of Christ.

In the sermon he said that Christianity was a challenge to the secular world and to other religions. He believes that in Russia the church is witnessing greater miracles than in any other country. Russia is referred to in the Bible as the 'land of the north', for example in the book of the prophet Jeremiah (16.14–15):

> However, the days are coming, declares the Lord, when men will no longer say, 'As surely as the LORD lives, who brought us up out of Egypt', but they will say, 'As surely as the LORD lives, who brought the Israelites up out of the land of the north and out of all the countries where he had banished them'. For I will restore them to the land I gave to their forefathers (NIV).

Hathaway received power from God as a young child (1 Pet 1.5), when he was blessed in an act of dedication by George Jeffreys, as Jeffreys visited his home. He believes that faith is the greatest gift and that God has protected him, even though there have been attempts on his life. He believes that Jesus is the healer because 'it is in the atonement'. His faith has been tested (1 Pet 1.7), but he has come through the tests (Heb 11.1). This is because faith is about trust and he trusts in God. He even broadcasts into Germany from Russia, where there are 6 million viewers on a Sunday morning. In the European Union a broadcaster cannot declare that salvation is in the name of Jesus, but since he broadcasts from Russia, he is not limited by this ruling. At the moment there is a revival in Russia and it will come to England. It will be the last great revival before the return of Jesus and it will happen through Russia, with the evidence of miracles.

In many ways, David Hathaway is a contemporary example of the sort of eschatological fervour that many early Pentecostals demonstrated. To understand his theology, it is important to consider early Pentecostal material, which displays many similar characteristics.

Early and Classical Pentecostalism

The American Pentecostal revival at the Azusa Street Mission, Los Angeles, 1906–1909, led by William J. Seymour, linked the outpouring of the Spirit to the belief that this was occurring in 'the last century of the second Christian millennium. This seemed to signal the imminent return of the Lord. Time was running out, and people needed to be saved!' (Robeck, 2006: 235). The use of the language of 'latter rain' (Joel 2.23) suggested that the final act of the church was taking place and the 'full gospel' needed to be preached. This anticipation of the second coming of Jesus Christ was also linked to the gift of speaking in tongues because of the belief that this gift provided a missionary language enabling the evangelism of people in foreign lands. Thus, the Azusa Street Mission's newspaper, *The Apostolic Faith* (1906–1908), illustrated this understanding when it stated:

> The gift of languages is given with the commission, 'Go ye into all the world and preach the Gospel to every creature.' The Lord has given languages to the unlearned Greek, Latin, Hebrew, French, German, Italian, Chinese, Japanese, Zulu and the languages of Africa, Hindu and Bengali and dialects of India, Chippewa and other languages of the Indians, Esquimaux, the deaf mute language and, in fact the Holy Ghost speaks all the languages of the world through His children. (*The Apostolic Faith*, 1906)

Robeck describes the process that took place in the Mission when someone spoke in what was considered a foreign language.

> Essentially, when someone spoke in a tongue, the mission followed a four-step procedure. First, they attempted to identify the language. Second, if they felt they had identified it, they sought to establish whether the speaker believed he or she had received a missionary 'call'. Third, if the tongues-speaker claimed to have received such a call, the mission staff tried to discern whether the call was genuine and whether the person was ready and willing to go. Finally, if the person testified to a readiness to go, and the mission discerned the necessary gifts and call, then they gave the candidate the money to reach the foreign field, and he or she left town within days, if not hours. (Robeck, 2006: 239)

This description suggests the coalescence of a number of beliefs in early American Pentecostal missiology, namely: the outpouring of the Spirit signalled that the second coming of the Lord Jesus was imminent, that there was a harvest of souls to be gathered in before his return, and that missionary tongues was the key to this worldwide revival (cf. McQueen, 2009). The Lord Jesus was expected to return before the missionaries would be expected home: they were missionaries of the 'one-way ticket' (Synan, 1997: 127).

When we turn to the early British Pentecostal movement, we see similar views reported in *Confidence* (e.g. 1908c, 1909a): speaking in tongues is understood as the ability to speak foreign languages on the mission field. However, the editor (Boddy) does not appear to subscribe to this view (*Confidence*, 1908b, 1908f). Within a short time it was realised that these missionaries could not really speak the foreign language and the belief began to be qualified (Anderson, 2007: 61). Nevertheless, eschatology, the emphasis on the second coming of Christ, and its impact on the urgency of the mission of the church was maintained (Anderson, 2004: 217–220; 2007: 219–223). As Faupel (1996) states, '[t]he belief in the imminent premillennial return of Christ proved to be the primary motivation for evangelization and world mission' (21).

Following on from existing Holiness and revivalist traditions, it is arguable that the expectation of the imminent return of Christ was *the* significant aspect to the theology of *Confidence* and that the other features must be seen as fitting into this overarching concern (Cartledge, 2008a; cf. Walsh, 2010). Many of the issues of *Confidence* begin with the words of new songs, emerging from the context of praise and worship. By far the most dominant theme is the second coming of Christ, as illustrated by titles such as: 'The Bride is Getting Ready', 'Caught Up', 'The Midnight Cry', 'Be Ye also Ready', 'He is Coming', 'Soon', 'Surely I Come Quickly', 'The Coming of the Lord', 'Behold, I Come!', and 'When our King Comes'. Visions, sermons and addresses, articles, extracts from books, as well as criticisms of the precise date of the Rapture and Tribulation, suggest a definite preoccupation with the eschatological.

The eschatological expectation of an imminent return of Christ was signalled in the very first issue of *Confidence*, where the Pentecostal experience was likened to the promised 'Latter Rain', to speed the ripening of the harvest before the End (based on Dt 11. 10–15; Faupel, 1996: 30–32). The waiting church is experiencing 'sublime and supernatural preparations' for the moment, as the midnight cry of 'Behold the Bridegroom cometh; go forth to meet him' is 'echoed and re-echoed in holy joy from land to land by thousands of Spirit-inspired voices'. It is 'a watch of Spirit-enkindled love and worship, of welcome and expectation; a watch of Spirit-empowered service and co-operation in the divine programme so blessedly nearing fulfilment' (*Confidence*, 1908a).

The first Sunderland Conference was regarded as an auspicious occasion, because to gather together so many people in such short a time suggested that the 'Latter Rain' outpouring was a foretaste of what God was going to do in preparation for the return of Jesus (*Confidence*, 1908d). At the evening meeting of 10 June 1908, Miss Barbour from Wimbledon proclaimed that the End was near because certain signs had been given: (1) the biblical dates point to about 1914 (based on specific OT calculations); (2) the Jewish people are returning to the Land as never before; and (3) the Lord is revealing directly to the hearts of people that he is coming soon. This was followed by an address delivered by Miss Elizabeth Sisson from the USA who stated that as soon as his people are ready the Lord will come. At the moment the Bride is not ready, just as the first fruits of the harvest are not yet displayed (*Confidence*, 1908e; cf. Faupel, 1996: 22).

Boddy identified the seven signs that indicate the imminent return of Christ. These are: (1) the end of the times of the Gentiles, when they rule Jerusalem (estimated as 2,520 years from the reign of Nebuchadnezzar until somewhere between 1913–16, with a possible margin of 35 years); (2) the return of the Jews to the Holy Land, which is beginning to happen; (3) the fulfilment of the dream of Daniel (Dan 2.31–35), resulting finally in the democratic age; (4) the Apostasy in Christian lands where Christianity is discredited; (5) great earthquakes around the world; (6) the gospel preached to every nation, and now we are living in the greatest missionary age since Pentecost; and (7) the Latter Rain outpoured, which has literally increased in Palestine every decade in the past 50 years as a type of an outpouring before the 'last Harvest'. All these signs indicate the fact that 'Jesus is coming soon' (Boddy, 1910b).

The 'day of the Lord' is described as containing a number of scenes in sequence. These include: (1) the watchnight, the waiting for the coming of Christ by his faithful; (2) in the morning of the 'last day', the Lord comes and the first resurrection of the saints takes place; (3) afterwards in heaven the saints are rewarded and there is the marriage supper of the Lamb; on earth there is the Tribulation led by the figures of Satan, the Anti-Christ and the False prophet, with possible successive translations of the saints; (4) at noon the Lord descends onto the Mount of Olives with his saints and the battle of Armageddon takes place, with Jesus being victorious; (5) the millennial reign of Christ begins from Jerusalem to whole of the world; (6) in the evening there is a short revival by Satan before his utter destruction with his supporters; (7) the closing scenes of the last day see the second resurrection of the impenitent dead and those who are still in the grave before the Great White Throne; and the eternal ages commence with a new heaven and a new earth, when God is all in all and those who love the Lord will receive their crowns of righteousness (Boddy, 1910c). In another article Boddy offers a similar version, with a diagram depicting 'The Seven Ages of the World's History and the Soon Coming of the Lord' (Boddy, 1911, 1914). The 'day' is given further time allocations, with the tribulation lasting between 2.5 years and 40 years (the diagram has 3.5 or 7 or more years!). This demonstrates that he believed in a version of pre-tribulation premillennialism based upon the dispensationalism of John Nelson Darby, made popular through the Scofield Reference Bible of 1909. That is, the rescue or rapture of the saints will occur prior to the tribulation, followed by the battle of Armageddon and the millennial reign of Christ on earth (Faupel, 1996: 29, 97–98; Anderson, 2004: 218–219; Kay, 2009: 39–40).

The experience of Pentecost was sometimes associated with the anticipation of the rapture, as noted by Pastor Paul in 1911. It led him to look for the coming of the Lord very soon, just like a bride waiting for the bridegroom. He likened tongues to 'the veil', so that when he is singing in tongues in his heart it is as if he has his veil and feels enclosed within it. Just as tongues edify the speaker, so to look on Jesus as the coming bridegroom edifies the bride. We live at the time of the midnight cry, 'Behold, the bridegroom comes!' (Paul, 1911). A conversation printed in September of 1911 suggests that the 'heavenly anthem' (singing in tongues) is so evocative of heaven itself that there is a view that the saints will be speaking or singing in tongues when the rapture occurs and thus find themselves singing in the air (*Confidence*, 1911).

The Assemblies of God denomination in the UK is an inheritor of this early Pentecostal theology (Gee, 1924, 1927; Coates, 1928; Horton, 1934; Carter, 1934; Vale, 1935; Woodford, 1939). Up to end of the twentieth century it still adhered to 'the pre-millennial second coming of the Lord Jesus Christ', even if the heightened sense of expectation had faded (Hollenweger, 1972: 520; Kay, 1998: 56; 2000b: 95). But its current formal statement of faith on the subject reads as follows:

> 3. We believe in the Virgin Birth, Sinless Life, Miraculous Ministry, Substitutionary Atoning Death, Bodily Resurrection, Triumphant Ascension and Abiding Intercession of the Lord Jesus Christ and in His personal, visible, bodily return in power and glory as the blessed hope of all believers (Isa. 7:14; Matt. 1:23; Heb. 7:26; 1 Pet. 2:22; Acts 2:22, 10:38; 2 Cor. 5:21; Heb. 9:12; Luke 24:39; 1 Cor. 15:4; Acts 1:9; Eph. 4:8–10; Rom. 8:34; Heb. 7:25; 1 Cor. 15:22–24, 51–57; 1 Thess. 4:13–18; Rev. 20:1–6).[3]

What is interesting about this statement is that it is set within the life and ministry of Jesus Christ rather than the mission of the church. It is also interesting for what is not described: premillennialism is now missing. The return of Christ is now described in much less imminent terms, and while 'personal, visible, bodily' in 'power and glory' are still used, there is a lack of urgency so characteristic of the earlier movement. This is the outcome of a debate between a convinced but non-exclusivist premillennial position (Hyde, 2002), which sees it as one among a number of possible eschatological positions, and a more traditional exclusivist Pentecostal position (Garrard, 2003). Clearly, the less precise and more inclusive position has won the day, at least for the moment.

A fascinating parallel discussion can be found in the British Elim Pentecostal denomination as described by James J. Glass (1996), and this has insights applicable to the Assemblies of God and British Pentecostalism more generally. Traditionally, as noted above, the second coming of Christ was associated with a particular interpretation of certain biblical texts (Mt 24.30; 1 Thess 4.15; 2 Pet 3.3–10). It was associated with fulfilled Old Testament prophecy, especially concerning the restoration of the Jews to the Holy Land (Isa 66; Zech 14; Mt 24.32–34; Lk 21.24), the rapture (1 Thess 4.13–18), the great tribulation (Rev 7.14; 13.5; Dan 7.25; 9.27) and the return of Christ for his millennial reign (Isa 11; Rev 20; cf. Smyth, 1976). However, by 1994 premillennialism had been discarded from the denomination's statement of faith. Glass suggests that there had always been some dissent regarding this doctrine throughout the movement but it was never strong enough to influence change (Glass, 1996: 137). The recent generation of leaders was more widely read and was influenced by Reformed theology. He suggests that change began in the 1980s, as the imminent return of Christ seemed less plausible because not only had the first generation of Pentecostals deceased but the second generation was also dying out. Previous signs of the End (World War II, the Suez crisis and the Cuban missile crisis) had not ultimately fulfilled prophecy. Both the Charismatic Renewal movement and the Restoration (House Church) movement influenced Pentecostals directly: no longer were other churches apostate, as the Spirit was clearly manifest in their worship and in signs and wonders (cf.

---

[3]   http://www.aog.org.uk/church_interest.asp; accessed on 3 January 2008.

Warrington, 2008: 312). Premillennial pentecostal pessimism was influenced by restorationist optimism and engagement with the world (Glass, 1996: 141). The kingdom of God was considered a present reality rather than something that would arrive at an imminent, but future, millennium reign. Contact with, and influence by, these very different strands of theology eroded the traditional Pentecostal position. The change in doctrinal statement signals that it has been relegated to a secondary, rather than a primary, doctrine; and hence should not be considered a restriction to fellowship (145).

Finally, these doctrinal changes can be usefully placed alongside a recent survey. Kay's analysis (2000b) of the beliefs and attitudes of Pentecostal ministers from the Assemblies of God, Elim, Apostolic and Church of God denominations (N = 930) shows that almost all believe that Jesus will physically return at some point in the future (99%). Most believe that there will be a millennial reign by Christ on earth (88%) and that the church will be raptured (69%), although just under a half think that Christians will not suffer during the great tribulation (47%), presumably because they have been raptured. On the basis of this data, Kay divided the groups into two: (1) those believing that the church will be raptured prior to the tribulation (designated R for non-tribulation rapturists, N = 279), and (2) those believing that the church will not be raptured prior to the tribulation (designated T for non-rapture tribulationists, N = 35). The T group tended to be younger and better educated than the R group. They also tended to place greater emphasis on the use of charismatic gifts both by themselves and within their congregations. Kay attempts to explain this picture by saying that although Pentecostals do expect biblical prophetic texts to be fulfilled, they are wary (because of previous failures, e.g. 1914!) to speculate about historical figures and specific dates. Instead, there is a form of common sense being applied to the situation by those anticipating the tribulation: they ride out the storm by doing 'the simple things that make up their fervent Christian lives' (Kay, 2000b: 111).

Millennialism and Millenarian Discourse

There have been a variety of accounts of Pentecostal eschatology, even if a number of themes remain constant. For the purpose of this discussion, I shall focus on three analyses offering different perspectives, namely that Pentecostal eschatology be understood by means of mood, worldview and rhetoric.

Harvey Cox's (1996) analysis of Pentecostal spirituality is one that will be returned to by scholars because of its simplicity and resonance, even if it is not unproblematic. He attempts to categorise Pentecostalism as a form of primal spirituality or *homo religiosus* (Cox, 1996: 83). Under this classification, it contains primal speech (glossolalia), piety (visions, dreams, healing and dance) and hope (millennial outlook). It is the third of these features that is important for this discussion.

For Cox, Pentecostals are like other Christians who anticipate the *eschaton*, but for Pentecostals it has already begun to arrive (112). In the midst of Pentecostal communities there already exists an egalitarianism and fellowship that foreshadows the new heaven and the new earth. For many African American Pentecostals at the beginning of the twentieth century, it was the overcoming of racial distinctions that was a sign of the coming of the eschatological kingdom (113). For Cox, the expectation of the second coming of Jesus Christ is not primarily a doctrine but a *mood* (116). It is a 'millennial sensibility' that significant change is underway. In a sense, millennial forms of religion signal a change in a particular culture.

> They [millennial movements] signal moments of change and transition. They enable the person or society to touch base with the past and with their deepest symbolic roots in order to be better prepared to take the next – sometimes frightening – step into the future. But the rhetoric of such movements cannot be taken literally. It needs to be interpreted both in the light of the mythic structure within which movements are located and in relation to the environing culture. The earnest fellow with the placard warning us that the end is near may have something important to tell us, but the end may not be what he thinks it is. The pentecostal movement and the religious renaissance of which it is a part embody not just a popular protest against the reigning assumptions of our time, but also outline an alternative, a heavenly city to replace the earthly one. (Cox, 1996: 117)

Cox believes that, in the context of a transition from modernity to postmodernity, Pentecostalism succeeds because it brings hope to people whom society has disregarded. We live in a world in which the doomsday prophets are just as likely to be scientists as religious types. This sense of significant cosmic change is something that Pentecostals live with, even if the fervour of early twentieth-century expectation has waned. Nevertheless, 'Pentecostalism has become a global vehicle for the restoration of primal hope' (119). This is especially the case for Pentecostals in the non-western world, the estimated 87% of Pentecostals who live below the poverty line (Barrett and Johnson, 2002: 284). For them, it is good news that change is coming, whereas for those comfortable with their lot it might be considered bad news. Early American Pentecostalism announced an imminent coming of Jesus Christ, but today this voice is rather muted. '[T]oday many middle-class [P]entecostal congregations appear very much at ease with the status quo'. Now they seem confident not that Jesus is coming soon, but that he is probably not, and that therefore nothing will interrupt their pursuit of success and self-indulgence (Cox, 1996: 317–318). For Cox, this produces a difficult dilemma: lack of eschatology yields comfort and consumer religion, but short-term apocalypticism makes it difficult to address long-term issues (e.g. the environmental crisis). He sees this tension resolved in the Pentecostals who teach that the world will be transformed, not decimated, that times and dates are unimportant and that 'Jesus promised His kingdom to the poor and to those who suffer for righteousness sake' (319).

Margaret Poloma's (2001) discussion of Pentecostal eschatology observes the kind of early beliefs noted above (pre-tribulation premillennialism) and that the outpouring of the Spirit was understood as being a direct fulfilment of end-time prophecy (166–167). Such prophecy belongs to a Pentecostal *worldview* that incorporates miracles, modern technology and postmodern mysticism. It is expected that during the end times there will be a 'release of the prophetic', although for many this is interpreted in terms of personal and congregational practices rather than apocalypticism (169). This form is a 'charism' available to the Spirit-baptised and developed as a prophetic office of the five-fold ministry (170). It is prophecy that has prepared the Pentecostal movement for its latest revival, whether Toronto, Pensacola or Florida, and Poloma sees this as one of its important functions. It is these revivals that demonstrate an eschatological dimension, as it is perceived that 'God is on the move' and it could just be the final push before the End, even if doomsday prophecy is missing (179–182). These revivals are, of course, linked to a 'harvest of souls', and such a harvest, as with the early Pentecostals, is associated with the second coming of Jesus Christ (185).

Stephen Hunt's (2009) analysis of the most recent American revival, the Florida 'outpouring' associated with Todd Bentley, builds on the work of Poloma. The revival, beginning in April 2008 in Lakeland, Florida, was understood as fulfilling prophetic expectations. While Toronto had emphasised intimacy with God, and Pensacola stressed repentance, Lakeland focused on healing and evangelism. Even though the revival was threatened prematurely when Bentley was forced to withdraw from leadership in late 2008, the revival showed signs of continuing into 2009. Hunt explains how prophecies given within Pentecostal and Charismatic church circles concerning forthcoming revivals (by Marc Dupont, Paul Yonggi Cho and Todd Bentley) were matched by events on the ground, with the expectation that a 'great end-time revival' would spread to the rest of the world. Extending Poloma's analysis, Hunt suggests that when public predictive prophecy is understood as being fulfilled it engenders hope and provides a model for further prophetic activity. These prophecies in turn play a role in the 'myths that tell the narrative of revivalism', which, of course, bolster the worldview that expects evangelistic efforts to precipitate the coming of the kingdom (Hunt, 2009: 45). Furthermore, this is made more plausible when such places of revival also become sites for global pilgrimage, again supporting the expectation of a worldwide revival prior to the End, endorsed by the charismatic personality at the centre of the revival: Todd Bentley (39–41).

Damian Thompson's study (2005) of the Elim Pentecostal church, Kensington Temple (hereafter KT), in London provides an important source of information for this discussion. He agrees that Pentecostals could be said to understand themselves as living in the end times (Thompson, 2005: 39). But he observes that the early Pentecostal fervour, associated with the outpouring of the Latter Rain, as a direct preparation for the second coming, has generally faded (47). The expectation resurfaces from time to time as revivals break out and there is an upsurge in the claims to the miraculous. Indeed, there are Pentecostals who are preoccupied with the end times and the associated popular prophetic literature, but these must be understood as a minority group (57). Rather, following Poloma, he agrees that prophecy is integral to the Pentecostal worldview but he considers it to be more in terms of personal and corporate spirituality than as predictive of the Last Days (56; Poloma, 2001: 169). Nevertheless, he acknowledges that revivalism, with which Pentecostalism has always been associated, contains eschatology within it. Any move of the Holy Spirit that results in large numbers of conversions and miracles will inevitably be linked to the imminent return of Christ, as noted above. Of course, greater claims to prophecy and healing amount to a high-risk strategy, as expectations are raised and these are problematic when they cannot be sustained.

His study suggests that Colin Dye, the senior pastor at KT, is a high-energy charismatic leader, who takes risks and uses revivalist impulses such as the Toronto Blessing and stresses charismatic phenomena and healing, even when espoused by popular American evangelists who also advocate a 'health and wealth' gospel (Thompson, 2005: 74). But there are limits to these risks and even excitement associated with specific charismatic manifestations has to be managed, so that dissonance is reduced (75). Thompson argues that the congregation at large functioned with a common sense rationality to discern claims made by speakers. The societal norms of acceptable behaviour were also at work in the church and this has the effect of moderating attitudes (80). This means that the high-tension, risk-taking approach of Dye is both modified by him (playing down the significance of charismatic phenomena on occasions) and by members of the congregation who operate an underlying rationality or common sense to such things.

Thompson observes the change in the doctrinal statement from earlier Elim Pentecostal theology, which was dispensational premillennialism similar to that found in the pages of *Confidence* magazine, to a short contemporary statement. It reads: 'We believe in the personal, physical and visible return of the Lord Jesus Christ to reign in power and glory' (defined in 1994; Thompson, 2005: 84). Colin Dye and his assistant, Bruce Atkinson, both believe in post-tribulation premillennialism as demonstrated by Atkinson's sermon series, which stands in tension with this official denominational position.[4] Thompson conjectures that perhaps it is an example of Atkinson being given a degree of liberty to speculate personally on prophetic texts; or perhaps it is that the subject does not matter enough to be treated as essential doctrine (89)? Maybe it simply reflects the flexibility of the Elim Pentecostal denomination? Thompson's fieldwork suggested to him that the second coming of Christ plays less of a role than it did for early British Pentecostalism. It is often ignored or downplayed. This suggests that the tension between Pentecostals and society on this matter has been relieved with the diminishing of such beliefs (90). However, it is also the case that it could be

---

[4]   See: http://www.elim.org.uk/elim_members/articles.asp?categorycode=ART00988 &ID=ART00988; accessed on 11 November 2009.

revived by individuals and groups at a future point in history. The KT bookshop stocks millenarian literature that is clearly at odds with the views of the leadership and this allows minority positions to be supported.

Most of the KT members surveyed in 1999 or interviewed by Thompson simply lacked interest in apocalypticism and did not wish to speculate regarding the second coming of Jesus Christ (95–96). There was a general feeling that those people who emphasised apocalyptic ideas, especially date-setting, were extreme or eccentric. Not only had previous predictions proved to be wrong, but the generation who believed in them had themselves died out (100). However, Thompson also discovered that there was some willingness to 'toy conversationally with conspiracy belief', for example that the European Union is controlled by a satanic computer, or that supermarket barcodes conceal the number of the beast (55, 101). Explanatory millenarianism was far more popular than the predictive type. Thompson makes a distinction between what he calls predictive and explanatory millenarianism. Predictive millenarianism is a high-tension strand that includes doomsday prophecy. Every prophecy about the end of the world has obviously failed, causing disappointment and the need for remedial ideological work to account for the failure (24). This would include the expectations of early British Pentecostalism noted above. Explanatory millenarianism, however, does not predict a certain date but attempts to make sense of the unsatisfactory state of contemporary society. Therefore, adherents of this view say it is likely that Jesus Christ will return in their lifetime but decline to speculate as to when this will be (27). This type of millenarianism is a form of rhetoric that helps to make sense of contemporary society and the evil 'signs of the times' (30). It is a low-tension strategy, which allowed the group to accommodate itself to the routine of life and push the expectation of imminence to the intermediate future. For most members of the church, they neither ignored apocalyptic ideas nor used them in any significant manner (105). Thus, apocalyptic rhetoric is used to affirm a particular understanding of history and the nature of contemporary society (13, 110). This was especially the case for 'white church members born outside the Pentecostal or evangelical community' who 'were more likely to express belief in the imminent return of Christ than those brought up within it' (140).

In summary, Thompson theorises that subjective common sense rationality was used to minimise the cognitive dissonance created by apocalyptic expectations. These ideas did not disappear; instead they were reconciled with everyday life, 'thereby lowering subcultural deviance' (168). To quote Thompson on this point:

> ... Debbie Mowbray and her friends told each other that 'Jesus is coming soon';
> but this assertion had little effect on their daily routine because it owed more
> to the rhetorical convention than to conviction. This is not to say that church
> members did not hold firm beliefs (though they tended not to be millenarian
> ones); rather, we need to recognize that their expressions of belief were often
> moulded to fit argumentative strategies and, as such, were influenced by all sorts

of factors – including, in many cases, the calculation of risk. (Thompson, 2005: 172)

Thompson borrows from the work of Stephen O'Leary (1994), who suggests that apocalyptic belief should be best analysed as *rhetoric* because it is a form of explanation and a response to evil. As O'Leary describes rhetoric, it is more than empty talk or literary technique.

> As understood by its most astute interpreters from Aristotle to Kenneth Burke, rhetoric is a social practice of 'public, persuasive, constitutive, and socially constituted utterance'; it is a discipline located at the intersection of aesthetics, politics, and ethics; it is a method of enquiry whose object is to discover how audiences are moved or persuaded through the interplay of style, form, content and context in texts both spoken and written. (O'Leary, 1994: 4)

O'Leary links this form of discourse to the age-old lament that society is in moral decline, with lack of respect for the elders, war and immorality, even as human knowledge develops and grows (5). He argues that apocalyptic discourse functions as a 'symbolic theodicy', offering a 'mythical and rhetorical' solution to the problem of evil that 'focuses attention on specific interpretive practices' (14–15). Time and evil are dominant themes that are linked by a third, namely authority. Therefore, the nature of this present time and its relationship to a future End is interpreted in relation to the problem of evil. How these interpretations are validated depends on the nature of authority that is appealed to in support of the particular interpretation (91).

Reflection

Members of the HPC community reflect the same position as the members of KT. They believe in the second coming and that it could well occur in their lifetime, but they are not high-risk takers, unlike the evangelist David Hathaway and the church leader Colin Dye. They are, to some extent, comfortable with their lives in the UK. They live in the West not the East, with relatively settled lives rather than dramatic, exciting but unpredictible lives, tending to be educated and younger rather than passionate and older ('re-FIRED'). In a sense David Hathaway is the one who has maintained the old Pentecostal premillennial fervour, but it is a frontier excitement, hence he operates on the edge of western society in Russia. He compares favourably with the American revivalists and can be seen as exhibiting the millennial worldview. This contrasts remarkably with HPC members, many of whom have made the journey in the opposite direction. Many have come from extremely perilous non-western contexts in Africa, seeking social mobility and safety rather than risk and danger. They have adapted well to their new environment, which means taking a low-risk strategy to eschatology, thereby integrating rather than being alienated by their host Christian church culture and secular society.

This accommodation has been identified by many commentators, including Hollenweger back in 1972.

> The fact that the attention and concern of Pentecostal believers is directed towards the event of Christ's second coming makes them indifferent to the political and social problems of the world. It works as a palliative which prevents them from despairing in the wretched circumstances in which they live ... As social conditions improve the fervent expectation of the imminent second coming disappears. It is still taught in theory, but is no longer a matter of experience. (Hollenweger, 1972: 417)

Since Hollenweger wrote this comment, the truth is that both main British Pentecostal denominations have shifted their official doctrinal positions. Under influence from Evangelical scholarship, including a-millennialism (the view that the millennial reign is symbolic of the present age being initiated by the fulfilled work of Christ who reigns in the heavenlies now), which is associated with figures such as John Stott (Edwards and Stott, 1988: 308–309). Other forms of charismatic Christianity and, of course, social mobility have also undermined its privileged position. Many Pentecostal leaders still believe in a premillennial eschatology, but only as one possible option alongside others, hence it has been relativised. As Hollenweger predicted, they teach it but it no longer informs their experience. So now and then, the old-time Pentecostal preacher is used to demonstrate that it is still an authentic, if minority, option.

The early Pentecostal belief in missionary tongues was shown to be unfounded, even if xenolalia is still a dominant belief in the movement (Cartledge, 2002a, 2006b). Today, it could be said that missionary tongues is best demonstrated by the use of multi-media to preach the gospel. This is clearly demonstrated by the ministry of Hathaway, who uses TV, the internet, radio, magazines and literature to communicate in many different languages to people all over the world. It is truly global, even if specific countries are targeted for eschatological reasons, namely the belief that revival will spread from Russia to the rest of Europe, including the UK, and then to the rest of the world. These media are themselves products of globalisation and in themselves contribute to globalisation (Coleman, 2000: 166–186). Pentecostalism is a religion made to travel (Dempster et al., 1999), and what better way than through various contemporary media. The fact that Hathaway can also visit a local church in the UK means that the local and the global connect: it is 'glocal'. HPC connects to, and is part of, a worldwide Pentecostal movement via the process of globalisation, especially through the media and migration (Coleman, 2000: 4–5). The eschatology brought by this global connection offers a tension (it is more high risk and contains predictive prophecy) but also feeds the Pentecostal mood, worldview and, to some extent, its local rhetoric. This is where the juxtaposition noted by Thompson is also present at HPC (Thompson, 2005: 70), even if the high-risk strategy is represented by a visiting preacher.

My analysis of HPC discourse is that it resonates strongly with the KT findings. As Cox has suggested, it is positive and hopeful in mood, rather than pessimistic. Members seek to make sense of the problems in this world, the problem of evil, by means of eschatology as a rhetoric of explanation. They are less concerned with the imminent return of Christ and the need to go out to all the world and preach the gospel. They see themselves as having already done this as part of the reverse mission from the South to the North (rather than from the East to the West). Instead, they appear willing to support evangelists like Hathaway to do it on their behalf. Thus, they could be said to support a form of vicarious religion, at least in this respect (Davie, 2007). I was intrigued by one preacher who suggested that many of the congregation from other parts of the world should consider going home in order to preach the gospel to their own people. This caused something of a reaction and the pastors intervened to reassure the members that all were welcome to stay and they only supported such a challenge if individuals felt called by God to return. It would appear that returning home for good could be considered a high-risk strategy. Like KT members, HPC members use apocalyptic language as a form of rhetoric to explain the nature of current problems in society, as *possible* signs of the End approaching in a vague sense, rather than definite signs that the End is imminent. However, the use of prophecy to bolster particular locations of revival, such as Toronto, Pensacola or Lakeland, is lacking. There is no UK centre that is pointed to as a fulfilment of revival prophecy, that would function as a sign of the End. This clearly contrasts with Hathaway's claim that Russia is 'the' locus of revival, which will usher in the end of the world, even as his claim stands in tension with American Pentecostals who (interestingly) claim exactly the same thing!

Clearly, mood, worldview and rhetoric are not exclusive categories. Rather they can be seen as providing different emphases: hope associated with cultural shift, a worldview focusing on the prophetic expectation linked to revivalism and rhetoric or explanations regarding the state of society. David Hathaway clearly falls within the second category and the HPC members inhabit the third, which is likely to be more typical of the view within the congregation more generally. Given that the ordinary eschatology of the HPC members is of a more low-key explanatory variety that expects Christ to return sometime in the future, which is soonish, but perhaps not that soon, what kind of rescripted eschatology is possible? It is here that I turn to a Pentecostal scholar who has attempted to engage with the subject in a fresh way, in order to reinvigorate his own tradition.

Pentecostal Eschatology

In order to provide further material towards the task of rescripting, a key Pentecostal theologian, Peter Althouse, will be considered. He has attempted to frame a dialogue between himself and four other Pentecostal theologians (Steven Land, 1993; Eldin Villafañe, 1993; Miroslav Volf, 1991, 1996; and Frank Macchia, 1993a, 1993b,

1996) in relation to the work of Jürgen Moltmann (esp. 1996). After introducing each of the four Pentecostals and outlining the contribution that Moltmann makes to the subject of eschatology, he proceeds to identify areas of importance. This is because for Moltmann and these other Pentecostals eschatology can be understood as central to their general theological endeavour and as underpinning it. They have all shifted eschatology away from a focus on the *parousia* to the transformation of creation in the kingdom of God (Althouse, 2003: 162). This dialogue provides the greatest potential for rescripting from within and from outside of Pentecostal scholarship. He suggests four areas that contribute resources for rescripting.

There is both continuity and discontinuity with the future kingdom of God, which has already begun to arrive in the person of Jesus Christ and through the continued ministry of the Holy Spirit (162–169). The outpouring of the Spirit in the here and now is therefore a sign of eschatological hope. It is a hope that is both in continuity with creation and in anticipation of the new creation. It is a sign of the inbreaking of the kingdom that awaits its final consummation at the *eschaton*. This is demonstrated in the liberation of the oppressed in this world through the transformation of socio-political structures as well as concrete experiences of marginalisation. The concept and language of 'apocalyptic' should not be associated with the complete destruction of the world because there must be continuity with the new creation. The kingdom of God is therefore present in some measure within history, if hidden, even as it continues to break into history from outside. Pentecost and the *parousia* are therefore two poles in God's revelation of his eschatological kingdom. Within the tension this polarity brings, healings can be seen as 'a prolepsis of the resurrection of the dead and the healing of creation' (167). This means that social liberation is also an important aspect of the inbreaking of the kingdom of God, and tongues can be understood as a sacrament of this ongoing event. Therefore, the sacrament of tongues contains within itself the tension between the now and not yet of eschatology (Cartledge, 2002a: 197–203).

Early Pentecostals associated the eschatological outpouring of the Latter Rain as a sign and preparation for the imminent return of Christ. Thus, there is an intimate connection between Jesus Christ, the Holy Spirit and the kingdom of God. The *charismata* of the Spirit do not point to the Spirit but to Christ and his kingdom. Pentecostals demonstrate a functional Christology by focusing on Christ's work (justification, sanctification, baptism in the Spirit, healing and the second coming). This enables pneumatology and Christology to be integrated, or, in Moltmann's terms, to display perichoretic unity. This unity is framed within a social trinitarianism that is both historical and eschatological. Althouse suggests that there is an implicit Spirit-Christology to liberation: namely, the charismatic Christ. 'The Spirit universalizes the reign of God through the mediation of the crucified and risen Christ' (Althouse, 2003: 172). The gifts of the Spirit, through which God's reign is made manifest, are not just about ministry in the worship service but are also gifts for the world of work. Indeed, a pneumatology of work suggests that they become the basis for our working lives, enabling us to perform many tasks. 'Although the basis of individual work is the *charismata* of the Spirit, cumulative work will be transformed and incoporated by the Spirit in the new creation' (174). This means that work can be understood as an anticipation of, as well as a participation in, the new creation. Pentecostals display a Spirit-Christology, especially associated with signs and wonders. Their Christology accentuates the 'theophanic' qualities of eschatology as they interrupt the everyday. It is these interruptions that also signal the transcendence and freedom of God, for they are ambivalent and cannot be fully grasped because God is Wholly Other, even if they also point towards the renewal of creation (177).

There is a political significance to eschatology. In the early American Pentecostal movement, the racial and gender prejudices of society were challenged (179). People from very many different backgrounds worshipped together in expectation of the unity of the people of God at the *eschaton*. Althouse's reflection on Moltmann and Volf highlights three principles in relation to economics: (1) freedom of individuals created *imago dei*, (2) satisfaction of basics needs especially for the poor, and (3) protection of nature from irreparable damage, all of which will be 'judged by the new creation' (180). Socio-economic justice is not merely a secular pursuit but needs people of faith to bring to bear the values of the kingdom of God. The embrace of the other who is different is an eschatological act of reconciliation and foreshadows the dwelling of the Trinity within the new creation. Thus, love and justice combine. 'Love is the basis for human rights and dignity. Love is also the basis of justice, for when there is justice there is also love' (182). However, this engagement is a corollary of, and is subsequent to, the transformation of the believer. It includes healing, not just in an individual human sense, but in a wider creational sense, as the Spirit works to liberate the world from social and systemic evil.

The cosmic nature of eschatology and the transformation of creation is significant for this discussion (186). With the inbreaking of the kingdom of God into world history begins the transformation of the whole of creation. It is God's act of judgment on sin and death, which can be demonstrated by the church through its social ministries to the poor and vulnerable. New life in the Spirit is for both body and soul, which is why Pentecostal worship demonstrates considerable kinesthetic activity: hand-waving, clapping, swaying, dancing, singing and laughing, eating and drinking, and greeting one another in the name of Jesus. Even if the world can be viewed negatively, a cosmic eschatology does not abandon the world but always seeks its transformation as indicative of the salvation that is to come. '[T]he new creation will be a recapitulation of all creation' (190). Salvation will be experienced by the whole of creation and there will be no personal salvation apart from creation. 'Creation is intended to glorify God, so the destruction of creation would disgrace God' (191). The gift of tongues is based in the cross of Christ that represents the suffering of creation not just of one person, and the resurrection, that great reversal, also indicates that salvation has come, that the presence of cosmic glory has already been received and points forward to the indwelling of God in creation.

Rescripting Ordinary Theology

The HPC testimonies could be rescripted in order to see the second coming as linked more to hope than to evil. Rather than focusing upon evil and the problems in society, and thus using explanatory millenarianism as a 'holding strategy', attention could be given to the concept of hope in the face of difficulties. The End is principally about the glory of the Lord rather than the destruction of his enemies. Although the church will have a central role in the *eschaton*, the theatre of God's glory will be the whole of creation, and eschatologically it is the renewed earth that will be focus of the presence of the Lord. Of course, the *eschaton* has already been inaugurated in the person of Christ. It is not something that is only in the future; the future has appeared in the past and is within Pentecostals in the present. The end time is as much about the now as it is about the future, for the future is here. The *eschaton* will concern the re-creation of the natural order: a new heavens and a new earth will be in continuity with the old, hence a renewed creation. As creatures, they are part of that creation being renewed by the Spirit, so Pentecostal spirituality is not necessarily against creation, or other-worldly, but it lies at the intersection between the earth and the heavens, because as Pentecostals speak in tongues they utter an eschatological cry: human sounds are inspired by the Spirit of God to groan in unity with the creation that longs for its release (Rom 8.26). Therefore, there will be a great deal of continuity with life after the second coming of Christ, as well as major discontinuities. Everyday life and the ordinary are very much part of God's plans for the future because they will be redeemed by Christ, who is in them by his Holy Spirit. The experience of the Holy Spirit is a sign of hope, which is a powerful means of transforming individuals, groups, communities and societies.

The HPC narrative could be rescripted in relation to the functional Christology of Pentecostalism. There is a real emphasis in Pentecostalism on the Spirit but this translates very quickly into functional Christology, with little ontological understanding. In certain respects this also appears to be the case for the members of HPC. It is not clear just how the Spirit and Christ are interrelated in their narratives. They are, at times, merely juxtaposed. Once again we observe an overall lack of trinitarian grammar, as noted above, which means that eschatology cannot be framed in this way. The discussion above suggests that a social trinitarianism can provide a framework in which to understand the relationship between the persons of the Trinity and the ways in which the persons of Christ and the Spirit are connected. While the eschatological reign of God is understood as inaugurated by Christ, it continues through the work of the Spirit in both the church and the world.

For Pentecostal Christians, with the accent on the gifts of the Spirit, there is a danger that *charismata* are expected to be operative on Sunday and in mid-week prayer meetings but cannot be expanded to include the world of work itself. Rather, this discussion suggests that work is an activity and domain in which, and through which, the end time Spirit can operate in order to prepare for the consummation of all things, but also as a blessing to the workers as they participate in the inaugurated kingdom. However, as with all of these things, qualifications are important and one is especially significant. Namely, that the transcendence of God cannot be domesticated by experiences of the *eschaton* via the Spirit now, whether in a church building or *charismata* in the work place. This is because God cannot be made wholly immanent, for he is Wholly Other. There is always a transcendent and ambiguous reality to experiences of God this side of the *eschaton*. This is not always acknowledged in ordinary discourse, with its accent on faith and reception 'now', but it could be framed differently, allowing for greater mystery in the ways in which the Spirit is spoken about.

At HPC there is a clear acceptance of people from very different backgrounds, cultures and languages. They display within themselves the prolepsis of the *eschaton* as there is real unity in their worship and life together. Unfortunately, this unity as an eschatological reality is not really explained as it could be. More could be made of its eschatological nature, the inbreaking of the kingdom of God as it is displayed in multi-racial and gender harmony. Certainly the church treats each person with dignity and considers the needs of people both within and outside of the church, but, again, more could be said in relation to the environment, which is missing within the narratives. A greater involvement in the socio-economic issues of the locality would signal not only the interest of a church community but also a willingness to work with 'the other' who is different. Such an engagement in local socio-economics means that the community would demonstrate both love and justice. And, as Land (1993) highlights, this conscious engagement must start within the life of the transformed believer, who is empowered to live for Christ in the world. More could be made of the eschatological nature of the transforming power of the Spirit for socio-economic engagement in the world. This could also be seen as a means of proclaiming the gospel to the nations: the transformation of all things in Christ. Indeed, the overarching HPC soteriology of healing could be applied not just to individual Christians as they are incoporated into the church but also to the whole of creation as it is liberated in preparation for the *eschaton*. This theology of healing is rooted in the atonement and is proleptic of the healing of the whole creation eschatologically (cf. Dermawan, 2003; Gabriel, 2007).

The HPC narrative could also be rescripted by suggesting that the social action of the church can be reconfigured not merely as pre-evangelism but as an act of judgment empowered by the Spirit, which speaks to the poor and vulnerable saying that their life is not what God intended. Their life will be transformed eschatologically and acts of kindness are ways of participating now in that which will come. This is also demonstrated in the holistic approach to ministry, whether that ministry is on a Sunday morning, or through the handing out of Christmas parcels. HPC already demonstrates a holistic approach to ministry, but this can always be accentuated and interpreted in the light of the resurrection of the Son of God. Just as Christ reigns in the heavenlies in a resurrection body, so the church experiences a foretaste of resurrection in holistic salvation through embodied worship and ministry. This means that although the world is fallen and sinful,

God is breaking into this world and is using both the community that is HPC, and individuals, to effect transformation. Personal conversion stories and communal salvation stories could be reframed in relation to the whole of creation and the whole of society as being caught up in the salvific purposes of God. God will not abandon the earth to destruction but will redeem it, just as he has redeemed those who experience the Spirit of God in corporate and personal worship. Indeed, the glory that is foreshadowed in the experience of Pentecostal worship is also an anticipation of the honour of God. There will be no shame in the presence of the God who is all in all (1 Cor 15.28), so HPC should confidently acclaim the honour of God in its narratives and in its praxis. The use of tongues-speech is a praxis that signifies both the weakness of humanity, and indeed the whole of creation, and at the same time the power of the Spirit in not just the individual but also the cosmos. Members of HPC might gain a sense of awe and humility by understanding that by speaking in tongues they participate in a sign of the End that has already begun to arrive, as on the day of Pentecost. There is also a sense in which the ministry of Hathaway opens up another dimension to glossolalia, as 'missionary tongues' is not conceived as spontaneous unlearned xenolalia but as carefully organised multi-lingual media. In this sense it can be seen as a means of gospel proclamation.

Summary

Historically, Pentecostals believed that they had a responsibility to preach the good news of Jesus Christ to the ends of the earth and that the outpouring of the Spirit, as on the day of Pentecost, was not only an enduement of power for witness but also a sign of the soon return of Christ the king. The conversation with the members of the church confirmed the view that it was still important to witness to the ends of the earth and that Jesus was coming soon, but it was unclear how soon his return would be. There are signs that the time is close, including war, violence and abuse, but no date can be predicted. This was contrasted with the evangelist, David Hathaway, a visitor to the church, who uses the media to proclaim the gospel to over 134 countries around the world. He firmly believes that Jesus Christ is coming very soon. As a sign of his return, he claims that revival has started already in Russia and it will spread to the rest of Europe and the world, ushering in the return of the king. Early Pentecostalism adhered to a premillennial eschatology made famous through the Scofield Bible of 1909, but this has now been dropped in favour of a more open posture. In the UK it reflects a low-risk expectation and strategy that uses eschatological language to explain the present evil in society rather than the high-risk strategy of predictive prophecy and revivalism. It could be suggested that HPC members largely adopt this explanatory millenarianism, which offers rhetoric for understanding contemporary society and the church's role within it (Thompson, 2005). The outpouring of the Spirit can be seen as a sign of eschatological hope, with the events of healing, interracial and gender harmony and ecological care functioning as anticipatory signs of a renewed created order. It is suggested that rather than focusing upon the evil in society HPC members might give attention to the hope that the Pentecostal message brings, because the future has already arrived in the person of Christ and continues to be mediated through the person of the Spirit. *Charismata* are also signs of the inaugurated kingdom of God and a means of participation in the renewal of creation. These gifts can be understood as functioning outside of the church context within the world of work and thus become a blessing to others outside of Sunday worship services. This renewed understanding could lead to a concern for socio-economic issues both locally and globally and the inauguration of the justice of God, especially for the most disadvantaged in society.

Chapter 9

Conclusion

This project has investigated the ordinary theology of classical Pentecostal Christians in the British Assemblies of God tradition by means of a congregational study using qualitative research. It has used a practical-theological methodology that not only maps out the beliefs, values and practices of adherents, but also engages in a critical dialogue with theoretical perspectives. It has applied the metaphor of 'rescripting' to this process of theological engagement, by which is meant a disciplined and attentive interaction with the verbatim testimony, the focus group and congregational material, and which treats the discourse that emerges as a form of script. This script is subsequently reflected upon using the resources of history, theology and social science in order to suggest modifications to the script, hence rescripting, that remain authentic to the original script. Insights gained through this research can now be applied back to the congregation so that both stakeholders and academics can appreciate the value of this kind of knowledge. Therefore, recommendations for renewed congregational praxis can now be made that display *both* continuity with the ordinary theology of believers *and* discontinuity through the rescripting process. In addition, further reflection arising from this research can synthesise the various themes and construct a proposal directed towards Pentecostal ecclesiology. To conclude, I shall also note what I regard as the main contribution that this research makes to scholarship, followed by some recommendations for future research.

Recommendations for Renewed Congregational Praxis

The investigation has enabled a rescription of the ordinary theology of members of HPC. Although the rescriptions primarily refer to the ordinary theology, by linking the different themes and using the ordinary accounts as interpretative lenses through which to view the congregation as a whole, it is possible to address the broader praxis of the church. Therefore, within the paradigm of practical theology, it is essential to attempt to address the 'so, what?' question in relation to this particular congregation. The following recommendations are suggestions for the church to consider in order to develop its praxis as an ecclesial community. Recommendations are made with respect to the key themes and I have restricted myself to two per theme.

Worship

(1) To consider adopting an explicitly trinitarian grammar within its oral worship liturgy. This could be provided by an introduction and blessing, hymnody and eucharistic liturgy, as well as celebrating the doctrine of the Trinity annually with a sermon on the subject. Indeed, a sermon series on the doctrine of the Trinity and how it shapes and frames Christian experience in general would be a very worthwhile exercise. It has been argued that trinitarian theology is required in order to account for the mystical experience in Christian theological language: baptism of the Spirit *into* the presence of the Father and the Son. The church might consider how it could implement a carefully worded form of liturgical language that emphasised the trinitarian nature of the experience of baptism in the Spirit. Perhaps, it could be accompanied by a short statement as to the meaning of baptism in the Spirit as a trinitarian event.

(2) To consider building on the existing innovation in local hymnody and develop a broader range of cultural forms, as well as addressing a greater range of human experience before God, such as lament, with the Psalms as an example of such a genre. The older generation of Pentecostals used the well-known hymnody associated with Methodism, thus some of this classical hymnody could be used but set to contemporary musical settings.

Conversion

(3) To consider developing a wider network with other Christian traditions, which would enhance the opportunities for other Christians to affiliate institutionally with HPC. At the moment it would appear that it has networks with a fairly limited Evangelical group. Association with a broader group would enhance its profile and allow easier transfer of potential new members.

(4) To consider its rites of commitment within the church. Not everyone will want to be baptised for a second time, if they have been baptised as an infant. Perhaps there could be options for membership, including an associate member status, which did not require full adherence to the statement of faith. Such a stance might make conversion or church membership easier for some enquirers.

Baptism in the Spirit

(5) To consider that the experience is likely to be post-conversion but will carry over aspects of conversion-initiation into expressions of the experience, such as repentance, seeking God, and generally being part of a broader process of integration into the fellowship of a Pentecostal church. Therefore, diversity of experience among its members should be expected and celebrated.

(6) To consider that baptism in the Spirit is clearly symbolised by a number of actions, including glossolalia, and these may change over time and place (cf. Twelftree, 2009: 99). Although the church will necessarily have to agree to the formulation of the doctrine by the denomination (including the phrase, 'essential, biblical evidence'), greater flexibility of expression locally might be explored in the light of experiential diversity. This move would not only be biblical (after all, glossolalia is missing as a sign from the major accounts in Acts 8.17 and 9.18, and clearly unessential there) but also pastorally helpful. It would also fit better with Pentecostal testimony rather than the judicial language of 'evidence', as if the experience were on trial, which it is no longer.

Healing

(7) To consider how the ministry of healing in the congregation can be understood as a mark of the church, and in this sense its symbolic or sacramental value can be enhanced as a key ritual. It is a major liturgical practice, in which many, if not all, of the members of the church participate and administer to one another. It is also a crucial event through which visitors and fringe members can be brought closer to the heart of the church fellowship. The quality of the relationships of the members in the church is a key indicator of how healing as a soteriological metaphor is embodied, and, in particular, how the margins of the church are managed as indicators of inclusion/exclusion. If salvation is to be extended to everyone as a universal invitation, then analysis of who does and does not benefit from this ministry would illuminate the boundary markers of the church. In other words, does it function as a means of integration into the community of the church or not?

(8) To consider how it can extend the salvific metaphor of healing to all areas of life, including the healing of relationships within the wider community and society. There is a clear focus on physical healing and, while this should not be diminished, it can be expanded to include other forms of healing in terms of relationships with other groups and support for other sectors of Birmingham society. The confidence that members have about their faith can be used to explore ways of engaging with the wider community through clear, practical and concrete steps. There are existing community practices, especially the engagement with the local schools, that can be built upon and extended. These may include developing links with different client groups such as the elderly and young people, as well as local shopkeepers and the business community. Members could be encouraged to engage in some form of community action as a part of their ongoing discipleship. This would strengthen the commitment to their own faith, as well as acting as a witness to their conversion in the wider world.

Life and Witness

(9) To consider how the church can develop its model of intra-Christian hospitality, as immigrants from around the world are successfully integrated within its community. It already shares its premises with other Pentecostal groups. This hospitality of resources could be shared more widely. Its experience of integrating immigrants could also be shared with other faith communities in order to support those migrating to the UK. Indeed, there are existing networks in the city that would benefit from a Pentecostal testimony in this area.

(10) To consider how the church can identify sectors of public life that it can engage for the common good, for example the local media and government. This would enable its distinct witness to be seen and heard in sectors of society that, as yet, it does not reach, and who are thus lacking the impact of its 'faith capital' (Furbey et al., 2006). It would also be a means of dispelling suspicion and fear of these sectors. Change will be impossible without first engaging in a conversation that leads to mutual understanding. A positive view of gifts of the Spirit, as signs of the outpouring of the Spirit as on the day of Pentecost, can be translated into a positive understanding of work. This might mean educating members to consider work as a Christian vocation within the economy of salvation. Ministry is not something that is contained within the worship service but spills out into the whole of life, especially working life. This positive view of the nature of work could enable the church in its relationships with the business communities in the area.

World Mission and the Second Coming

(11) To consider how the impact of such a positive eschatological worldview can lead to practical steps to participate in the redemption of the whole of creation, and how they can be understood as signs of the coming of the End. This could be translated into practical steps that demonstrate ecological concern. For example, the church might consider supporting the agenda of eco-awareness groups by aiming to cut its energy usage by 10%; it could also encourage its members to do so in their own homes.[1] Alternatively, the church might consider a theology of creation in worship and through community action days, making an explicit link between the action of God in creation, in life-giving and sustenance, and in the new birth and the new creation. This has the potential of building bridges with other community groups in the area, for example in relation to ecology.

(12) To consider how the gift of glossolalia can be understood as a sign both of weakness and of power, and, as such, symbolising the 'not yet' as well as the 'now' of God's reign. As an extension of the missionary gift of tongues the church might consider how its work can be extended through the use of different

---

[1] See http://www.1010uk.org/; accessed on 25 September 2009.

language media, thus representing in a new way the medium of tongues as a means of communicating its beliefs and values. It could also consider the greater usage of media, especially the internet, as a means of communicating its distinctive Pentecostal testimony.

Towards a Pentecostal Ecclesiology

From an analysis of the previous thematic chapters, five key features emerge linking the different themes and enabling the articulation of a constructive proposal towards Pentecostal ecclesiology. These features are: praise, healing, ministry, hospitality and hope. They are used to reconfigure the ordinary theology of HPC as expressed through its purpose statements (see chapter 1). Thus, celebrating God's presence in worship is developed by means of praise; love expressed in ministry is developed in two directions: healing and ministry through the use of *charismata*; incorporating God's family into fellowship is developed via a community of hospitality; and communicating God's Word in evangelism, together with education and discipleship, is elaborated as a pilgrimage of hope. This proposal offers something of a contrast with some previous attempts at developing a Pentecostal ecclesiology (e.g. Thomas, 1998; cf. Warrington, 2008: 131–179), while enabling comparisons with others (e.g. Chan, 2000a, 2000b; Yong, 2005). It is an example of ecclesiology constructed 'from below', a congregational ecclesiology (Healy, 2000: 181), rooted in ordinary theological discourse of the ecclesial lifeworld. Nevertheless, it uses biblical, theological and 'ideal' categories that transcend the purely local and are applicable (as theological theory) to other Pentecostal contexts and ecclesial settings (cf. Clifton, 2007: 215, 217).

Temple of Praise

Paul in his first letter to the Corinthians asks whether the church members realise that they are themselves God's temple, that God's Spirit lives in them, and that they are therefore sacred (1 Cor 3.16; cf. Eph 2.21–22). When this is allied to the day of Pentecost and the fact that the first disciples, having received the gift of the Spirit (Acts 2.4), declared the wonders of God in other tongues (Acts 2.11), we have a focus on praise as the primary action of the living temple of the church. Pentecostals begin their worship with praise and they end their worship with praise: it is an *inclusio* both to the nature of Pentecostal worship in the narrow sense of worship 'services' and in the broader sense of worship through the whole of one's daily life. Of course, Paul had in mind the nature of the church as a people of sacrifice, which is why he can use cultic language and extend it to this broader domain when he writes about the offering of Christians as 'living sacrifices', which are holy and pleasing to God (Rom 12.1). Therefore, worship in its narrow and broad sense can be understood as capturing the Pentecostal preoccupation with praise as constitutive of the church. Pentecostals are a people of praise!

For Pentecostals, praise, in the narrow sense of a worship service, is characterised by a genuine orality and spontaneity, which can nevertheless draw upon the treasures of the church's ancient traditions but translate them into extemporary forms that are culturally relevant to their various contexts. In this way an historic trinitarian hymnody and liturgical grammar can inform Pentecostal orality. It is inevitable that songs will capture not only the awe and wonder of the transcendent God but the intimacy and power of the immanent Spirit at work in the community, thereby stressing the narrative of encounter (Ward, 2005a: 202–204; Cartledge, 2006a; Warrington, 2008) and 'the presence of the living God' (Pinnock, 2006: 157). But alongside these songs of transcendence and immanence should be placed songs of lament and periods of silence (Hudson, 1998; Ellington, 2000, 2007; Hardy and Ford, 1984: 20–21). These practices will better reflect the struggles of the community and give greater authenticity to the nature of praise in different forms. It is also the case that the joy and celebration of worship and praise can spill out into the community and wider society for the good of all. Praise is not just about what we offer to God directly but what we offer to God indirectly through lives lived in the wider world. 'Led by the foundational witness of the apostles and prophets (Eph 2.20), we are "living stones" that are "being built into a spiritual house to be a holy priesthood, offering spiritual sacrifices acceptable to God through Jesus Christ" (1 Peter 2.5)' (Macchia, 2006: 203). In this sense, praise is offered when the living temple is gathered together and also when it is dispersed. It is proleptic of the *eschaton* when God will both receive worship and dwell intimately with his people (Rev 4. 9–11; 21.3).

Household of Healing

The letter of James suggests that the household of faith should be engaged in general prayer, praise and prayer specifically for the sick (Jas 5.13–14). Another metaphor that is often used for the church is household (Eph 2.19; 1 Tim 3.15); and household codes are used by Paul in his addresses to the church (e.g. Col 3.18–4.1). It is likely that Luke regarded the early church community as based upon the social structure of the Greco-Roman household, as a 'basic unit of social care and responsibility' (Twelftree, 2009: 63). At the centre of the Pentecostal household is a shared belief in the healing power of God, not just in a physical sense but in a fully holistic sense. If humanity's problem is sin-sickness, alienation and frailty, then the Pentecostal answer is to understand that Christ's atoning sacrifice provides the means for not just the forgiveness of sins, which is a narrow understanding of salvation, but a holistic full gospel that revolves around healing and reconciliation, including the 'acquisition of God's life and deliverance' (Coulter, 2008: 449). Therefore, the household of faith will offer prayer for healing, support for the needy, relief of the burdens carried by the oppressed, address issues surrounding sin, as well as emotional, spiritual and physical problems. This is understood as present in the earthly healing ministry of Jesus, the head of, and doctor in, the house, whose anointed ministry continues through the household as the Spirit enables (Pinnock, 2006: 151; Williams, 2002: 119–120).

In this household of healing there will be opportunity for the narrative of God's healing power to be shared by means of testimony. But alongside these positive stories of transformed lives will be placed testimonies of lament, suffering, struggle and pain. In this way, the 'now and not yet' of the kingdom of God is given explanatory privilege, enabling greater participation by those on the margins who are not healed, but live with disability or illness. This means that healing is understood as a broad soteriological category that is always qualified by the eschatological: the first-fruits have arrived but the full harvest is yet to come and we live between the two eras. Nevertheless, there are theophanic signs of God's glory and these are celebrated in praise, worship and service. Indeed, a central rite is the sacrament of Holy Communion, in which the healing of humanity and the whole of creation is celebrated as its inauguration is remembered in the cross and resurrection of Christ (Chan, 2000a: 189). Such remembrance is also empowering, as it is allied to the contemporary experience of healing, harmony, unity and love within the household of faith: God's blessing of *shalom*. The sacrament is an eschatological foretaste of this healing and unity in the heavenly banquet as the *epiclēsis* 'calls for his (Christ's) coming for table fellowship in anticipation of the coming of the kingdom' (Kärkkäinen, 2002: 140). Drawing upon the ancient eucharistic traditions of the church would enable Pentecostals to strengthen their theology of healing by seeing the rite of Holy Communion as *pharmakon* or medicine (Kärkkäinen, 2002: 142; Theron, 1999: 58).

Members of Ministry

Paul uses another metaphor for understanding the church in its internal and external ministry, namely the human body (1 Cor 12.12–13; Rom 12.5; cf. Eph 5.25–28). The one Spirit has baptised believers from many different backgrounds into one body and has given each 'the one Spirit to drink' (12.13, NIV). Therefore, the many different members are united pneumatologically into this one body. Each member needs the other for the healthy functioning of the whole body (12.14–17, 19–21). It is God who has designed the body just as it is and has given the different roles to the different parts of the body (12.18). Every member of the church is a member of this body, which is the body of Christ (12.27); and each member has a function or ministry in, with and to that body. If Christ 'instituted' the church, then the Holy Spirit 'constituted' the church (Kärkkäinen, 2002: 86). The work of the Spirit is to be understood primarily in relation to the corporate body, rather than its individual members (Chan, 2000a: 180). As such 'the church is not only ... the people of God and body of Christ but also the "charismatic fellowship of the Spirit"' (Yong, 2005: 151; cf. Kärkkäinen, 2002: 109–122).

This metaphor of members of a body, which are united in a ministry as the body that belongs to Christ, provides the context for the use of *charismata* in Paul's thinking (1 Cor 12.28–31). In the context of worship services and *diakōnia* in and to the world, the church is comprised of members who minister with joy and gladness the healing that they themselves have received and enjoy through their reconciliation with God. Thus, *charismata* are not merely giftings for the elite, but for all, and they are not restricted to the 'prayer ministry times' or altar calls within the church but are taken out into the world of work. Members display the *charismata*, the gifts of God's grace, as they embody in their actions the presence of the Holy Spirit (Boone, 1996). Therefore, *charismata* are not simply located in the church but are a very 'constituting feature of the church – its charism' (Coulter, 2007: 82; Volf, 1998: 228–233). Indeed, '[t]he flow of manifestations constitutes the life and growth of the community' (Pinnock, 2006: 160). The believers exercise a ministry that is bestowed upon all, as the egalitarian Spirit uses *every* member for the glory of the triune God. But it is a differentiated ministry because God has given different gifts to different individuals (12.28–30). This includes the ministry of pastoral oversight and leadership, which some are called to perform as a *charism* (Kärkkäinen, 2002: 115). All aspects of this ecclesial ministry are empowered by the presence of the Spirit in the life of the believer through conversion (including baptism) and subsequent occasions or moments of encounter (including the baptism in the Spirit), be they sacramental or charismatic.

Community of Hospitality

The early church devoted itself to the apostles' teaching, to fellowship (*koinōnia*), the breaking of bread and to prayer (cf. Twelftree, 2009: 128–132). They witnessed signs and wonders, were together and held everything in common, giving to those in need and the 'Lord added to their number daily those who were being saved' (Acts 2.47, NIV). This picture suggests a close-knit community, sharing a level of commonality yet being open to newcomers and enquirers, visitors and guests. For contemporary ecclesiology it could be translated into the practices of traditioning through attention to the Scriptures, positive interpersonal relationships, fellowship around the Lord's table in each other's homes, and a generosity whereby those in need were supported and cared for. In this context of learning, pastoral care and hospitality, signs and wonders are seen and new Christians are integrated into a hospitable community. It 'is, therefore, both a reflection and an extension of God's own hospitality – God's sharing of the love of the triune life with those who are dust' (Hütter, 2002: 219).

The church is the *ekklēsia* of God (Acts 8.1; 20.28; Eph 5.25), gathered together in community yet facing out towards society. Pentecostals are often understood to be informal in their style and highly relational in their focus, prioritising flexible networks over settled or rigid structures. Unfortunately, they are often insular, being suspicious of other denominations and unwilling to engage in ecumenical relationships at local, national and international levels (Warrington, 2008: 169–170). Their strengths need to be translated into an interest towards and an openness to other Christian traditions because of the distinctive witness they can offer to these traditions; and because of what they might learn from them regarding how they, too, have understood the teaching of the apostles. In this sense it needs to be more conscious of catholicity, which is normally regarded as a mark of the church (Chan, 2000a: 184–187; Yong, 2005: 127, 143–146; Macchia, 2006: 224–229). Openness to others within the Christian tradition might be facilitated by a greater recognition of very different baptismal practices even within Pentecostalism itself (Robeck and Sandidge, 1990: 509–512; Hunter, 2002: 947). This recognition might facilitate the transfer of membership into Pentecostalism through rites of reception other than baptism, as well as recognition that there are a variety of signs of Spirit baptism, not just glossolalia. Given the global nature of Pentecostalism, it is expected that Pentecostal ecclesiology will pay attention to cultural diversity issues and prize 'the many tongues of Pentecost' within the unity of the community, thus being a sign of intercultural reconciliation. It will provide a 'home from home' for those on the journey, as well as a bridge for the integration of immigrants into local cultures. In this context of care and support, it will reach out and provide hospitality to those of different faiths or none, without compromising its faith in the lordship of Jesus Christ.

Pilgrims of Hope

The account of the two disciples on the road to Emmaus is often cited as an example of how Christian discipleship is a journey of discovery (Lk 24.13–35). It is only at the end of the journey that the presence of the resurrected Christ is revealed, even though he had accompanied them all along. When this is brought alongside the narrative of the day of Pentecost, it can be recognised that the presence of the Holy Spirit mediates to the disciples the presence of the resurrected Christ, but now in a universal sense: 'Pentecost is Easter for everyone' (Smail, 1978: 2; Cartledge, 2008b: 98). This experience is both illuminating and empowering. The disciples understood just how Christ had reversed the impact of sin and death, but also how the Spirit enabled them to look upwards and outwards, to anticipate the new creation demonstrated in the resurrection of Christ and now available to all through the presence of the Spirit. Just as in the *missio dei* the Father sent the Son and the Father (and the Son) sent the Spirit to be with the disciples (Jn 14–16, 20.21), so the Spirit sends out the pilgrims on the road of mission in the world (Acts 1.8). And this hope is proclaimed in the gospel message itself, and as an interpretation of what it is that is seen and heard in the lives of Pentecostals (Acts 2.14–41). It is this pilgrimage towards the consummation of the *eschaton* that characterises Pentecostals as people, or indeed pilgrims, of hope (Chan, 2000a: 193–196). They are on a soteriological journey into the very presence of God: a *via salutis*.

As pilgrims of hope, Pentecostals understand that their own personal redemption is past (Titus 3.4–7), present (1 Cor 1.18) and future (Rom 5.9), even as the redemption of the cosmos is also past, present and future. Once again the future reign of God, which gives hope, has impacted individuals and communities in the present reality so that theophanic qualities are seen in their lives through baptism in the Spirit and subsequent empowering. This leads to a commitment to live for Christ and his kingdom, to be set apart for the purposes of God and not to be distracted. The hope and joy of worship can be translated into concrete action in the world, such as proclaiming the Christian message, feeding the poor, helping the marginalised and engaging with the power structures of the world for the sake of justice (Dempster, 1995). The commitment to justice comes from the belief that Jesus Christ is the ultimate righteous judge of all the earth and will do right. To extend a hand of hope to the hopeless in society is an eschatological judgment on the sinfulness of society, and not to do so is to collude with the sinfulness of the church. This work of engagement and transformation is empowered by prayer, especially prayer in the Spirit (Rom 8.26), as glossolalia is an eschatological cry of the heart for the liberation of the children of God. It is also a work that is committed to the whole of creation, which will be redeemed for the glory of God. The Pentecostal *via salutis* is just one aspect of this cosmic redemption as they live not only between the 'now and not yet' of the eschatological reign of Christ, but also between the twin domains of heaven and earth. Ultimately, the coming of Christ is an event of hope fulfilled; and it is this hope which Pentecostals display through concrete actions in the world today.

Integrating Framework

Those familiar with academic theological discourse may have realised that a number of doctrines have been woven into the above account. For the sake of clarity and in order to appreciate how they integrate the above features, they are stated here.

As well as being shaped by concrete categories mediated through a rescripted ordinary theology, Pentecostal ecclesiology is shaped by ideal categories. In particular, trinitarian theology frames its identity. This is because *koinōnia* between the three persons is at the heart of the divine Trinity, such that any participation in the divine life through the ministry of the Holy Spirit will mean that it flows into, and energises, human relations and actions. '[A] trinitarian ecclesiology in which God, being himself a communion of love whose power is not dictatorial but interactive and shared, calls forth a community to share his glory (Jn 17.24–26)' (Pinnock, 2006: 154). It also reflects the *missio dei* as the church participates in the salvific missions of the persons of the Godhead (Althouse, 2009). It is an ecclesiology that is focused upon the person and work of Christ who reveals the nature of the Trinity, as the one God is differentiated through recognition that this person of Christ is also the second person of the Trinity. This divine-human person reconciles humanity with God and gives a focus to the work of God in redemption. In this way Pentecostals proclaim both his role as Saviour and Lord. This Christological focus also grounds trinitarian theology in soteriology and acts as a counter to abstract speculation (LaCugna, 1991; Hunt, 1997). It is an identity that is energised by an experience of the Spirit, who mediates the very presence of both the Son and the Father (1 Jn 1.3; Turner, 2004), and who constitutes the church for the sake of the world. Finally, it is an ecclesiology that is shaped by the reign or kingdom of God, and this includes the eschatological tension that it brings. The church is caught between the inaugurated and consummated rule of God and, as such, constantly witnesses the tension in its life and work. This means that while it worships, prays for healing, exercises *charismata* and delivers hospitality, it is also on a journey into the very presence of Almighty God. It has not arrived, the journey continues, but one day there will be a grand homecoming. In the meantime, it anticipates the glory that will be revealed and strives to be faithful to the vocation it has received.

Contribution

It can be suggested that this research makes a significant contribution in a number of respects. It is the first study to use a practical-theological approach to investigate the ordinary theology of a Pentecostal congregation in a sustained and in-depth manner. It extends my version of the empirical-theological paradigm within practical theology (Cartledge, 2002a, 2003), thus demonstrating its continued relevance. This is significant both for research in practical theology, which has lacked any real attention to Pentecostalism, and for Pentecostal and Charismatic studies, which has only a limited record of empirical-theological research (Cartledge, 2010). It explores contemporary verbatim testimony as a mode of theological discourse and a unique source for theological reflection; and it is the first study to apply the notion of theological rescripting to ordinary discourse. It offers insights into the relationship between religion and society in the British context at this current time and suggests ways in which these might be further explored. It also engages with contemporary Pentecostal ecclesiology, providing an alternative model rooted in the concrete rather than the ideal church, and in this sense offers a critique of current scholarship, opening up a new avenue of debate: namely, the ways in which congregational studies can contribute to the development, or rescripting, of more systematic ecclesiological categories.

Future Research

In conclusion, some suggestions are made for future research in practical-theological studies of Pentecostal and Charismatic Christianity.

1. This study could be replicated in terms of methodology: other Pentecostal traditions could be studied in a similar congregational and qualitative manner, paying attention to the ordinary theology of adherents.
2. The findings from the key themes – worship, conversion, baptism in the Spirit, healing, life and witness, world mission and the second coming – could be operationalised and tested by means of a congregational questionnaire survey. The sample could be drawn from churches in the Assemblies of

God, Elim and the Apostolic traditions, as well other Pentecostal traditions in the UK.

3. The issues that have been identified as contextual to Birmingham could be researched more widely amongst other Christian churches in the city. This could include the so-called mainstream denominations as well as the newer independent churches.

4. The integration of immigrants into established British denominations is underdeveloped in the literature and this is an important social issue in the light of increased migration around the world.

5. One of the key issues to emerge from this study is the relationship of Christianity to other religions and how there is a concern amongst ordinary Pentecostals after the terrorist assaults in recent years. Further research could consider how both Christians and members of other religious traditions perceive each other, whether there are regional, ethnic and significant theological differences within (not just between) these religious traditions, and what steps might be taken in order to establish greater mutual understanding.

6. This approach to the study of ordinary Pentecostal theology could be applied in intercultural and comparative studies of global Pentecostalism, in order to ground such studies empirically across diverse cultural expressions.

7. Pentecostals have often considered testimony as an important feature of their spirituality. This study confirms this understanding and illustrates how contemporary testimony can be a source for theological reflection. Future work can build on insights from this study by examining more fully the notion of testimony as a legitimate theological mode.

Appendix A

The Statement of Fundamental Truths (1924)

The Scriptures, known as the Bible, are the inspired Word of God; the infallible and all-sufficient rule for faith, practice and conduct. This statement of Fundamental Truths is not intended as a creed of the Church, but as a basis of unity for a full Gospel Ministry (1 Cor 1–10), and we do not claim that it contains all truth in the Scriptures.

1. The Bible is the inspired word of God. 2 Tim 3.15–16; 1 Pet 2.2.
2. The unity of The One True and Living God who is the Eternally self existent "I Am" Who has also revealed Himself as One Being in three Persons, Father, Son, and Holy Spirit. Deut 6.4; Mark 12.29; Matt 28.19.
3. The fall of man, who was created pure and upright, but fell by voluntary transgression. Gen 1.26–31; 3.1–7; Rom 5.12–21.
4. Salvation through faith in Christ, Who died for our sins according to the Scriptures, was buried, but was raised from among the dead on the third day according to the Scriptures, and through His blood we have Redemption. Tit 2.11; Rom 10.8–15; Tit 3.5–7; 1 Cor 15.3–4.
5. The baptism by immersion in water is enjoined upon all who have really repented and have truly believed with all their hearts in Christ as Saviour and Lord. Matt 28.19; Acts 10.47–48; Acts 2.38–39.
6. The baptism of the Holy Spirit, the initial evidence of which is speaking with other tongues. Acts 2.1–4; Acts 10.44–46; 11.14–16; Acts 19.6.
7. Holiness of life and conduct in obedience to the command of God. "Be ye holy for I am holy." 1 Peter 1.14, 15, 16; Heb 12.14; 1 Thess 5.23; 1 John 2.6; also 1 Cor 13.
8. Divine Healing – Deliverance from sickness is provided for in the Atonement. Isaiah 53.4–5; Mat 8.16–17.
9. The Breaking of Bread. This is enjoined upon all believers until the Lord comes. Luke 22.14–20; 1 Cor 11.20–34.
10. The premillennial second coming of the Lord Jesus Christ himself is the blessed hope set before all believers. 1 Cor 15.22–24; 1 Thess 4.13–18; 1 Cor 15.51–57.
11. The everlasting punishment of all who are not written in the Book of Life. Rev 20.10–15.
12. The Gifts of the Holy Spirit and the offices as recorded in the New Testament. Eph 4.7–16; 1 Cor 12.

Source: Redemption Tidings, July 1924, 1, 1: 19

Appendix B

The Statement of Faith (2004)

1. We believe that the Bible (i.e. the Old and New Testaments excluding the Apocrypha), is the inspired Word of God, the infallible, all sufficient rule for faith and practice (2 Tim. 3:15–16; 2 Peter 1:21).

2. We believe in the unity of the One True and Living God who is the Eternal, Self-Existent "I AM", Who has also revealed Himself as One being co-existing in three Persons – Father, Son and Holy Spirit (Deut. 6:4; Mark 12:29; Matt 28:19; 2 Cor. 13:14).

3. We believe in the Virgin Birth, Sinless Life, Miraculous Ministry, Substitutionary Atoning Death, Bodily Resurrection, Triumphant Ascension and Abiding Intercession of the Lord Jesus Christ and in His personal, visible, bodily return in power and glory as the blessed hope of all believers (Isa. 7:14; Matt. 1:23; Heb. 7:26; 1 Pet. 2:22; Acts 2:22, 10:38; 2 Cor. 5:21; Heb. 9:12; Luke 24:39; 1 Cor. 15:4; Acts 1:9; Eph. 4:8–10; Rom. 8:34; Heb. 7:25; 1 Cor. 15:22–24, 51–57; 1 Thess. 4:13–18; Rev. 20:1–6).

4. We believe in the fall of man, who was created pure and upright, but fell by voluntary transgression (Gen. 1:26–31, 3:1–7; Rom. 5:12–21).

5. We believe in salvation through faith in Christ, who, according to the Scriptures, died for our sins, was buried and was raised from the dead on the third day, and that through His Blood we have Redemption (Titus 2:11, 3:5–7; Rom. 10:8–15; 1 Cor. 15:3–4). This experience is also known as the new birth, and is an instantaneous and complete operation of the Holy Spirit upon initial faith in the Lord Jesus Christ. (John 3:5–6; James 1:18; 1 Pet. 1:23; 1 John 5:1).

6. We believe that all who have truly repented and believed in Christ as Lord and Saviour are commanded to be baptised by immersion in water (Matt. 28:19; Acts 10:47–48; Acts 2:38–39).

7. We believe in the baptism in the Holy Spirit as an enduement of the believer with power for service, the essential, biblical evidence of which is the speaking with other tongues as the Spirit gives utterance (Acts 1:4–5, 8, 2:4, 10:44–46, 11:14–16, 19:6).

8. We believe in the operation of the gifts of the Holy Spirit and the gifts of Christ in the Church today (1 Cor. 12:4–11, 28; Eph. 4:7–16).

9. We believe in holiness of life and conduct in obedience to the command of God (1 Pet. 1:14–16; Heb. 12:14; 1 Thess. 5:23; 1 John 2:6).

10. We believe that deliverance from sickness, by Divine Healing is provided for in the Atonement (Isa. 53:4–5; Matt. 8:16–17; James 5:13–16).

11. We believe that all who have truly repented and believe in Christ as Lord and Saviour should regularly participate in Breaking of Bread (Luke 22:14–20; 1 Cor. 11:20–34).

12. We believe in the bodily resurrection of all men, the everlasting conscious bliss of all who truly believe in our Lord Jesus Christ and the everlasting conscious punishment of all whose names are not written in the Book of Life (Dan. 12:2–3; John 5:28–29; 1 Cor. 15:22–24; Matt. 25:46; 2 Thess. 1:9; Rev. 20:10–15).[1]

---

[1]   See www.aog.org.uk/church interest.asp; accessed on 31 January 2008. Cited with permission.

Appendix C
The Pattern of Worship

Major Units	Minor Links	Location

1. Welcome, Preparation to worship
   Greeting, Prayer, Exhortation
   Testimony
   Scripture reading/s
		Platform

2. Songs
   Phase 1: Upbeat (2–3)
   Phase 2: Quieter/reflective ones
	Praise shouts
	Exhortations
		Platform
		Plat./Main
		Plat./Main

3. Response
   Prophecy/Tongues and int./Sing in
tongues
     Ministry
       Thanksgiving
       (Prayer
       Testimony
       Clap offering)
	Interpretation
	Instructions
		Main
		Between
		Plat. to Main
		Main to Plat.

4. Communion
   Prayers over the elements
   Song/music in background
   Interpretation of its significance
   Spontaneous Bible reading/prayer
   Community-building actions
     Turn to the person next to you
	Song links
	Interpretation
	Congregation
	Instruction
		Between
		Platform
		Main
		Main
		Platform

5. Notices/Family business/Offertory
   DVD
   Family information
   Collection and prayer
	Song links
	
	Prayer for Preacher
		Platform
		
		Platform
		
		Platform

6. Sermon [Response if not at 3]	Song links	*Platform* *Platform*

Major Units	**Minor Links**	**Location**

7. Closure
  (Normally abrupt because of time)
    Prayer
    Statement
      Invitation to tea/coffee in
minor hall and service at 6.30pm
		Platform

References

Pentecostal Periodicals

The Apostolic Faith, 1906–1908

(*The Azusa Street Papers: A Reprint of the Apostolic Faith Mission Publications, Los Angeles, California (1906–1908)*, ed. William J. Seymour, Together in the Harvest Publications, P.O. Box 2090 Foley, AL 36536, USA, 1997).
(1906), 'The Old Time Pentecost', I, 1: 1.

Confidence, 1908–1926

(Published digitally by Tony Cauchi, Revival Library, King's Centre, High Street, Bishop's Waltham, SO32 1AA, UK, 2006)
(1908a), 'The Bridegroom Cometh', 1: 19.
(1908b), 'The Gift of Tongues', 2: 4–5.
(1908c), 'Tongues in the Foreign Field. Interesting Letters.' Supplement to *Confidence*, 2: 1–3.
(1908d), 'The Sunderland Conference, June 1908', 3: 12–13.
(1908e), 'The Near Coming of the Lord', 3: 17–18.
(1908f), 'Speaking in Tongues at Caesarea', 7: 22–23.
Boddy, Alexander A. (1908), 'Rules for Whitsuntide Conventions', 1: 2.
(1909a), 'Experience and Observations', II, 1: 7–8.
Boddy, Alexander A. (1909), 'Born from Above', II, 4: 95–98.
Boddy, Alexander A. (1910a), 'Health in Christ', III, 8: 175–179.
Boddy, Alexander A. (1910b), 'Seven Signs of His Coming', III, 12: 281–283, 287–288.
Boddy, Alexander A. (1910c), 'The Day of the Lord', III, 12: 288–289.
Paul, Jonathan (1911), 'The Bride and Her Heavenly Bridegroom', IV, 7: 152–153.
(1911), 'Tongues in the Air', IV, 9: 204.
Boddy, Alexander A (1911), 'The Second Advent: Our Blessed Hope', IV, 10: 228–229.
(1914), 'A Chart of the World's Ages and the Coming of the Lord', VII, 4: 70–71.
Boddy, Alexander A. (1914), 'Healing by Faith', VII, 6: 110–111, 113–114.
(1922) 'The Heavenly Birth', 131: 54–56.
(1926) Our Need for the New Creation', 141: 173–174.

Prophetic Vision

Hathaway, David (2008, Winter), 'The World Changed!', 50: 2–3.

Redemption Tidings, 1924–1939

(Published digitally by Tony Cauchi, Revival Library, King's Centre, High Street, Bishop's Waltham, SO32 1AA, UK, 2005)
Gee, Donald (1924), 'Jesus is Coming Again', 1, 1: 9–10.
(July 1924), 'The Statement of Fundamental Truths', 1, 1: 19.
Parr, John Nelson (1927a), 'Letters to New Converts', 3, 2: 6–7.
Parr, John Nelson (1927b), 'Letters to New Converts', 3, 3: 9
Gee, Donald (1927), 'Questions and Answers: "The Latter Rain"', 3, 4: 9.
Parr, John Nelson (1927c), 'Letters to New Converts', 3, 5: 2.
Coates, R.D. (1928), 'Discerning the Signs of the Times', 4, 7; 3–4.
Barratt, T.B. (1929), 'Holiness', 5, 6: 4–5.
Sykes, Seth (1931), 'Singing Souls to Christ', 7, 2: 4–5.
Gee, Donald (1931), 'Sanctification and Inspiration', 7, 3: 2–3; 7, 4: 5–6.
Carter, John (1932), 'The New Birth', 8, 7: 6–7.
Thomson, Cunningham (1934a), 'Regeneration, or the New Birth: Positive and Practical Evidences Relating Thereto', 10, 4: 6–7.
Vale, Garfield (1934), 'Topical Studies. Study XIV. Sanctification', 10, 4: 12.
Horton, Harold (1934), 'Blessed Hope of the Coming of the Lord', 10, 7: 1–2.
Carter, Howard (1934), 'The Second Advent of Christ', 10, 14: 1–2.
Thomson, Cunningham (1934b), 'Regeneration: The New Birth Defined', 10, 17: 6.
Thomson, Cunningham (1934c), 'Regeneration: The Trinity Employed in our Sonship', 10, 20: 2–3.
Squire, F.H. (1935), 'The Full Gospel of Jesus Christ', 11, 4: 3–4.
Vale, Garfield (1935), 'Christ's Second Coming', 11, 22: 14–15.
Gee, Donald (1936), 'Instructed in the Songs of the Lord', 12, 18: 4–5.
Carter, Howard (1937), 'Changed from Glory to Glory. The True Process of Sanctification', 13, 2: 5–6.
Gee, Donald (1937), 'Singing in the Spirit', 13, 3: 12–13.
McAlister, H. (1937), 'The Healing Christ', 13, 18: 2–3.
Sherlock, Chas. E. (1937a), 'II. Sanctification', 13, 19: 5–6.
Sherlock, Chas. E. (1937b), '13. Divine Healing', 13, 23: 3–4.
Comstock, E. (1938), 'Diving Healing – Is It for Today?', 14, 20: 5–6.
Boffey, G.H. (1939), 'The Pentecostal Testimony and Other Religious Bodies', 15, 19:5–6.
Cooper, Leslie (1939), 'Sanctification and the Baptism with the Holy Spirit', 15, 23: 1–2.
Woodford, L.F.W. (1939), 'His Coming Again', 15, 25: 3–5.

Church and Denomination Material

Butcher, John W. (n.d.), Base One: The Way to Church Membership, based on Rick Warren's Purpose Driven Church Christian Life and Service Seminars; see: www.saddlebackresources.com/en-US/MinistryTools/ClassMaterials/ClassMaterials.htm; accessed on 9 November 2009.

Garrard, David J. (2003), 'The Importance of Keeping the Premillennial Rider in any Statement of Faith regarding the Second Coming of Christ', A Discussion Paper submitted to the General Council of the Assemblies of God, The Donald Gee Centre, Mattersey Hall, nr. Doncaster.

Hyde, Bob (2002), 'Do Pentecostals Need to Be Premillennial?' A Discussion Paper submitted to the General Council of the Assemblies of God, The Donald Gee Centre, Mattersey Hall, nr. Doncaster.

Petts, David (2001), Letter to the Executive Council of the Assemblies of God, concerning a proposal to revise article 10, The Donald Gee Centre, Mattersey Hall, nr. Doncaster.

Redemption Hymnal (1951, reprinted 1952, 1954, 1960, 1964), London: Elim Publishing House; London: Assemblies of God Publishing House.

Websites

Assemblies of God (UK)
http://www.aog.org.uk/
Assemblies of God World Fellowship:
http://www.agcongress.org/01_abot/abt_agfellowship.html
Elim Pentecostal Church:
http://www.elim.org.uk/elim
Evangelical Alliance UK:
http://www.eauk.org/
Hockley Pentecostal Church:
http://www.hockleypentecostal.com/about/
http://www.youtube.com/watch?v=YCStZJhzZ4g
http://www.flickr.com/photos/faster1974/2859880733/
Worldwide Pentecostal Fellowship:
http://www.worldwidepf.com/go/default/index.cfm

Articles and Books

Albrecht, Daniel E. (1997), 'Pentecostal Spirituality: Ecumenical Potential and Challenge', *Cyberjournal for Pentecostal-Charismatic Research*, 2: 1–40.

Albrecht, Daniel E. (1999), *Rites in the Spirit: A Ritual Approach to Pentecostal/ Charismatic Spirituality*, Sheffield: Sheffield Academic Press.

Albrecht, Daniel E. (2004), 'Anatomy of Pentecostal Worship: A Pentecostal Analysis', in Wonsuk Ma and Robert P. Menzies (eds.), *The Spirit and Spirituality: Essays in Honour of Russell P. Spittler*, London: T & T Clark, pp. 70–82.

Aldridge, Alan (2000), *Religion in the Contemporary World: A Sociological Introduction*, Cambridge: Polity Press.

Alexander, Kimberly Ervin (2006), *Pentecostal Healing: Models in Theology and Practice*, Blandford Forum, Dorset: Deo Publishing.

Allen, David (1990), 'Signs and Wonders: The Origins, Growth, Development and Significance of Assemblies of God in Great Britain and Ireland 1900–1980', PhD thesis, University of London.

Allen, David (2007), *The Neglected Feast: Rescuing the Breaking of Bread*, Nottingham:Expression Publications.

Allen, Gillian and Wallis, Roy (1976), 'Pentecostalists as a Medical Minority', in Roy Wallis and Peter Morley (eds.), *Marginal Medicine*, London: Peter Owen, pp. 110–137.

Althouse, Peter (2003), *Spirit of the Last Days: Pentecostal Eschatology in Conversation with Jürgen Moltmann*, Sheffield: Sheffield Academic Press.

Althouse, Peter (2009), 'Towards a Pentecostal Ecclesiology: Participation in the Missional Life of the Triune God', *Journal of Pentecostal Theology* 18: 230–245.

Ammerman, Nancy T. (2007), *Everyday Religion: Observing Modern Religious Lives*, Oxford: Oxford University Press.

Amoah, Michael (2004), 'Christian Musical Worship and "Hostility to the Body": The Medieval Influence Versus the Pentecostal Revolution', *Implicit Religion* 7, 1: 59–75.

Ancel, Alfred (1974), *Theology of the Local Church in Relation to Migration*, Staten Island, NY: Center for Migration Studies.

Anderson, Allan (2004), *An Introduction to Pentecostalism: Global Charismatic Christianity*, Cambridge: Cambridge University Press.

Anderson, Allan (2007), *Spreading Fires: The Missionary Nature of Early Pentecostalism*, London: SCM.

Arrington, French (2003), *Encountering the Holy Spirit: Paths of Christian Growth and Service*, Cleveland, TN: Pathway.

Arweck, Elisabeth and Stringer, Martin (2002), *Theorizing Faith: The Insider/ Outsider Problem in the Study of Ritual*, Birmingham: University of Birmingham Press.

Astley, Jeff (2002), *Ordinary Theology: Looking, Listening and Learning in Theology*, Aldershot: Ashgate.

Astley, Jeff and Christie, Ann (2007), *Taking Ordinary Theology Seriously*, Cambridge: Grove Books, Pastoral Series 110.

Audi, Robert (2000), *Epistemology: A Contemporary Introduction to the Theory of Knowledge*, 2nd edn, London: Routledge.

Barrett, D.B. and Johnson, T.M. (2002), 'Global Statistics' in S.M. Burgess and E.M. van der Maas (eds.), *The New International Dictionary of Pentecostal and Charismatic Movements*, Grand Rapids, MI: Zondervan, pp. 284–302.

Barth, Karl (1956), *Church Dogmatics, Volume 1: The Doctrine of the Word of God. Prolegomena to Church Dogmatics, Part 2*, G.T. Thomson and Harold Knight (trans.), G.W. Bromiley and T.F. Torrance (eds.), Edinburgh: T & T Clark.

Bebbington, David W. (1989), *Evangelicalism in Modern Britian: A History from 1730s to 1980s*, London: Unwin Hyman.

Beckford, James A. (1983), 'The Restoration of "Power" to the Sociology of Religion', *Sociological Analysis* 44: 11–33.

Beidelman, Thomas O. (1974), 'Social Theory and the Study of Christian Missions in Africa', *Africa* 44: 235–249.

Beidelman, Thomas O. (1981), 'Contradictions between the Sacred and Secular Life: The Church Mission Society in Ukaguru, Tanzania, East Africa, 1876–1914', *Comparitive Studies in Society and History* 23: 73–95.

Beidelman, Thomas O. (1982), *Colonial Evangelism*, Bloomington: Indiana Press.

Beilby, James and Eddy, Paul R. (eds.) (2006), *The Nature of the Atonement: Four Views*, Downers Grove, IL: InterVarsity Press.

Berger, Peter L. (1969), *Sacred Canopy*, Garden City, NY: Doubleday.

Berger, Peter L. (1977), *Facing Up to Modernity*, New York: Basic Books.

Bevans, Stephen B. (2002), *Models of Contextual Theology*, revised and expanded edn, Maryknoll, NY: Orbis Books.

Blumhofer, Edith (1993), *Aimee Semple McPherson: Everybody's Sister*, Grand Rapids, MI: Eerdmans.

Boone, R. Jerome (1996), 'Community and Worship: Key Components of Pentecostal Christian Formation', *Journal of Pentecostal Theology* 8: 129–142.

Bowie, Fiona (2000), *The Anthropology of Religion*, Oxford: Blackwell.

Brown, Callum G. (2009), *The Death of Christian Britain: Understanding Secularisation 1800–2000*, 2nd edn, London: Routledge.

Bryman, Alan (2004), *Social Research Methods*, Oxford: Oxford University Press.

Cameron, Helen, Richter, Philip, Davies, Douglas and Ward, Frances (2005), *Studying Local Churches: A Handbook*, London: SCM.

Camery-Hoggatt, Jerry (2005), 'The Word of God in Living Voices: Orality and Literacy in the Pentecostal Tradition', *Pneuma: The Journal of the Society for Pentecostal Studies* 27, 2: 225–255.

Cartledge, Mark J. (1994), 'Charismatic Prophecy: A Definition and Description', *Journal of Pentecostal Theology* 5: 81–122.

Cartledge, Mark J. (1995), 'Charismatic Prophecy', *Journal of Empirical Theology*, 8, 1: 71–88.

Cartledge, Mark J. (1996), 'Empirical Theology: Towards an Evangelical-Charismatic Hermeneutic', *Journal of Pentecostal Theology* 9: 115–126.

Cartledge, Mark J. (1998a), 'The Future of Glossolalia: Fundamentalist or Experientialist?', *Religion*, 28, 3: 233–244.

Cartledge, Mark J. (1998b) 'Interpreting Charismatic Experience: Hypnosis, Altered States of Consciousness and the Holy Spirit?', *Journal of Pentecostal Theology*, 13: 117–132.

Cartledge, Mark J. (1998c), 'Practical Theology and Empirical Identity', *European Journal of Theology*, 7, 1: 37–44.

Cartledge, Mark J. (1999a) 'Tongues of the Spirit: An Empirical-Theological Study of Charismatic Glossolalia', PhD thesis, University of Wales.

Cartledge, Mark J. (1999b), 'The Socialisation of Glossolalia', in Leslie J. Francis (ed.), *Sociology, Theology and the Curriculum*, London: Cassell, pp. 125–134.

Cartledge, Mark J. (1999c), 'The Symbolism of Charismatic Glossolalia', *Journal of Empirical Theology*, 12, 1: 37–51.

Cartledge, Mark J. (1999d) 'Empirical Theology: Inter- or Intra- Disciplinary?', *Journal of Beliefs & Values* 20, 1: 98–104.

Cartledge, Mark J. (2000), 'The Nature and Function of New Testament Glossolalia', *Evangelical Quarterly*, 72, 2: 135–150.

Cartledge, Mark J. (2002a), *Charismatic Glossolalia: An Empirical-Theological Study*, Aldershot: Ashgate.

Cartledge, Mark J. (2002b), 'Practical Theology and Charismatic Spirituality: Dialectics in the Spirit', *Journal of Pentecostal Theology*, 10, 2: 107–124.

Cartledge, Mark J. (2002c), *Testimony: Its Importance, Place and Potential*, Cambridge: Grove Books, R9.

Cartledge, Mark J. (2003), *Practical Theology: Charismatic and Empirical Perspectives*, Carlisle: Paternoster.

Cartledge, Mark J. (2004), 'Affective Theological Praxis: Understanding the Direct Object of Practical Theology', *International Journal of Practical Theology*, 8, 1: 34–52.

Cartledge, Mark J. (2006a), *Encountering the Spirit: The Charismatic Tradition*, London: Darton, Longman & Todd.

Cartledge, Mark J. (2006b), 'The Practice of Tongues Speech as a Case Study: A Practical-Theological Perspective', in Mark J. Cartledge (ed.), *Speaking in Tongues: Multi-disciplinary Perspectives*, Milton Keynes: Paternoster, pp. 206–234.

Cartledge, Mark J. (2008a), 'The Early Pentecostal Theology of *Confidence Magazine* (1908–1926): A Version of the Five-Fold Gospel?', *Journal of the European Pentecostal Theological Association*, 28, 2: 117–130.

Cartledge, Mark J. (2008b), '*Theological Renewal* (1975–1983): Listening to an Editor's Agenda for Church and Academy', *Pneuma: The Journal of the Society for Pentecostal Studies*, 30, 1: 83–107.

Cartledge, Mark J. (2008c), 'Pentecostal Experience: An Example of Practical-Theological Rescripting', *Journal of the European Pentecostal Theological Association*, 28, 1: 21–33.

Cartledge, Mark J. (2010) 'Practical Theology', in Allan Anderson, Michael Bergunder, André Droogers and Cornelius van der Laan (eds.), *Studying Global Pentecostalism: Theories and Methods*, Berkeley: University of California Press, pp. 348–376.

Casanova, José (1994), *Public Religions in the Modern World*, Chicago: University of Chicago Press.

Chan, Simon (2000a), 'Mother Church: Toward a Pentecostal Ecclesiology', *Pneuma: The Journal of the Society for Pentecostal Studies* 22, 2: 177–208.

Chan, Simon (2000b), *Pentecostal Theology and the Christian Spiritual Tradition*, Sheffield: Sheffield Academic Press.

Christie, Ann and Astley, Jeff (2009), 'Ordinary Soteriology: A Qualitative Study' in Leslie J. Francis, Mandy Robbins and Jeff Astley (eds.), *Empirical Theology in Texts and Tables: Qualitative, Quantitative and Comparative Perspectives*, Leiden: Brill, pp. 177–196.

Clifton, Shane (2007), 'Pentecostal Ecclesiology: A Methodological Proposal for a Diverse Movement', *Journal of Pentecostal Theology*, 15, 2: 213–232.

Coady, C.A.J. (2000), *Testimony: A Philosophical Study*, Oxford: Clarendon Press.

Coleman, Simon (2000), *The Globalisation of Charismatic Christianity: Spreading the Gospel of Prosperity*, Cambridge: Cambridge University Press.

Conn, Walter (1986), 'Adult Conversions', *Pastoral Psychology* 34: 225–236.

Corten, André and Marshall-Fratani, Ruth (eds.) (2001), *Between Babel and Pentecost: Transnational Pentecostalism in Africa and Latin America*, London: Hurst & Company.

Cotterell, Peter (2006), 'Conversion and Apostasy: The Case of Islam', in Christopher Partridge and Helen Reid (eds.), *Finding and Losing Faith: Studies in Conversion*, Milton Keynes: Paternoster, pp. 190–205.

Coulter, Dale M. (2007), 'The Development of Ecclesiology in the Church of God (Cleveland, TN): A Forgotten Contribution?', *Pneuma: The Journal of the Society for Pentecostal Studies* 29, 1: 59–85.

Coulter, Dale M. (2008), '"Delivered By the Power of God": Toward a Pentecostal Understanding of Salvation', *International Journal of Systematic Theology*, 10, 4: 447–467.

Cox, Harvey (1996), *Fire from Heaven: The Rise of Pentecostal Spirituality and the Reshaping of Religion in the Twenty-first Century*, London: Cassell.

Creswell, John W. (1998), *Qualitative Inquiry and Research Design: Choosing Among Five Traditions*, London: Sage.

Cruchley-Jones, Peter (ed.) (2008), *God at Ground Level*, Oxford: Peter Lang.

Csordas, Thomas J. (1997), *The Sacred Self: A Cultural Phenomenology of Charismatic Healing*, 2nd edn, Berkeley: University of California Press.

Csordas, Thomas J. (2001), *Language, Charisma, and Creativity: Ritual Life in the Catholic Charismatic Renewal*, Basingstoke: Palgrave.

Davie, Grace (1994), *Religion in Britain Since 1945*, Oxford: Blackwell.

Davie, Grace (2004), 'A Reply to Francis and Robbins', *Implicit Religion* 7, 1: 55–58.

Davie, Grace (2007), *The Sociology of Religion*, London: Sage.

Davis, Caroline Franks (1989), *The Evidential Force of Religious Experience*, Oxford: Clarendon Press.

De Matviuk, Marcela A. Chaván (2002), 'Latin American Pentecostal Growth: Culture, Orality and the Power of Testimony, *Asian Journal of Pentecostal Studies*, 5, 2: 205–222.

Dempster, Murray A. (1995), 'Evangelism, Social Concern, and the Kingdom of God', in Murray A. Dempster, Byron D. Klaus and Douglas Petersen (eds.), *Called and Empowered: Global Mission in Pentecostal Perspective*, Peabody, MA: Hendrickson.

Dempster, Murray A., Klaus, Byron D., and Petersen, Douglas (eds.) (1999), *The Globalization of Pentecostalism: A Religion Made To Travel*, Carlisle: Regnum and Paternoster.

Dermawan, Agustinus (2003), 'The Spirit in Creation and Environmental Stewardship: A Preliminary Pentecostal Response toward Ecological Theology', *Asian Journal of Theology*, 6, 2: 199–217.

Dey, Ian (1993), *Qualitative Data Analysis: A User-Friendly Guide for Social Scientists*, London: Routledge.

Dingemans, Gijsbert D.J. (1996), 'Practical Theology in the Academy: A Contemporary Overview', *The Journal of Religion*, 76, 1: 82–96.

Dreyer, Jaco S. (2009), 'Establishing Truth from Participation and Distanciation in Empirical Theology', in Leslie J. Francis, Mandy Robbins and Jeff Astley (eds.), *Empirical Theology in Texts and Tables: Qualitative, Quantitative and Comparative Perspectives*, Leiden: Brill, pp. 3–25.

Dunn, James D.G. (1970), *The Baptism in the Holy Spirit: A Re-examination of the New Testament Teaching on the Gift of the Holy Spirit in Relation to Pentecostalism Today*, London: SCM.

Dunn, James D.G. (1975), *Jesus and the Spirit: A Study of the Religious and Charismatic Experience of Jesus and the First Christians as Reflected in the New Testament*, London: SCM.

Dunn, James D.G. (1996), *The Acts of the Apostles*, Epworth Commentaries, Peterborough: Epworth Press.

Edwards, David and Stott, John (1988), *Essentials: A liberal-evangelical dialogue*, London: Hodder & Stoughton.

Ellington, Scott A. (2000), 'The Costly Loss of Testimony', *Journal of Pentecostal Theology* 16: 48–59.

Ellington, Scott A. (2001), 'History, Story, and Testimony: Locating Truth in a Pentecostal Hermeneutic', *Pneuma: The Journal of the Society for Pentecostal Studies* 23, 2: 245–263.

Ellington, Scott A. (2007), 'The Reciprocal Reshaping of History and Experience in the Psalms: Interactions with Pentecostal Testimony, *Journal of Pentecostal Theology* 16, 1: 18–31.

Epstein, Seymour (1985), 'The Implications for Cognitive-Experiential Self-Theory for Research in Social Psychology and Personality', *Journal for the Theory of Social Behaviour* 15: 283–310.

'Evangelization, Proselytism and Common Witness: The Report from the Fourth Phase of the International Dialogue (1990–1997) between the Roman Catholic Church and Some Classical Pentecostal Churches and Leaders' (1999), *Pneuma: The Journal of the Society for Pentecostal Studies* 21, 1: 11–51.

Faupel, D. William (1996), *The Everlasting Gospel: The Significance of Eschatology in the Development of Pentecostal Thought*, Sheffield: Sheffield Academic Press.

Fisher, Harriet and Reeve, Olive (n.d.), *Still It Flows: The Story of the Pentecostal Church at Hockley Birmingham*, Lytham, Lancs: Lord's Publishers.

Flinn, Frank K. (1999), 'Conversion: Up from Evangelicalism or the Pentecostal and Charismatic Experience', in Christopher Lamb and M. Darrol Bryant (eds.), *Religious Conversion: Contemporary Practices and Controversies*, London: Cassell, pp. 51–72.

Forrester, Duncan B. (2000), *Truthful Action: Explorations in Practical Theology*, Edinburgh: T & T Clark.

Francis, Leslie J. and Robbins, Mandy (2004), 'Belonging without Believing: A Study in the Social Significance of Anglican Identity and Implicit Religion among 13–15 Year-Old Males', *Implicit Religion* 7, 1: 37–54.

Furbey, Robert, Dinham, Adam, Farnell, Richard, Finneron, Doreen, and Wilkinson, Guy (2006), *Faith as Social Capital: Connecting or Dividing?*, Bristol: The Polity Press and the Joseph Rowntree Foundation.

Gabriel, Andrew K. (2007), 'Pneumatological Perspectives for a Theology of Nature: The Holy Spirit in Relation to Ecology and Technology', *Journal of Pentecostal Theology*, 15, 2: 195–212.

Gallagher Robert L. (2006), 'The Holy Spirit in the World: In Non-Christians, Creation and Other Religions', *Asian Journal of Pentecostal Studies*, 9, 1: 17–33.

Gallay, Paul with Jourjon, Maurice (1974), *Grégoire de Nazianze Lettres Théologiques: Introduction, Texte Critique, Traduction et Notes*, Paris: Les Éditions du Cerf.

Gallup (2009), *The Gallup Coexist Index 2009: A Global Study of Interfaith Relations: With an In-depth Analysis of Muslim Integration in France, Germany, and the United Kingdom*, Washington, DC: Gallup, Inc.

Gee, Donald (1935), *Upon All Flesh: A Pentecostal World Tour*, Springfield, MI: Gospel Publishing House.

Gee, Donald (1944), *Why Pentecost?*, London: Victory Press.

Gelpi, Donald, J. (1982), 'Conversion: The Challenge of Contemporary Charismatic Piety', *Theological Studies* 43: 606–628.

Gerloff, Roswith (2008), 'Churches of the Spirit: The Pentecostal/Charismatic Movement and Africa's Contribution to the Renewal of Christianity', in Afe Adogame, Roswith Gerloff and Klaus Hock (eds.), *Christianity in Africa and the African Diaspora*, London: Continuum, pp. 208–220.

Gill, Robin (2003), 'The Future of Religious Participation and Belief in Britain and Beyond', in Richard K. Fenn (ed.), *The Blackwell Companion to Sociology of Religion*, Oxford: Blackwell, pp. 279–291.

Gillespie, V. Bailey (1991), *The Dynamics of Religious Conversion*, Birmingham, AL: Religious Education Press.

Gilpin, G. Wesley (1976), 'The Place of the Pentecostal Movement Today', in P.S. Brewster (ed.), *Pentecostal Doctrine*, private publication by P.S. Brewster, pp. 113–126.

Glass, James J. (1996), 'Eschatology: A Clear and Present Danger – A Sure and Certain Hope', in Keith Warrington (ed.), *Pentecostal Perspectives*, Carlisle: Paternoster, pp. 120–146.

Gold, Malcom (2006), 'From the "Upper Room" to the "Christian Centre": Changes in the Use of Sacred Space and Artefacts in a Pentecostal Assembly', in E. Arweck and W. Keenan (eds.), *Materializing Religion: Expression, Performance and Ritual*, Aldershot: Ashgate, pp. 74–88.

Gräb, Wilhelm and Charbonier, Lars (2009) (eds.), *Secularization Theories, Religious Identity and Practical Theology*, Berlin: LIT Verlag.

Graham, Elaine, Walton, Heather and Ward, Frances (2005), *Theological Reflection: Methods*, London: SCM.

Graham, Elaine, Walton, Heather and Ward, Frances (2007), *Theological Reflection: Sources*, London: SCM.

Green, Laurie (1999), 'Oral Culture and the World of Words', *Theology* CII, 809: 328–335.

Hardy, Daniel W. and Ford, David F. (1984), *Jubilate: Theology in Praise*, London: Darton, Longman & Todd.

Hathaway, Malcolm R. (1996), 'The Role of William Oliver Hutchinson and the Apostolic Faith Church in the Formation of British Pentecostal Churches', *Journal of the European Pentecostal Theological Association* 16: 40–57.

Healy, Nicholas M. (2000), *Church, World and the Christian Life: Practical-Prophetic Ecclesiology*, Cambridge: Cambridge University Press.

Heirich, Max (1977), 'Change of Heart: A Test of Some Widely Held Theories about Religious Conversion', *American Journal of Sociology* 83: 653–680.

Heitink, Gerben (1993), *Practical Theology: History, Theory, Action Domains*, Grand Rapids, MI: Eerdmans.

Hewer, Chris (2003), 'The Multireligious Multicultural Society: A Case Study of Birmingham, England', in Viggo Mortensen (ed.), *Theology and the Religions: A Dialogue*, Grand Rapids, MI: Eerdmans, pp. 67–71.

Hine, Virginia H. (1970), 'Bridge Burners: Commitment and Participation in a Religious Movement', *Sociological Analysis* 31: 61–66.

Hollenweger, Walter J. (1972), *The Pentecostals: The Charismatic Movement in the Churches*, London: SCM.

Hollenweger, Walter J. (1997), *Pentecostalism: Origins and Developments Worldwide*, Peabody, MA: Hendrickson.

Hudson, D. Neil (1998), 'Worship: Singing a New Song in a Strange Land', in K. Warrington (ed.), *Pentecostal Perspectives*, Carlisle: Paternoster, pp. 177–203.

Hunt, Anne (1997), *The Trinity and the Pascal Mystery: A Development in Recent Catholic Theology*, Collegeville, MN: The Liturgical Press.

Hunt, Stephen (2009), 'The Florida "Outpouring" Revival: A Melting Pot for Contemporary Pentecostal Prophecy and Eschatology?', *PentecoStudies: Online Journal for the Interdisciplinary Study of Pentecostalism and Charismatic Movements* 8, 1: 37–57.

Hunter, Harold D. (2002), 'Ordinances, Pentecostal' in S.M. Burgess and E.M. Van der Mass (eds.), *The New International Dictionary of Pentecostal and Charismatic Movements – Revised and Expanded Edition*, Grand Rapids, MI: Zondervan, pp. 947–949.

Hütter, Reinhard (2002), 'Hospitality and Truth: The Disclosure of Practices in Worship and Doctrine', in Miroslav Volf and Dorothy C. Bass (eds.), *Practicing Theology: Beliefs and Practices in Christian Life*, Grand Rapids, MI: Eerdmans, pp. 206–227.

Inbody, Tyron (1992), 'History of Empirical Theology', in Randolph Crump Miller (ed.), *Empirical Theology: A Handbook*, Birmingham, AL: Religion Education Press, pp. 11–35.

Ipgrave, Michael (2006), 'Conversion, Dialogue and Identity: Reflections on the British Context', in Christopher Partridge and Helen Reid (eds.), *Finding and Losing Faith: Studies in Conversion*, Milton Keynes: Paternoster, pp. 3–22.

James, William (1925), *The Varieties of Religious Experience: A Study in Human Nature*, 35th edn, New York: Longmans, Green and Co. (orig. 1902).

Jarvis, R. and Fielding, A.G. (1971), 'The Church, Clergy and Community Relations', in Alan Bryman (ed.), *Religion in Birmingham: Essays in the Sociology of Religion*, Birmingham: University of Birmingham, pp. 85–98.

Kalu, Ogbu (2008), *African Pentecostalism: An Introduction*, Oxford: Oxford University Press.

Kärkkäinen, Veli-Matti (2002), ed. Amos Yong, *Toward a Pneumatological Theology: Pentecostal and Ecumenical Perspectives on Ecclesiology, Soteriology, and the Theology of Mission*, Lanham, NY: University Press of America.

Kärkkäinen, Veli-Matti (2004), *Trinity and Religious Pluralism: The Doctrine of the Trinity in Christian Theology of Religions*, Aldershot: Ashgate.

Kay, William K. (1989), 'A History of the British Assemblies of God', PhD thesis, University of Nottingham.

Kay, William K. (1998), 'Assemblies of God: Distinctive Continuity and Distinctive Change', in Keith Warrington (ed.), *Pentecostal Perspectives*, Carlisle: Paternoster.

Kay, William K. (2000a), *Pentecostals in Britain*, Carlisle: Paternoster.

Kay, William K. (2000b), 'Pre-Millennial Tensions: What Pentecostal Ministers Look Forward to', in Martyn Percy (ed.), *Calling Time: Religion and Change at the Turn of the Millennium*, Sheffield: Sheffield Academic Press, pp. 93–113.

Kay, William K. (2006), 'Pentecostal Perspectives on Conversion', in Christopher Partridge and Helen Reid (eds.), *Finding and Losing Faith: Studies in Conversion*, Milton Keynes: Paternoster, pp. 103–119.

Kay, William K. (2007), *Apostolic Networks in Britain: New Ways of Being Church*, Milton Keynes: Paternoster.

Kay, William K. (2008), 'Pentecostal and Charismatic Churches: Minorities that Resist Secularisation', in Hans-Georg Ziebertz and Ulrich Riegel (eds.), *Europe: Secular or Post-Secular?*, Berlin: LIT Verlag, pp. 127–142.

Kay, William K. (2009), *SCM Core Text: Pentecostalism*, London: SCM.

Kay, William K. and Dyer, Anne E. (2004), *Pentecostal and Charismatic Studies: A Reader*, London: SCM.

Kimmel, Allan J. (2007), *Ethical Issues in Behavioural Research: Basic and Applied Perspectives*, Oxford: Blackwell.

Knight, Henry H., III (1993), 'God's Faithfulness and God's Freedom: A Comparison of Contemporary Theologies of Healing', *Journal of Pentecostal Theology* 2: 65–89.

Kreider, A. (1999), *The Change of Conversion and the Origin of Christendom*, Harrisburg, PA: Trinity Press International.

Krueger, Richard A. (1988), *Focus Groups: A Practical Guide for Applied Research*, London: Sage.

Labanow, Cory E. (2009), *Evangelicalism and the Emerging Church: A Congregational Study of a Vineyard Church*, Aldershot: Ashgate.

LaCugna, Catherine M. (1991), *God for Us: The Trinity and Christian Life*, New York: HarperCollins.

Land, Steven J., Moore, Rick, D., and Thomas, John Christopher (1992), 'Editorial', *Journal of Pentecostal Theology* 1: 3–5.

Land, Steven J. (1993), *Pentecostal Spirituality: A Passion for the Kingdom*, Sheffield: Sheffield Academic Press.

Laurentin, René (1977), *Catholic Pentecostalism*, London: Darton, Longman & Todd, 1977.

Littlewood, David (2010), 'Dancing in the aisles with Hockley's dynamic duo!', *Heroes of the Faith – Pilot Issue*, January: 32–33.

Lofland, John and Stark, Rodney (1965), 'Becoming a World-Saver: A Theory of Conversion to a Deviant Perspective', *American Sociological Review* 30: 862–875.

Lord, Andy (2003), 'Principles for a Charismatic Approach to Other Faiths', *Asian Journal of Pentecostal Studies* 6, 2: 235–246.

Lynch, Gordon (2006), 'Beyond Conversion: Exploring the Process of Moving Away from Evangelical Christianity', in Christopher Partridge and Helen Reid (eds.), *Finding and Losing Faith: Studies in Conversion*, Milton Keynes: Paternoster, pp. 23–38.

Macchia, Frank D. (1993a), *Spirituality and Social Liberation: The Message of the Blumhardts in the Light of the Wuertemberg Pietism*, Metuchen, NJ: Scarecrow Press.

Macchia, Frank D. (1993b), 'Tongues as a Sign: Towards a Sacramental Understanding of Pentecostal Experience', *Pneuma: The Journal of the Society for Pentecostal Studies*, 15, 1: 61–76.

Macchia, Frank D. (1996), 'Tongues and Prophecy: A Pentecostal Perspective' in Jürgen Moltmann and Karl-Josef Kuschel (eds.), *Pentecostal Movements as an Ecumenical Challenge*, Concilium 3, London: SCM.

Macchia, Frank D. (2002), 'Theology, Pentecostal' in S.M. Burgess and E.M. Van der Mass (eds.) *The New International Dictionary of Pentecostal and Charismatic Movements*, revised and expanded edn, Grand Rapids, MI: Zondervan, pp. 1121–1141.

Macchia, Frank D. (2006) *Baptized in the Spirit: A Global Pentecostal Theology*, Grand Rapids, MI: Zondervan.

MacNutt, Francis (1974), *Healing*, Notre Dame, IN: Ave Maria Press.

Marshall, I. Howard (1991), *The IVP New Testament Commentary Series: 1 Peter*, Leicester: IVP.

Martin, David (2005), *On Secularization: Towards a Revised General Theory*, Aldershot: Ashgate.

Martin, David (2006), 'Undermining Old Paradigms: Rescripting Pentecostal Accounts', *PentecoStudies: Online Journal for the Interdisciplinary Study of Pentecostal and Charismatic Movements*, 5, 1: 18–38.

Massey, Richard D. (1987), '"A Sound and Scriptural Union": An Examination of the Origins of the Assemblies of God of Great Britain and Ireland during the Years 1920–1925', PhD thesis, University of Birmingham.

Massey, Richard D. (1992), *Another Springtime: The Life of Donald Gee, Pentecostal Leader and Teacher*, Guildford: Highland Books.

McGuire, Meredith B. (1977), 'Testimony as a Commitment Mechanism in Catholic Pentecostal Prayer Groups', *Journal for the Scientific Study of Religion* 16, 2: 165–168.

McGuire, Meredith B. (1988), *Ritual Healing in Suburban America*, New Brunswick, NJ: Rutgers University Press.

McGuire, Meredith B. (1990), 'Religion and the Body: Rematerializing the Human Body in the Social Sciences of Religion', *Journal for the Social Scientific Study of Religion* 29, 3: 283–296.

McGuire, Meredith B. (1992), *Religion: The Social Context*, 3rd edn, Belmont, CA: Wadsworth.

McGuire, Meredith B. (1996), 'Religion and Healing the Mind/Body/Self', *Social Compass* 43, 1: 101–116.

McGuire, Meredith B. (2008), *Lived Religion: Faith and Practice in Everyday Life*, Oxford: Oxford University Press.

McQueen, Larry (2009), 'Early Pentecostal Eschatology in the Light of *The Apostolic Faith*, 1906–1908', Paper presented to the 38th Annual Meeting of the Society for Pentecostal Studies, Eugene, OR, 17pp.

Menzies, William W. and Menzies, Robert P. (2000), *Spirit and Power: Foundations of Pentecostal Experience*, Grand Rapids, MI: Zondervan.

Moltmann, Jürgen (1978), *Church in the Power of the Spirit*, London: SCM.

Moltmann, Jürgen (1996), *The Coming of God: Christian Eschatology*, London: SCM.

Newbigin, Lesslie (1989), *The Gospel in a Pluralist Society*, London: SPCK.

O'Leary, Stephen D. (1994), *Arguing the Apocalypse: A Theory of Millennial Rhetoric*, Oxford: Oxford University Press.

Olubunmi, Christopher (1981), 'Christ Apostolic Church of Nigeria: A Suggested Pentecostal Consideration of its Historical, Organisational and Theological Developments, 1918–1975', PhD thesis, University of Exeter.

'On Becoming a Christian: Insights from Scripture and the Patristic Writings with Some Contemporary Reflections' (2007), *Cyberjournal for Pentecostal-Charismatic Research* 18: 1–99; http://www.pctii.org/cyberj/cyberj18/2007RC_Pent_Dialogue.pdf; accessed on 27 August 2009.

Osmer, Richard R. (2004), 'Johannes van der Ven's Contribution to the New Consensus in Practical Theology', in Chris A.M. Hermans and Mary E. Moore (eds.), *Hermeneutics and Empirical Research in Practical Theology: The Contribution of Empirical Theology by Johannes A. van der Ven*, Leiden: Brill, pp. 149–167.

Osmer, Richard R. (2008), *Practical Theology: An Introduction*, Grand Rapids, MI: Eerdmans.

Parker, Stephen E. (1996), *Led by the Spirit: Toward a Practical Theology of Pentecostal Discernment and Decision Making*, Sheffield: Sheffield Academic Press.

Parry, Robin (2005), *Worshipping Trinity: Coming Back to the Heart of Worship*, Milton Keynes, Paternoster.

Percy, Martyn (1996), *Words, Wonder and Power*, London: SPCK.

Percy, Martyn (1997), 'Sweet Rapture: Subliminal Eroticism in Contemporary Charismatic Worship', *Theology and Sexuality* 6: 71–106.

Percy, Martyn (2000), 'Introduction', in Martyn Percy (ed.), *Previous Convictions: Conversion in the Present Day*, London: SPCK, pp. ix–xviii.

Petts, David (1993), 'Healing and the Atonement', PhD thesis, University of Nottingham.

Petts, David (1998), 'The Baptism in the Holy Spirit: The Theological Distinctive', in Keith Warrington (ed.), *Pentecostal Perspectives*, Carlisle: Paternoster, pp. 98–119.

(The) Pew Forum on Religion & Public Life (2006), *Spirit and Power: A 10-Country Survey of Pentecostals*, Washington, DC: The Pew Forum; www. pewforum.org; accessed on 20 September 2009.

Pinnock, Clark (1992), *A Wideness in God's Mercy: The Finality of Jesus Christ in a World of Religions*, Grand Rapids, MI: Zondervan.

Pinnock, Clark (1996), *Flame of Love: A Theology of the Holy Spirit*, Downers Grove, IL: InterVarsity Press.

Pinnock, Clark (2006), 'The Church in the Power of the Spirit: The Promise of Pentecostal Ecclesiology', *Journal of Pentecostal Theology* 14, 2: 147–165.

Plüss, Jean-Daniel (1987), 'How Public Are Public Testimonies? A Short Reflection on Liturgical Practice', *European Pentecostal Theological Association Bulletin* 6, 1: 4–12.

Plüss, Jean-Daniel (1988), *Therapeutic and Prophetic Narratives in Worship: A Hermeneutic Study of Testimonies and Visions – Their Potential and Significance for Christian Worship and Secular Society*, Frankfurt am Main: Peter Lang.

Plüss, Jean-Daniel (1999), 'Globalization of Pentecostalism or Globalization of Individualism? A European Perspective', in Murray W. Dempster, Byron D. Klaus and Douglas Petersen (eds.), *The Globalization of Pentecostalism: A Religion Made to Travel*, Oxford: Regnum Books, pp. 170–182.

Poewe, Karla (1999), 'Charismatic Conversion in the Light of Augustine's *Confessions*', in Christopher Lamb and M. Darrol Bryant (eds.), *Religious Conversion: Contemporary Practices and Controversies*, London: Cassell, pp. 191–206.

Poloma, Margaret M. (1989), *The Assemblies of God at the Crossroads: Charisma and Institutional Dilemmas*, Knoxville, TN: University of Tennessee Press.

Poloma, Margaret M. (2001), 'The Millenarianism of the Pentecostal Movement', in Stephen Hunt (ed.), *Christian Millenarianism: From the Early Church to Waco*, London: C. Hurst & Co., pp. 166–186.

Poloma, Margaret M. (2003), *Main Street Mystics: The Toronto Blessing & Reviving Pentecostalism*, Walnut Creek, CA: AltaMira Press.

Poloma, Margaret M. and Hood, Ralph W. (2008), *Blood and Fire: Godly Love in a Pentecostal Emerging Church*, New York: New York University Press.

Rambo, Lewis R. (1993), *Understanding Religious Conversion*, London: Yale University Press.

Rambo, Lewis R. and Farhadian, Charles E. (1999), 'Converting: Stages of Religious Change', in Christopher Lamb and M. Darrol Bryant (eds.), *Religious Conversion: Contemporary Practices and Controversies*, London: Cassell, pp. 23–34.

Reichenback, Bruce R. (2006), 'Healing View', in James K. Beilby and Paul R Eddy (eds.), *The Nature of the Atonement: Four Views*, Downers Grove, IL: InterVarsity Press, pp. 117–142.

Richie, Tony (2010), 'Speaking by the Spirit: A Wesleyan-Pentecostal Theology of Testimony as a Model for Interreligious Encounter and Dialogue in the USA with Global Implications', PhD thesis, University of Middlesex.

Robeck, Cecil M., Jr. and Sandidge, Jerry L. (1990), 'The Ecclesiology of *Koinōnia* and Baptism: A Pentecostal Perspective', *Journal of Ecumenical Studies* 27, 3: 504–534.

Robeck, Cecil M., Jr. (2006), *The Azusa Street Mission and Revival: The Birth of The Global Pentecostal Movement*, Nasville, TN: Thomas Nelson.

Robeck, Cecil M., Jr. (2008), '"On Becoming a Christian": An Important Theme in the International Roman Catholic–Pentecostal Dialogue', *PentecoStudies: An Interdisciplinary Journal for Research on the Pentecostal and Charismatic Movements* 7, 2: 1–28.

Robson, Colin (2002), *Real World Research*, 2nd edn, Oxford: Blackwell.

Romain, Jonathan A. (2000), *Your God Shall Be My God: Religious Conversion in Britain Today*, London: SCM Press.

Sanders, Cheryl J (1997), 'African-American Worship in the Pentecostal and Holiness Movements', *Wesleyan Theological Journal* 32, 2: 31–35; http://wesley.nnu.edu/wesleyan_theology/thejrnl/31-35/32-2-6.htm; accessed on 29 May 2008.

Savage, Sara (2000), 'A Psychology of Conversion – From All Angles', in Martyn Percy (ed.), *Previous Convictions: Conversion in the Present Day*, London: SPCK, pp. 1–18.

Schreiter, Robert J. (1985), *Constructing Local Theologies*, London: SCM.

Sequeira, Debra-L. (1994), 'Gifts of Tongues and Healing: The Performance of Charismatic Renewal', *Text and Performance Quarterly* 14: 126–143.

Smail, Thomas A. (1978), 'Spiritual Renewal and the Resurrection of Christ', *Theological Renewal* 8: 2–6.

Smith, James K.A. (1997), 'The Closing of the Book: Pentecostals, Evangelicals and the Sacred Writings', *Journal of Pentecostal Theology*, 11: 49–71.

Smyth, John C. (1976), 'The Signs of the Times', in P.S. Brewster (ed.), *Pentecostal Doctrine*, private publication by P.S. Brewster, pp. 381–390.

Solivan, Samuel (1998), 'Interreligious Dialogue: An Hispanic American Pentecostal Perspective', in S. Mark Heim (ed.), *Grounds for Understanding: Ecumenical Resources for Responses to Religious Pluralism*, Grand Rapids, MI: Eerdmans, pp. 37–45.

Spittler, Russell P. (2002), 'Glossolalia', in S.M. Burgess and Eduard M. van der Mass (eds.), *The New International Dictionary of Pentecostal and Charismatic Movements*, revised and expanded edn, Grand Rapids, MI: Zondervan, pp. 670–676.

Stake, Robert E. (1995), *The Art of Case Study Research*, London: Sage.

Steven, James H.S. (1997), 'Charismatic Hymnody in the Light of Early Methodist Hymnody', *Studia Liturgia* 27: 217–234.

Steven, James H.S. (2002), *Worship in the Spirit: Charismatic Worship in the Church of England*, Carlisle: Paternoster.

Stringer, Martin D. (1999), *On the Perception of Worship*, Birmingham: University of Birmingham Press.

Stringer, Martin D. (2005), *A Sociological History of Christian Worship*, Cambridge: Cambridge University Press.

Stringer, Martin D. (2008), *Contemporary Western Ethnography and the Definition of Religion*, London: Continuum.

Stronstad, Roger (1999), *The Prophethood of All Believers: A Study in Luke's Charismatic Theology*, Sheffield: Sheffield Academic Press.

Swinton, John and Mowat, Harriet (2006), *Practical Theology and Qualitative Research*, London: SCM.

Synan, Vinson (1997), *The Holiness-Pentecostal Tradition: Charismatic Movements in the Twentieth Century*, 2nd edn, Grand Rapids, MI: Eerdmans.

Tan-Chow, May Ling (2007), *Pentecostal Theology for the Twenty-First Century*, Aldershot: Ashgate.

Ter Haar, Gerrie (2001), *African Christians in Europe*, Nairobi: Acton Publishers.

Theron, Jacques P.J. (1999), 'Towards a Practical Theological Theory for the Healing Ministry in Pentecostal Churches', *Journal of Pentecostal Theology*, 14: 49–64.

Thomas, John Christopher (1998), 'Pentecostal Theology in the Twenty-First Century', *Pneuma: The Journal of the Society for Pentecostal Studies*, 20, 1: 3–19.

Thomas, John Christopher (2005), 'Healing in the Atonement: A Johannine Perspective', *Journal of Pentecostal Theology* 14, 1: 23–39.

Thomas, A.J. (2009), 'Empirical Theology, African Pentecostals and an "Evangelical-Charismatic Hermeneutic"', *Practical Theology in South Africa* 23, 3: 46–66.

Thompson, Damian (2005), *Waiting for Antichrist: Charisma and Apocalypse in a Pentecostal Church*, Oxford: Oxford University Press.

Tidball, Derek (2006), 'The Social Construction of Evangelical Conversion', in Christopher Partridge and Helen Reid (eds.), *Finding and Losing Faith: Studies in Conversion*, Milton Keynes: Paternoster, pp. 84–102.

Turner, Bryan S. (1992), *Regulating Bodies*, London: Routledge.

Turner, Max (2004), 'The Churches of the Johannine Letters as Communities of "Trinitarian" *Koinōnia*', in Wonsuk Ma and Robert P. Menzies (eds.), *The Spirit and Spirituality: Essays in Honour of Russell P. Spittler*, London: T & T Clark, pp. 53–61

Turner, Max (2007), *The Holy Spirit and Spiritual Gifts: Then and Now*, reprint of 2nd edn, Milton Keynes: Paternoster, (orig. 1996).

Turner, Victor, (1969), *The Ritual Process: Structure and Anti-Structure*, London: Routledge & Kegan Paul.

Turner, Victor (1987), *The Anthropology of Performance*, New York: PAJ Publications.

Twelftree, Graham H. (2009), *People of the Spirit: Exploring Luke's View of the Church*, London: SPCK.

Ukah, Asonzeh F.-K. (2009), 'Contesting God: Nigerian Pentecostals and Their Relations with Islam and Muslims', in David Westerlund (ed.), *Global Pentecostalism: Encounters with Other Religious Traditions*, London: I.B. Tauris, pp. 93–114.

Ullman, Chana (1989), *The Transformed Self: The Psychology of Religious Conversion*, New York: Plenum Press.

Van der Ven, Johannes A. (1993), *Practical Theology: An Empirical Approach*, Kampen: Kok Pharos.

Vanhoozer, Kevin J. (2005), *The Drama of Doctrine: A Canonical-Linguistic Approach to Christian Theology*, Louisville, KT: Westminster John Knox Press.

Villafañe, Eldin (1993), *The Liberating Spirit: Toward an Hispanic American Pentecostal Social Ethic*, Grand Rapids, MI: Eerdmans.

Volf, Miroslav (1991), *Work in the Spirit: Toward a Theology of Work*, Oxford: Oxford University Press.

Volf, Miroslav (1996), *Exclusion and Embrace: A Theological Exploration of Identity, Otherness and Reconciliation*, Nashville, TN: Abingdon Press.

Volf, Miroslav (1998), *After Our Likeness: The Church as the Image of the Trinity*, Grand Rapids, MI: Eerdmans.

Wainwright, Geoffrey (1980), *Doxology: The Praise of God in Worship, Doctrine and Life – A Systematic Theology*, London: Epworth Press.

Wakefield, G. (2006), *Conversion Today*, Cambridge: Grove Books.

Wakefield, G. (2007), *Alexander Boddy: Anglican Pentecostal Pioneer*, Milton Keynes: Paternoster.

Walker, Andrew (1988), *Restoring the Kingdom: The Radical Christianity of the House Church Movement*, 2nd edn, London: Hodder & Stoughton.

Walker, Tom W. (1976a), 'The Baptism of the Holy Spirit' in P.S. Brewster (ed.), *Pentecostal Doctrine*, private publication by P.S. Brewster, pp. 27–37.

Walker, Tom W. (1976b), 'The Recovery of Worship', in P.S. Brewster (ed.), *Pentecostal Doctrine*, private publication by P.S. Brewster, pp. 39–44.

Walsh, Tim (2010), 'Eschatology and the Fortunes of Early British Pentecostalism', *Theology* CXIII, 871: 31–43.

Wanless, Derek (2003), *Securing Good Health for the Whole Population: Population Health Trends*, Norwich: HMSO.

Ward, Pete (2005a), *Selling Worship: How What We Sing Has Changed the Church*, Milton Keynes: Paternoster.

Ward, Pete (2005b), 'Affective Alliance or Circuits of Power: The Production and Consumption of Contemporary Charismatic Worship in Britain', *International Journal of Practical Theology* 9: 25–39.

Ward, Pete (2008), *Participation and Mediation: A Practical Theology for the Liquid Church*, London: SCM.

Warrington, Keith (1998), 'Healing and Exorcism: The Path to Wholeness', in Keith Warrington (ed.), *Pentecostal Perspectives*, Carlisle: Paternoster, pp. 147–176.

Warrington, Keith (1999), 'Major Aspects of Healing within British Pentecostalism', *Journal of the European Pentecostal Theological Association* 19: 34–55.

Warrington, Keith (2003), 'The Role of Jesus as Presented in the Healing Praxis and Teaching of British Pentecostalism: A Re-Examination', *Pneuma: The Journal of the Society for Pentecostal Studies*, 25, 1: 66–92.

Warrington, Keith (2008), *Pentecostal Theology: A Theology of Encounter*, London: T & T Clark.

Weaver, F.C. (1972), 'The Assemblies of God', in Norman Tiptaft (ed.), *Religion in Birmingham*, Warley, Worcs: Norman Tiptaft.

Weller, Paul (2008), *Religious Diversity in the UK: Contours and Issues*, London: Continuum International.

Wenk, Matthias (2000), 'Conversion and Initiation: A Pentecostal View of Biblical and Patristic Perspectives', *Journal of Pentecostal Theology* 17: 56–80.

Westerlund, David (2009), 'Islam in Pentecostal Eyes: A Swedish Example' in David Westerlund (ed.), *Global Pentecostalism: Encounters with Other Religious Traditions*, London: I.B. Tauris, pp. 193–205.

Williams, Melvin D. (1974), *Community in a Black Pentecostal Church: An Anthropological Study*, Pittsburgh: University of Pittsburgh Press.

Williams, Tammy R. (2002), 'Is There a Doctor in the House? Reflections on the Practice of Healing in African American Churches', in Miroslav Volf and Dorothy C. Bass (eds.), *Practicing Theology: Beliefs and Practices in Christian Life*, Grand Rapids, MI: Eerdmans, pp. 94–120.

Wilson, Bryan R. (1961), *Sects and Society: A Sociological Study of Three Religious Groups in Britain*, London: William Heinemann.

Wilson, Bryan R. (1966), *Religion in Secular Society: A Sociological Comment*, London: C.A. Watts & Co..

Wilson, Bryan R. (1982), *Religion in Sociological Perspective*, Oxford: Oxford University Press.

Wilson, Bryan (2003), 'Salvation, Secularization, and De-moralization', in Richard K. Fenn (ed.), *The Blackwell Companion to Sociology of Religion*, Oxford: Blackwell, pp. 39–51.

Woodhead, Linda, Guest, Matthew and Tusting, Karen (2004), 'Congregational Studies: Taking Stock', in Matthew Guest, Karin Tusting and Linda Woodhead (eds.), *Congregational Studies in the UK: Christianity in a Post-Christian Context*, Aldershot: Ashgate.

Yin, Robert K. (1989), *Case Study Research: Design and Method*, London: Sage.

Yin, Robert K. (1993), *Applications of Case Study Research*, London: Sage.

Yong, Amos (1999), '"Not Knowing Where the Wind Blows …": On Envisioning a Pentecostal-Charismatic Theology of Religions', *Journal of Pentecostal Theology* 14: 81–112.

Yong, Amos (2000), *Discerning the Spirit(s): A Pentecostal-Charismatic Contribution to Christian Theology of Religions*, Sheffield: Sheffield Academic Press.

Yong, Amos (2003), *Beyond the Impasse: Toward a Pneumatological Theology of Religions*, Grand Rapids, MI: Baker Academic.

Yong, Amos (2005), *The Spirit Poured Out on All Flesh: Pentecostalism and the Possibility of Global Theology*, Grand Rapids, MI: Baker Academic.

Yong, Amos (2007), *Theology and Down Syndrome: Reimagining Disability in Late Modernity*, Waco, TX: Baylor University Press.

Yong, Amos (2008a), *Hospitality and the Other: Pentecost, Christian Practices, and the Neighbour*, Maryknoll, NY: Orbis.

Yong, Amos (2008b), 'The Inviting Spirit: Pentecostal Beliefs and Practices regarding Religions Today', in Steven M. Studebaker (ed.), *Defining Issues in Pentecostalism: Classical and Emergent*, Eugene, OR: Pickwick Publications, pp. 29–45.

Yong, Amos (2010), *In the Days of Caesar:Pentecostalism and Political Theology. The Cadbury Lectures 2009*, Grand Rapids, MI: Eerdmans.

Index